经济管理学术文库 • 管理类

基于GSA方法的多级库存优化问题研究

Optimization of (R, Q) Policies for Multi-Echelon Inventory Systems with Guaranteed Service

李 鹏／著

图书在版编目（CIP）数据

基于 GSA 方法的多级库存优化问题研究/李鹏著. —北京：经济管理出版社，2019.1
ISBN 978-7-5096-6305-9

Ⅰ. ①基… Ⅱ. ①李… Ⅲ. ①库存—仓库管理—研究 Ⅳ. ①F253

中国版本图书馆 CIP 数据核字（2019）第 008932 号

组稿编辑：杨国强
责任编辑：杨国强 张瑞军
责任印制：高 娅
责任校对：陈 颖

出版发行：经济管理出版社
（北京市海淀区北蜂窝 8 号中雅大厦 A 座 11 层 100038）
网 址：www. E-mp. com. cn
电 话：（010）51915602
印 刷：玉田县昊达印刷限公司
经 销：新华书店
开 本：720mm×1000mm/16
印 张：12.75
字 数：222 千字
版 次：2019 年 1 月第 1 版 2019 年 1 月第 1 次印刷
书 号：ISBN 978-7-5096-6305-9
定 价：68.00 元

前　言

随着经济的全球化发展，供应链结构变得日益复杂，集成供应链管理已成为企业在满足客户需求的同时降低企业成本的重要策略之一，这种变化使得学术研究人员和行业从业者在过去 20 年中越来越关注于多级库存管理。

本书系统研究了存在订货成本的多级库存系统优化问题。由于订货成本的存在，使得传统的供应链结构优化变得异常复杂。服务水平保证法（Guaranteed Service Approach，GSA）作为多级库存优化的重要方法之一，已形成了较为成熟的理论框架，然而由于其在设置系统安全库存时，没有考虑订货成本，极大地限制了这种方法的应用领域。本书针对带有订货成本的三类复杂多级库存系统——串型系统、装配型系统和分配型系统，提出拓展的 GSA 库存控制模型，以寻求最优的库存控制策略，使企业在满足顾客需求的同时实现成本最小化。为了验证模型的有效性，本书提出改进的动态规划算法，数据验证证明了算法的有效性。

Abstract

With the increasing complexity of supply chains led by economic globalization, integrated supply chain management has become an important strategy utilized by the firms to reduce the overall cost while meeting the customer service. This change has made academic researchers and industrial practitioners pay more and more attention to multi-echelon inventory management over the last two decades.

In this thesis, we study multi-echelon inventory systems with fixed order costs at each stock. Because of the existence of fixed order costs, the optimization of such system becomes very complicated. Recently, Guaranteed Service Approach (GSA) was used to set safety stock for multi-echelon inventory systems, but without fixed order costs. We extend the GSA to optimize (R, Q) inventory policies for multi-echelon inventory systems with Poisson demand and fixed order costs. Our objective is to find optimal (R, Q) policy for such a system so that its total cost is minimized while achieving a service level to customer. Three types of multi-echelon inventory systems, serial systems, assembly systems and two-level distribution systems are considered. For each type, we first establish a mathematical model for the optimization problem. Then, the model is solved by an iterative procedure based on two dynamic programming (DP) algorithms. One DP algorithm is used to solve the order size decision sub-problem and the other is used to solve the reorder point decision sub-problem of the model. Numerical experiments demonstrate the efficiency of the algorithms and the procedure.

General Introduction

A supply chain is a network of enterprises through which products are produced and delivered to end customers.Supply chain management (SCM) aims at optimizing a system wide performance of such a network by coordinating the flow and the storage of goods from raw material suppliers to distributors through manufacturers.In recent years, economic globalization, product proliferation and fast product innovation have significantly increased the complexity of supply chain management in many industries. Oneimportant issuein supply chain management is managing/controlling inventoriesat all stocks in a general supply network facing uncertain customer demands. The objective of this inventory management is to reduce inventory costs while assuring a given high service level to customers.

Traditionally, inventories at different stocks in a supply chain were managed independently, buffered by high inventories. Increasing competitive pressures and market globalization have forced firms to make more efforts to reduce their inventories while improving the customer service. This has been making academic researchers and industrial practitioners pay more and more attention to multi-echelon inventory management which takes the interactions between different stocks in a supply chain into consideration.

A supply chain with multiple stocks can be modeled as a multi-echelon inventory system, where the stocks are arranged in multiple echelons or levels and each stock is replenished from one or multiple stocks at a higher echelon. Multi-echelon inventory management adopts a global optimization approach. In such an approach, the inventory optimizations of all stocks are considered simultaneously, with an objective to minimize a system-wide cost while meeting requirements on customer service. Therefore, the key strategy of multi-echelon inventory management is efficient coordination of inventory policies among all participating companies in a supply chain.

In the literature, there are two competing approaches for inventory system optimization: Stochastic service approach (SSA) and guaranteed service approach (GSA). In SSA, safety stock is assumed to be the only buffer against demand variability. On the other hand, the GSA model assumes the safety stock is sized to cover demand variability up to a certain level, i.e., the maximum reasonable lead time demand level. If a demand exceeds this level, excessive part of the demand is treated by using extraordinary measures due to operating flexibility of the underlying system. Compared with the SSA, the GSA models the entire system in an approximate fashion but it allows a planner to make strategic and tactical inventory decisions based on a simplified model.

In the literature, most studies on multi-echelon inventory systems assume no fixed order cost at each stock or only the stock(s) at the highest echelon has (have) a fixed order cost. However, in practice, each stock usually has a fixed cost which may correspond to the order delivery cost or other quantity-independent costs. For a multi-echelon inventory system,if a fixed order cost incurs at each stock of, $(R,\ Q)$ policy or $(s,\ S)$ policy is usually used as the inventory policy of the system. Due to its simplicity and popularity in practice, we choose $(R,\ Q)$ policy rather than $(s,\ S)$ policy for controlling multi-echelon inventory systems with fixed order costs in this thesis. We study the optimization of$(R,\ Q)$ policy for multi-echelon inventory systems with stochastic customer demand and fixed order costs. Our objective is to find the optimal $(R,\ Q)$ policy for such a system so that its average system-wide total cost is minimized while satisfying a target service level to customers. Three types of multi-echelon inventory systems, serial systems, assembly systems and two-level distribution systems, are considered.

The existence of fixed order costs at each stock makes the inventory policy optimization of the multi-echelon inventory systems very difficult. The SSA, as a classical approach, was usually used to solve such optimization problem. However, due to the high complexity of the systems with fixed order costs, only approximate (heuristics) algorithms for finding near-optimal inventory policies were developed under the SSA.

On the other hand, under the assumption that excessive demand superior to a certain level is treated by operating flexibility, the GSA is able to model an inventory optimization problem as a deterministic mathematical programming problem, which can be solved more easily. In the literature, no previous work has used this approach to optimize multi-echelon inventory systems with fixed order costs at each stock. Therefore, in this thesis, we use the GSA to model and solve inventory optimization problems of multi-echelon inventory systems with fixed order costs. Different from the standard GSA which ignores the operating flexibility costs for using extraordinary measures to fulfill excessive demand, we develop a new GSA which considers operating flexibility costs and the effects of extraordinary measures on the material flows of the multi-echelon inventory systems in this thesis. In our study, maximum reasonable level of lead time demand is determined according to a service level to final customer.

The main contributions of this thesis include:

1) We extend the GSA to multi-echelon inventory systems with fixed order costs at each stock. Since all previous works on the GSA only deal with inventory systems without fixed order costs, this thesis is the first attempt to optimize multi-echelon inventory systems with fixed order costs under the framework of the GSA.

2) The standard GSA ignores the effect of operating flexibility on the material flow and the total cost of a multi-echelon inventory system. In this thesis, we extend the standard GSA by considering the effect and by including explicitly the operating flexibility costs in our inventory policy optimization models. In the models, the total cost of a multi-echelon inventory system not only includes fixed order costs, on-hand inventory holding costs, but also includes operating flexibility costs.

3) For each of the three types of multi-echelon inventory systems considered, we formulate a mathematical programming model for the inventory policy optimization problem under the framework of the GSA.

4) The consideration of the operating flexibility effects and costs makes our GSA model more complicated than the standard GSA model with an objective function depending on two service levels (α-service level and β-service level). We propose an iter-

ative procedure to solve the model based on the estimation of β-service level.

5) For given α-service level and β-service level, the inventory policy problem can be decomposed into two sub-problems: One is to determine the optimal order size Q of each stock (called Q-problem) and the other is to determine the optimal reorder point R of each stock (called R-problem). We develop dynamic programming algorithms for efficiently solving the two sub-problems.

6) The efficiency of the dynamic programming algorithms and the iterative procedure is evaluated by numerical experiments.

This thesis consists of six chapters. Chapter 1 introduces basic concepts of inventory management, the motivation of this research, and the specific problems studied in this thesis, and provide a literature review for multi-echelon inventory management research related to our work. Chapter 2 presents the basic terminology of multi-echelon inventory control as well as a standard GSA model that can help the readers to understand the GSA models to be developed in the upcoming chapters. In this chapter, we also discuss how to evaluate operating flexibility costs under the GSA. In chapter 3, we consider serial systems with Poisson customer demand and fixed order costs at each stock and develop a mathematical programming model and a solution approach for optimizing their (R, Q) policies under the GSA. The model takes into consideration both fixed order costs and operating flexibility costs and the solution approach is based on two dynamic programming algorithms we develop or adopt for two sub-problems of the model. The performances of the algorithms and the solution approach are evaluated by numerical experiments. Chapter 4 extends the model and the solution approach developed in Chapter 3 to assembly systems with numerical experiments for performance evaluation as well. In Chapter 5, we consider two-level distribution systems with one warehouse and multiple retailers. The analysis and optimization of such systems are more difficult than serial and assembly systems. We also develop a mathematical programming model and a solution approach for the optimization of the distribution system under the GSA. In addition, we consider five different types of integer-ratio constraints possibly imposed on the order sizes of the stocks of the system, and compare their effectiveness by computational experiments. Finally, Chapter 6 concludes the thesis and suggests some directions for further research.

Notations

Network

N	the number of stocks in a multi-echelon inventory system
i	stock index, i=1, ..., N
t	time index...,
$s\ (i)$	the set of immediate successor of stock i
$SUC\ (i)$	the set consisting of stock i and all its successors
$P\ (i)$	the set of the immediate predecessors of stock i
$PRE\ (i)$	the set consisting of stock i and all its predecessors

Demand

F	set of stocks facing external demand (customer demand)
λ_i	average demand rate of the customer demand at stock i, $i \in F$
$d_i\ (t)$	demand realization of stock i at time t, $i \in F$
$d\ [t-L_i,\ t)$	the lead time demand over L_i units of time of stock i, i=1, 2, ..., N
$\hat{d}\ [t-L_i,\ t)$	the lead time demand over L_i units of time fulfilled normally by a multi-echelon inventory system considered
$D_i\ (\tau)$	maximum reasonable lead time demand level over τ periods

Time parameters and variables

T_i	Production time of stock i
S_i	outbound service time of stock i
SI_i	inbound service time of stock i

L_i net lead time of stock i

M_i maximum replenishment time of stock i

s_i upper bound of the outbound service time of stock i when $i \in F$

Performance measures

h_i^e Unit echelon on-hand inventory holding cost at stock i

h_i Unit on-hand inventory holding cost at stock i

c_i fixed order cost for placing each order by stock i to its supplier

p operating flexibility cost for using extraordinary measures to fulfill each unit of excessive customer demand

α_i service level for stock i, which is defined as the probability of satisfying demand from the stock

β_i fill rate of stock i, which is the fraction of customer demandsatisfied directly form the stock

Inventory control and replenishment variables

$I_i\ (t)$ on-hand inventory of stock i,

$I_i^e\ (t)$ echelon on-hand inventory of stock i

$IL_i^e\ (t)$ echelon inventory level of stock i

$IP_i^e\ (t)$ echelon inventory position of stock i

$OO_i\ (t_1, t_2]$ the quantity of all orders placed by stock i from time t_1 to time t_2 (not including t_1), i=1, 2, ..., N.

Contents

List of Tables

List of Figures

Chapter 1
Introduction

1.1 Inventory Management

Products and services are usually delivered to end customers through a supply chain which is a network of organizations connected together through the products and services that separately and/or jointly add valuesto it. Many real-world supply chains, such as those found in automotive, electronics, and consumer packaged goods industries, consist of a large number of assembly and distribution operations realized in geographically dispersed facilities. One challenge for the management of such a supply chain is the effective management of its inventories located in multiple production and distribution facilities facing stochastic demand and uncertain supply of products with high inventory and transportation costs. According to a study, American companies spent almost 1 trillion dollars in supply-related activities in 2000 (or 10.1% of Gross Domestic Product), among which transportation costs constitute 58.6%, inventory costs 37.4% and management costs 4% of the total cost. Generally, inventory can represent from 20% to 60% of the total assets of manufacturing firms (Arnold, 2004). Therefore, the total capital investment in inventories is enormous, and the control of the capital tied up in raw material, work-in-progress, and finished goods offers a very important potential for improvement. Scientific methods for inventory management can give a significant competitive advantage.

Inventory management has a very important impact on the performance of an enterprise especially the financial health of its balance sheet. As indicated by a study of the Aberdeen Group (Viswanathan, 2007), inventory management was ranked on top of the list of investments in application-oriented software for companies in 2007. In 2008 the market for inventory management applications continued to increase by 4% over 2007 according to AMR research (Trebilcock, 2009), demonstrating that companies were making more efforts on improving their inventory management activities. An effective inventory management is particularly important in the current increasing competitive environment due to market globalization. In order to contain cost and free working capital, inventories need to be reduced without sacrificing the service level to customers. Inventory management aims at determining and controlling the inventory levels within physical inventory systems, so that the need for product availability and the need for minimizing the costs related to inventory are well balanced. As a matter of fact, inventory management may have conflicting objectives. One objective is to keep stock levels as low as possible to minimize costs and free working capitals as much as possible. Another objective is to provide a high service levelto customers in order to avoid the risk of lost sales in case of insufficient inventories.

It is seldom trivial to find the best balance between such goals, that is why we need to study inventory management. One important issue of inventory management is to find an optimal inventory policy to control the inventory replenishment of each stock in an inventory system so as to minimize the costs related to inventory, while maintaining a given target level to customers. Here, an inventory policy is a mechanism, which decides when a stock should place an inventory replenishment order and in which quantity it should order. The optimization of the inventory policy of the stock should consider its cost structure. In inventory systems, many costs may be involved such as:

- costs for ordering, material handling, and transportation;
- costs for capital tied up in the inventories;
- costs for not providing an adequate customer service.

Correspondingly, fixed order costs, inventory holding costs and backorder/penalty costs arise. Since the inventory policy decision has a very important impact on the costs, the research on the optimization of inventory policies is of great practical and academic significance.

1.2 Multi-Echelon Inventory Systems

A supply chain with multiple stocks is usually modeled as a multi-echelon inventory system, which is an inventory system with multiple stocks arranged in multiple echelons or levels, wherethe " echelon" of a stock refers to the position (level) at whichthe stock is located within the system. A multi-echelon inventory system is depicted as in Figure 1.1.

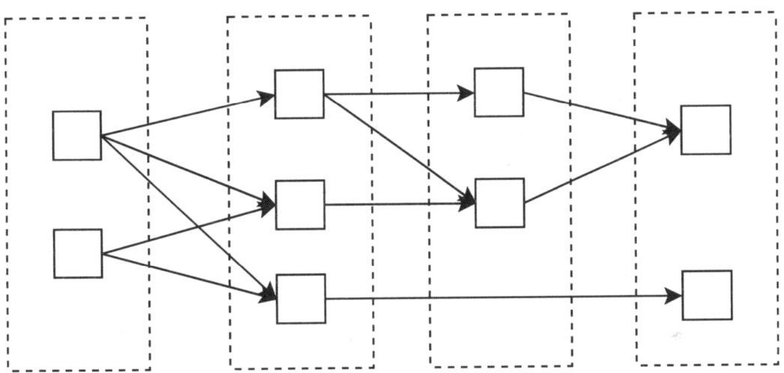

Figure 1.1 A multi-echelon inventory system

The main characteristics of a multi-echelon inventory system can be described as follows:

■ The system is composed of multiple stocks and each stock has a physical location;

■ All stocks are grouped into multiple echelons (levels);

■ Each stock at a lower echelon replenishes its inventory from one or multiple stocks at a higher echelon.

Intuitively, one can imagine a multi-echelon inventory system as something resembling a "network", in which the "nodes" are the stocks of the participating companies that are inter-connected in a supply chain (See Figure 1.1). Two nodes are connected through a directed link (arc) in the network if the upstream node is a supplier of the downstream node or in other words the downstream node is a customer of the upstream node. In real-world a multi-echelon inventory system may be more complex than the one depicted in Figure 1.1 that is really a chainrather than a network, because there may exist multiple suppliers and multiple customers for each stock in the system.

On the basis of network structure, multi-echelon inventory systems can be classified into serial systems, assembly systems, distribution systems and general systems. The simplest structure is that of serial systems, in which each echelon only has a single stock. A more complex structure is that of assembly systems, in which multiple components/subassemblies are assembled into a single subassembly or final product and consequently a stock may have multiple suppliers. In a distribution system, a supplier distributes (delivers) a product to multiple customers, andtherefore, the supplier can have multiple customers. In general case, amulti-echelon inventory system can include any of the above three structures as parts of the system (Zipkin, 2000).

Most consumer and industrial goods are distributed through multi-echelon inventory systems of one sort or another. Any enterprise with geographically-dispersed markets, production facilities, and material suppliers must rely on the performance of its multi-echelon inventory system to remain competitive. The management of multi-echelon inventory systems is thus a crucial part of supply chain management.

1.3 Multi-Echelon Inventory Management

Historically, the actorsina supply chain, i.e., manufacturers, warehouses, distributors, etc., planned and managed their inventories independently, and even in an enterprise its stocks at different echelons were planned independently or in a sequential way. Here, sequential planning means that the inventory planning of the stocks at each echelon only considers the inventory planning of its immediate downstream stocks. However, such individual or sequential planning approach completely neglects interdependencies between the stocks at two adjacent echelons. As a result, some stocks might hold excessive inventories whereas the others might frequently be in shortage, because the sequential approach does not well answer the following questions: Is it more costly to hold inventory at an upstream or a downstream echelon? How does the inventory planning of an upstream echelon affect the inventory planning of a downstream echelon? Which level of service should each stock in an upstream echelon provide to its internal customers (stocks in a downstream echelon) such that external customer demand can be satisfied according to a target service level?

Increasing competitive pressures and market globalization have forced firms to change their inventory planning and management strategies. To remain competitive and decrease inventory costs, they now work together to plan and mange their supply chainsin a coordinated way so that productscan be delivered to final customers at the least cost while achieving a high service level to final customers. This has been making academic researchers and industrial practitioners pay more and more attention to multi-echelon inventory management over the past two decades.

Multi-echelon inventory management adopts a global optimization approach. In such approach, all stocks (echelons) from the external suppliers to the end customers in a supply network are considered simultaneously, with the objective of minimizing a system-wide cost subject to constraints on customer service. Thus, the shortcomings of the sequential approach are overcome. It is reported that "It is not unusual for a global supply chain to see inventory levels reduced by as much as 15%-25%" (Ellis et al., 2009) due to effective multi-echelon inventory management.

There are two drivers for the advancement of multi-echelon inventory management. Firstly, the rapid development of information and computer technologies has made information available to all enterprises and all stocks across a supply chain possible, this has made the implementation of a multi-echelon inventory management application in such a supply chain possible. Secondly, multi-echelon inventory research in recent years has brought us models and methods that can capture and handle a broad variety of real inventory systems with a large number of stocks at multiple echelons.

1.4 Models and Methods Used for Multi-Echelon Inventory Management

In this section we provide an overview of models and methods for multi-echelon inventory management. This will help the reader to understand the materialsto be presented in later sections. In addition, we will briefly introduce different inventory policies used in the control of multi-echelon inventory systems.

1.4.1 Inventory Models

From a mathematical inventory theory perspective, the inventory modelsused can be classified into deterministic and stochastic inventory models.

Deterministic Inventory Models: A deterministic inventory model assumes that the demand is deterministic. Due to this assumption, the analysis of the model is considerably simplified. Stockout in a deterministic inventory model is usually not allowed. Deterministic inventory models can further be subdivided into static and dynamic models. The static models are usually derived from the classical economic order quantity (EOQ) which seeks for an optimal trade-off between fixed order costs and variable inventory holding costs. Multi-stage EOQ-type models exists. Such models can be used in the situations when the system conditions are stable and there are no fluctuations in the demand. To deal with the situations with deterministic time varying demand, various lot sizing models have been developed, which can be applied in different situations. The most widely used methods for single stock lot sizing are Wagner-Whittin method (Wagner and Whitin, 1958), Silver meal heuristics (Silver and Pyke, 1988), and part period balancing (Callarman and Hamrin, 1983). A review of lot sizing models for multi-echelon (level) systems can be found in Teunter (1998). Note that these deterministic models provide a basisfor treating inventory systems with uncertainty.

Stochastic Inventory Models: Stochastic inventory models which specify the demand as a stochastic process are more realistic compared with their deterministic counterparts. In spite of the fact that it has been known for a long time that there exists an optimal inventory policy under quite general conditions, optimal control parameters of the policy under the stochastic setting are hard to be computed, let alone applying such policy to real inventory systems. One reason for this is that the analysis of stochastic inventory models is usually very difficult. The cost functionsof most stochastic inventory models have been widely perceived as rather complex and too difficult to be evaluated analytically (Zheng, 1992). In the literature, a number of stochastic inventory models have been proposed; most of the models are stationary with an infinite horizon. Most previous studies on stochastic inventory models were focused on cost evaluation and on determining optimal control parameters for predetermined inventory policies. In contrast, results on optimal policy structures are rare. In most studiesthe demand is modeled as a Poisson process or compound Poisson process. Detailed information will be provided in section 1.6.

1.4.2 Inventory Policies

In inventory management, an inventory policy determines when the state of a stock must be reviewed, when the stock must place a replenishment order and in which quantity each order must be placed by the stock. Most frequently used inventory policies for multi-echelon inventory systems are base stock policy or order-up-to level policy, (R, Q) policy and (s, S) policy according to the consideration of fixed order costs or not in the system. Moreover, according to the different information used for order decision, existing inventory policies can be also classified into two groups: Installation inventory policies and echelon inventory policies. The former considers only local stock information whereas the latter can be used only when centralized information is available. Finally, inventory policies can be classified into continuous review policies and periodic review polices according to the nature of their inventory tracking. An inventory control system can be designed so that its inventory position is monitored continuously or periodically, which leads to a continuous review and a periodic review policy, respectively. Continuous review, also known as perpetual review, involves a system that tracks each stock and updates inventory counts every time an item is removed from inventory. On the other hand, periodic review involves counting and documenting inventory at specified times. Periodic review with a short review period is, of course, very similar to continuous review.

Base Stock Policy: Withthis policy, the inventory position of a stock is reviewed only after a certain predetermined time interval. An order is placed to restore the inventory position to a predetermined order-up-to-level. Therefore, thebase stock policy is also known as "Order up to level" policy because the order size is determined based on a predetermined order up to level. This policy is in common use in real inventory sys tems as it does not require continuous monitoring of the inventory status and thus makes it easy to be implemented, especially when computerized systems are not available for inventory planning. This policy is optimal in case that excess demand is backordered, the lead time is deterministic and no fixed order cost is charged.

Although base stock policy is very simple but this policy is optimal only when no fixed order cost is charged. For this reason, (R, Q) policy and (s, S) policywhich take account of fixed order costs are also used in multi-echelon inventory systems.

(R, Q) Policy: This policy operates as follows: when the inventory position of a stock declines to or below a reorder point R, an order of Q units is placed. When the inventory position is periodically reviewed, the stock may be necessary to order a multiple of Q unitsto raise its inventory position to above R. The considered policy is therefore also referred to as (R, nQ) policy, where N is the minimal positive integer such that the current inventory position plus nQ units to be ordered will be greater than R.

(s, S) Policy: This policy has two control parameters: The reorder point s and the order-up-to level S. When the inventory position of a stock declines to or below s, the stock places an order to bring its inventory position to the maximum level S. Compared with (R, Q) policy, (s, S) policy no longer orders a multiple of a given order size. If the reorder point is always hit exactly in case of continuous review and continuous demand, the two policies are equivalent provided $s=R$ and $S=R+Q$. Otherwise, the two policies are different.

In general, an inventory model using either (R, Q) policy or (s, S) policyhas a complex structure, this leads to a fact that few results exist for the optimization of such policy in the context of multi-echelon inventory systems except for approximate optimization procedures.Between the two policies, the use of (s, S) policy is more advantageous from a theoretical point of view. However, their cost differences are, in general, very small, and in practice it is often much easier to implement an (R, Q) policy. For this reason, we only consider (R, Q) policyin this thesis.

1.4.3 Inventory Optimization Approaches

Two competing approaches have been developed over the years for inventory system optimization. Although they solve the same inventory policy optimization problem in their core, they make different assumptions with regard to the role of safety stock. In the SSA model, safety stock is assumed to be the only buffer against demand variability. On the other hand, the GSA model assumes that safety stock is sized to cover demand variability up to a certain level only, i.e., the maximum reasonable lead time demand level. All demand variability exceeding this level is treated by using extraordinary countermeasures due to operating flexibility of the underlying system. The twoapproaches differ in demand treatment, replenishment strategy and service time characteristics.

Stochastic Service Approach (SSA): Most inventory models adopt the SSA. In the SSA,each stock maintains a sufficient inventory level in order to meet its stochastic demand. When the inventory level of a stock is not sufficient to meet the demand coming form its downstream stocks or final customers, unsatisfied demand is fully backlogged and will be filled later when on-hand inventory becomes available. This implies that the stock may have a stochastic delay to fill an unsatisfied demand, the service time of the stock, which is defined as the lead time for filling its demand is thus stochastic.

Guaranteed Service Approach (GSA): The GSA was originated from the work of Simpson (1958). In the GSA, each stock sets a deterministic service time for meeting any demand from its downstream stocks and guarantees that the demand can always be satisfied in the given service time. This approach assumes that excessive customer demand superior to a bound is treated by some extraordinary measures such as expediting and overtime. With this assumption, each stock can predict its maximum demand to fill and assure a given service time to its downstream stocks. Therefore, the service time of each stock in GSA is deterministic. In the GSA model, it is assumed that extraordinary measures besides safety stock exist to cope with demand variability, if the demand exceeds a certain maximum reasonable level. However, this "operating flexibility" of using extraordinary measures is not explicitly modeled in the standard GSA framework, and this becomes a major point of criticism for such approach. In order to counteract this criticism, in this thesis, we adopt an extended GSA model which explicitly considers the effect that operating flexibility measures have on the material flow and the total cost of a multi-echelon inventory system.

In summary, the stochastic service approach (SSA) employs a more complicated model that allows for a more exact and detailed understanding of the system. However, the model as well as solution techniques for it are not easy to develop and are computationally hard. The guaranteed service approach (GSA) models the entire system in an approximate fashion and allows a planner to make strategic and tactical decisions without the need to approximate portions of the system that are not captured by a simplified topological representation. For a detailed comparison of these two approaches, please see Graves and Willems (2003) and Humair and Willems (2006).

1.5 The Problems Studied in This Thesis

In this thesis, we study the inventory optimization in multi-echelon inventory systems with stochastic customer demand and fixed order costs. Because of existing fixed order costs at each stock, this optimization problem becomes more complicated, and most researchers have been developed an approximate optimal method rather than exact method. We consider three types of inventory system, such as serial, assembly and two-level distribution systems, our objective is to find optimal inventory policy so that the average system-wide total cost is minimized while achieving a target service level to customers.

Fixed order costs include the expense involved in placing an order for a quantity of material, such as the paper work cost for preparing the order and the costs for the in spection, packaging and delivery of the order. In practice, fixed order costs are often overlooked by companies as they only pay attention to inventory holding costs and backorder costs. However, when calculating the cost of ordering items, it is often a surprise to companies when they find out how much it actually costs to have an item of material purchased and available at their warehouse. Therefore, as an important part of system total costs, fixed order costs can not be ignored.

The high complexity of multi-echelon inventory systems with fixed order costs makes the optimization for their inventory policies very difficult. The SSA, as a classical inventory optimization method, was usually used to solve such problem. However, the stochastic model employed by this approach is usually hard to be solved because of its complicated structure and the stochastic nature of the service time of each stock in the model. As a result, most researchers only presented heuristic algorithms to solve such model, and these algorithms are usually quite complicated. On the other hand, by assuming that excessive demand superior to a certain level is treated by operating flexibility, the GSA is able to model an inventory policy optimization problem as a deterministic mathematical programming problem which is much easier to be solved. In addition, the latter approach can guarantee a deterministic service time of each stock to its customers. Therefore, we adopt the GSA to model and solve the inventory optimization problems considered in this thesis.

Previously, the GSA was only used to optimize multi-echelon inventory systems without fixed order cost. In this thesis, we have generalized this approach to the optimization of multi-echelon inventory systems with fixed order cost at each stock. Moreover, different from the standard GSA which ignores the costs of using extraordinary measures to fulfill excessive demand, our GSA has taken into account the operating flexibility costs.

As mentioned in Section 1.4, if fixed order costs occur at each stock, (R, Q) policy or (s, S) policy is usually used as the inventory policy to control the replenishment process of a multi-echelon inventory system. In this thesis, we choose (R, Q) policy because it is more simple than (s, S) policy and is more commonly used in practice.

In summary, this thesis has studied the optimization of (R, Q) policies for multi-echelon inventory systems with fixed order costs at each stock by using the GSA with the objective to minimize a system-wide total cost while achieving a given service level to end customers. The costs of such systems include not only fixed order costs and inventory holding costs, but also operating flexibility costs. In the past, none studied such problem by using the GSA.

1.6 Literature Review of Multi–Echelon Inventory Management

In this subsection we review the models and methods proposed in the literature for analysis and optimization of multi-echelon inventory systems, especially for the systems with fixed order costs. We first give a general introduction of the works in multi-echelon inventory management in subsection 1.6.1. Then, we focus on the current studies of multi-echelon inventory management using two optimization approaches: Stochastic service approach (in subsections 1.6.2, 1.6.3 and 1.6.4) and guaranteed service approach (in subsection 1.6.5). The comparison between the two competing approaches is discussed in subsection 1.6.6.

1.6.1 General Studies of Multi–Echelon Inventory Management

The study of multi-echelon inventory systems was originated by a pioneering work of Clark and Scarf (1960). In that work, they showed that an echelon base stock policy is optimal for a “pure” serial inventory system, in which the fixed order cost is charged only at the highest echelon. For the system with fixed order costs at each echelon, they pointed out that an optimal policy, if exists, may be complex and hard to implement.

Since 1960, a lot of research has been conducted to extend the work of Clark and Scarf. Federgruen and Zipkin (1984) generalized Clark-Scarf model to the infinite horizon case. Chen and Zheng (1994) provided a new proof of the results of Clark and Scarf by deriving lower bounds on the long-run costs of their model. A more detailed discussion of these results can be found in Zipkin (2000). Inderfurth (1991) and Minner (1997) proposed different dynamic programming algorithms for finding optimal echelon base stock policy of the Clark-Scarf model. Zangwill (1966, 1969) and Love (1972) presented discrete time dynamic programming models for periodic review, finite horizon serial systems with time-varying demand. Bessler and Veinott (1966) studied a general multi-echelon inventory system and examined the near-optimality of "myopic" one-period policies for the system. Recently, Sinha et al. (2011) provided a computationally simple and unified approach to finite- and infinite-horizon Clark-Scarf model. For these extensions, serial and assembly systems without fixed order costs of echelon base stock policies have been shown to be optimal. For distribution systems without fixed order costs, echelon base stock policies are optimal under the so-called balance assumption, but they are not optimal without that assumption (Van Houtum, 2006). Owing to the complex structure of the systems with fixed order costs at each echelon, most of researchers have focused on optimizing and evaluating simple batch ordering policies, such as (R, Q) policies. We will give an in-depth overview of the current studies on such problem in the latter subsections according to the different types of inventory systems.

Almost at the same time, Simpson (1958) proposed the guaranteed service approach to describe the dynamicsand the control of a serial inventory system without fixed order costs, in which each stock operates an installation base stock policy facing a random but bounded demand. Simpson's results showed that the optimal inventory policy for the serial system is an "all or nothing" policy, i.e., each stock either has no safety stock, or carries enough stocks to decouple the downstream stocks from the upstream stocks. Different extensions of Simpson's work for assembly and distribution systems will be introduced later.

Based on the two seminal papers by Clark and Scarf (1960) and Simpson (1958), two competing approaches have been developed over the years.

1.6.2 Stochastic Service Approach for Serial Inventory Systems

In this subsection, stochastic service approach for serial inventory systems is reviewed, especially for the systems with fixed order costs and operating (R, Q) policies. These works can be essentially be classified into two categories: Cost evaluation and optimization of inventory policies. Other related studies on serial systems will also be reviewed.

Cost Evaluation of (R, Q) Inventory Policy

For cost evaluation,Axsater (1998) considered a two-echelon serial system with continuous-review installation (R, Q) policies and proposed a method to exactly evaluate holding and shortage costs. Bodt and Graves (1985) first introduced echelon (R, Q) policies for a multi-echelon, serial system and presented an approximated model for the cost evaluation of the system. Axsater and Rosling (1993) have shown that echelon (R, Q) policies dominate installation (R, Q) policies for serial and assembly systems. For distribution systems, installation (R, Q) policies and echelon (R, Q) policies may, however, outperform each other in different situations. Chen and Zheng (1994) developed a procedure for exact performance evaluation of echelon (R, nQ) policies in serial systems. The procedure was applied to both continuous-review systems with compound Poisson demand and periodic-review systems with independent, identically distributed demands. In their procedure, a fixed order cost is charged for each replenishment rather than each order. Axsater (1997) proposed an alternative scheme for the cost evaluation of echelon (R, Q) policies, which applies the concept of matching supply units with demand which was originally used for the evaluation of installation stock policies.

Optimization of (R, Q) Inventory Policy

For policy optimization, Chen and Zheng (1998) developed an algorithm to find a near-optimal echelon (R, nQ) policy for serial systems with compound Poisson demand. Mitra and Chatterjee (2004) considered two-echelon serial systems for fast moving items and analyzed Bodt and Grave's model from the implementation point of view, and suggested a possible improvement of the model. Chen (2000) showed that if we ignore the fixed costs but order in fixed sizes, an echelon (R, Q) policy is optimal for serial and assembly systems and the optimal policy can be easily calculated. Shang and Song (2007) considered two stochastic serial inventory models; one assumes that there is a fixed order size at each echelon, and the other considers a fixed order cost only for external orders. They showed that the optimal echelon (*R*, *Q*) policies of the models can be approximated by a series of independent, single-stage optimal policies. Shang (2008) proposed a heuristic algorithm for finding near-optimal base order sizes for serial system models. Shenas et al. (2009) studied a continuous-review two-echelon serial system with Poisson demand. By considering the one-for-one replenishment policy, a special case of installation/echelon (*R*, *Q*) policy, they proposed a procedure for computing an optimal policy for the system by first solving a base stock policy to set the inventory position of the supplier. Yang et al. (2011) also considered a continuous-review two-echelon serial system with Poisson demand and an echelon (*R*, *Q*) policy, they derived a necessary condition for the optimality of an echelon (*R*, *Q*) policy and the quasi-convexity of the cost function for the system. Based on these properties, they designed a simple heuristic algorithm to find a near-optimal echelon (*R*, *Q*) policy for the problem. Dogru et al. (2008) considered a serial inventory system with a given fixed batch size per echelon and linear inventory holding and penalty costs. On the basis of new average cost formulas, they obtained newsvendor equations for the optimal reorder levels.

Some papers address (*R*, *nQ*, *T*) policies for the control of serial systems. Under such a policy, each stock reviews its inventory in every T period and orders according to an installation or echelon (*R*, *nQ*) policy. Shang and Zhou (2010) studied a periodic-review serial system controlled by echelon (*R*, *nQ*, *T*) policies with two types of fixed order costs: One associated with each order size of *Q* units ordered and the other incurred for each inventory review. They developed a simple heuristic for obtaining effective order sizes and reorder intervals. This heuristic is based on finding lower and upper bounds of the total cost function. They also provided a complete enumeration approach for finding the optimal order sizes and reorder intervals. Chao and Zhou (2009) studied a serial system with echelon (*R*, *nQ*, *T*) policies and fixed replenishment intervals. Since every stock places orders according to a regular schedule, fixed order costs were not considered. They derived the optimal inventory control policy, provided a distribution function solution for its optimal control parameters, and presented an efficient algorithm for computing those parameters. Shang and Zhou (2009) proposed a simple heuristic for generating a solution for echelon (*R, nQ, T*) policies by sequentially solving a deterministic demand problem, a sub-problem with fixed reorder intervals, and sub-problem with fixed order sizes. Van Houtum et al. (2007) considered a periodic-review serial inventory system with fixed replenishment intervals. For this system, they proved the optimality of base stock policy, derived newsvendor equations for the optimal base stock levels, and developed an efficient exact solution procedure for the case with mixed Erlang demands.

Other Studies on Serial Inventory Systems

Except for the above cited papers, Chen (1988) and Shang et al. (2010) studied the impacts of different information sharing/coordination mechanism on the performance of serial inventory systems controlled by installation/echelon (*R, nQ*) policies. Rezg et al. (2004) presented an integrated method for inventory control of a production line made up of *N* machines, they proposed a methodology combining the simulation and genetic algorithms to optimize inventory control policies. Sahin et al. (2008, 2009) studied a three-stage system where execution errors result in a discrepancy between the physical inventory and information system. They introduced a new cost component for the conventional Newsvendor model, capturing the cost of not satisfying an initial commitment due to inventory inaccuracy. Shang (2012) proposed a simple heuristic for determining stocking levels in a serial inventory system with non-stationary demand and no fixed order costs based on single-stage approximations. Gallego and Ozer (2003) and Huh and Janakiraman (2008) proposed a new heuristic and a new proof of the optimality of echelon base stock policies for serial inventory systems without fixed order costs in the framework of the Clark-Scarf model. Arslan et al. (2007) considered a single-product inventory system that serves multiple demand classes, and developed a model for cost evaluation and a heuristic for policy optimization under the assumptions of Poisson demand and a continuous-review (*R, Q*) policy with rationing. Axsater (2003) considered the problem of minimizing the holding costs under a fill rate constraint for a continuous-review serial system with discrete compound Poisson demand. The author showed that under some assumptions, the optimal policy is an echelon (R, nQ) policy and provided a simple procedure for the determination of the optimal policy. Huh and Janakiraman (2010) studied a periodic-review serial inventory system with lost sales and derived elementary properties of the vector of optimal order sizes in this system. They showed that the optimal order size at each stock is a decreasing function of the inventory at any downstream stock and an increasing function of the inventory at any upstream stock.

1.6.3 Stochastic Service Approach for Assembly Inventory Sys–tems

In this subsection, the stochastic service approach for assembly systems is generally presented. Compared with serial systems, assembly systems with stochastic demand attracted relatively less attention in the literature.

Schmidt and Nahmias (1985) characterized an optimal policy for a two-echelon assembly system under stochastic demand. Rosling (1989) extended Clark-Scarf model to assembly systems and showed that a general assembly systems without fixed order costs can be transformed equivalent into a serial system. Both papers assume no fixed order costs in their system considered. The inclusion of fixed order costs makes assembly systems with stochastic demand extremely difficult. Schwarz and Schrage (1975) proposed a near-optimal policy for an infinite horizon continuous-review assembly system with fixed order costs. Bodt and Graves (1985) considered inventory policies with fixed lot sizing for an assembly system with fixed order costs and developed an approximate method for finding near-optimal policies. Carlson and Yano (1986) presented a heuristic approach for a two-echelon assembly system with fixed order costs as well as upper and lower bounds on the optimal cost of the system. Chen (2000) showed that if we ignore the fixed order costs but order in fixed sizes, an (R, nQ) policy is optimal for assembly systems and the optimal policy can be easily calculated. Arda and Hennet (2006) analyzed an inventory control problem with Poisson demand, they showed that a base-stock policy coupled with a Bernoulli splitting process is easy to implement and leads to cost savings since it is generally profitable to dispatch the orders between several suppliers rather than to direct all the replenishment orders toward a single supplier.

Next, we restrict our attention to installation/echelon (*R*, *Q*) policies for assembly systems with fixed order costs. Many papers have studied the (*R*, *Q*) policy on policy evaluation and optimization (Hadley and Whitin, 1961; Veinott, 1965; Federgruen and Zheng, 1992; Rosling, 2002; De Bodt and Graves, 1985; Axsater and Rosling, 1993; Axsater, 1997; Chen and Zheng, 1994). Axsater (1997) suggested an alternative scheme for the evaluation of echelon (*R*, *Q*) policies, applying his concept of matching supply units with demand which was originally used for the evaluation of installation stock policies. A brief discussion of (*R*, *Q*) policies for assembly systems are given in Axsater and Rosling (1993) and Chen (2000). In practice, it is common to use a simple two-step approach to determine the order size *Q* and the reorder point R of an installation/echelon (*R*, *Q*) policy. In the first step, the stochastic demand is replaced by its mean and the order size *Q* is determined according to a standard EOQ model. In the second step, the reorder point *R* is determined with the given *Q*. Axsater (1996) and Gallego (1997) derived bounds for approximation errors when using such a method. Moreover, most of the previous work, which addressed (*R*, *Q*) policies, only presented heuristic algorithms rather than exact methods for cost evaluation and policy parameter optimization for assembly systems with fixed order costs.

1.6.4 Stochastic Service Approach for Distribution Inventory Systems

In this subsection, stochastic service approach for distribution systems is reviewed. We mainly focus on the current studies on two-level distribution systems with one-warehouse and multiretailers. In such systems, if all unsatisfied demands are backlogged and will be satisfied later, there exists an important extra issue that determines an allocation policy, which decides how to allocate the on-hand inventory of the warehouse to the retailer's orders when these orders cannot be all satisfied on time. In addition, if all unsatisfied demands are not allowed backlogged, the problem becomes a problem with lost sales. Due to the increased complexity of distribution systems caused by models with allocation policies or lost sales, inventory management in distribution systems becomes more complex than that of serial and assembly systems. In the following, we review the current studies in these two categories separately. We also distinguish installation policies from echelon policies in the following review.

Inventory Policies for Distribution Systems with Allocation Policy

In the literature, one common allocation policy is the first-come first-served (FCFS), which fills customer orders according to their arrival time. The adoption of this allocation policy can simplify the analysis of the distribution systems but it is generally not optimal (Axsater, 2007). Because the priority of FCFS is always given to the earliest backlogged order, Chen and Samroengraja (2000) also referred to this policy as the past priority allocation (PPA) policy. In addition, they introduced another allocation policy, called the current priority allocation (CPA) policy. This policy is used in the situation when the warehouse is unable to satisfy a retailer order immediately but at the same time has inventories earmarked for the other retailers' orders. In each period the ware house considers only the designated retailer and uses its on-hand inventory to fill the current as well as the backlogged orders from that retailer. Howard and Marklund (2011) considered a state-dependent myopic policy instead of the FCFS, which allows the allocation decisions to be postponed at a later point in time and based on the state of the system.

With these allocation policies, inventory models with one-warehouse, multiretailers were received a great attention in the literature. The majority of the models assumes independent demands across retailers and use base stock policies or continuous-review (*R*, *Q*) policies. Studies on base stock policies for distribution systems are referred to Graves (1985), Axsater (1990), Caglar et al. (2000), Gallego et al. (2007) and Axsater (2007).

Most previous studies with installation (*R*, *Q*) policies are focus on exact and approximate cost evaluation of such systems, as in Svoronos and Zipkin (1988) and Axsater (1993). A general overview of such studies before 2003 is given by Axsater (2003). Forsberg (1996) and Axsater (1998) presented different cost evaluation methods for the system with unit demand and general distribution inter-arrival times for customer orders. Cheung and Hausman (2000) presented an exact method for evaluating the steady-state performance of a warehouse in a two-level distribution system. Cachon (2001) provided an exact evaluation method for average inventory, backorders and fill rates for a two-level distribution system. Chen et al. (2001) considered a two-level distribution system under periodic-review installation (*R*, *nQ*) policies, and showed that under a certain condition, the inventory position at each location are stationary, uniformly distributed and independent of the inventory positions at other locations. Kiesmuller et al. (2004) developed an approximate evaluation method for a two-level distribution system with compound renewal demand. Axsater et al. (2007) assumed direct customer demand also occurred at the warehouse, and presented three cost evaluation techniques for such as system. All the above mentioned studies utilize installation and decentralized control policies.

Alternatively, in a system where system-wide information is available, echelon (*R*, *Q*) policies can be used. Chen and Zheng (1997) and Axsater (1997) considered two-level distribution systems with Compound Poisson demand, but controlled by echelon (*R*, *Q*) policies. Because when all facilities (the warehouse and the retailers) apply echelon (*R*, *Q*) policies, the structure of the inventory model of the distribution systems becomes more complicated. In order to simplify the analysis, some researchers studied new models for the system where the warehouse and the retailers use different inventory policies. For instance, Howard and Marklund (2011) considered distribution systems where the warehouse applies echelon (*R*, *Q*) policies and the retailers use base stock policies; they developed an exact cost evaluation method.

On the other hand, only few papers studied policy parameter optimization of the distribution systems with installation/echelon (*R*, *Q*) policies. Early work on approximate optimization can be found in Deuermeyer and Schwarz (1981), Moinzadeh and Lee (1986) and Lee and Moinzadeh (1987). More recently, Axsater and Rosling (1993) demonstrated that installation stock and echelon (*R*, *Q*) policies may outperform each other in different situations for distribution systems. Axsater and Juntti (1996) analyzed two-level distribution systems with stochastic demand by simulation, the results showed that echelon (*R*, *Q*) policies seem to dominate installation (*r*, *Q*) policies for long warehouse lead times, while the opposite is true for short warehouse lead times. Axsater

(2003) used a normal approximation of demands both for the retailers and the warehouse, and presented a simple technique for approximate optimization for the reorder points of the system. Axsater (2005) presented a simple technique for determining the backorder cost to decide its order point so that the sums of the expected costs are minimized.

Inventory Policies for Distribution Systems with lost sales

Research in the second category assumes that unsatisfied demands at the retailers are lost sales. Technically this may mean either a demand is lost as lost sales or it is expedited (i.e., satisfied by using some external measures). For two-level distribution systems, it is well known that the time between two successive orders from each retailer has an Erlang distribution if no sales are lost at any retailer. However, for a distribution system with lost sales at the retailers, there is no simple form for the probability distribution of the time between two successive orders from each retailer (Hill et al., 2007). That's why lost sales models are generally more difficult to analyze than the corresponding backorder models. For this reason, even though researchers started studying lost sales inventory models around 1960s, there were not many applications that considered such models. As in the first category, base stock policies are often chosen as inventory policies for two-echelon distribution systems with lost sales, which can be referred to Federgruen (1993), Nahmias and Smith (1994), Andersson and Melchiors (2001) and Haji et al. (2009) for a comprehensive review of the relevant research work on lost sales models. On the other hand, installation/echelon (R, Q) policies are generally not optimal inventory policies for lost sales models, but they are widely used in practice. Cost evaluation of lost sales models is mainly focused on systems with continuous review installation (R, Q) policies and Poisson demand. Seifbarghi and Akbari (2006) developed an approximate cost function which is used in finding near-optimal reorder point of a two-level distribution system with the order sizes of all its stocks are given. Hill et al. (2007) also considered a two-level distribution system with the retailers using installation (R, Q) policies (with an exogenously given Q) and the warehouse applying an $(SQ, (S-1)Q)$ policy, with non-negative integer S. They developed procedures for determining the average total stock in the system and for finding the optimal policy of the system. Bendre and Thorstenson (2008) analyzed the long-run average fill rate, inventory and ordering frequency and developed simple approximations for two-level distribution systems with installation (*R*, *Q*) policies and Poisson demand. Their approximation results were compared with the results obtained from simulations. To the best of our knowledge, the only paper considering lost sales models with parameter optimization stock (*R*, *Q*) policies is Al-Rifai and Rosseti (2007). They considered a two-level distribution system with the retailers controlled by installation (*R*, *Q*) policies for non-repairable items and approximately solved the optimization problem by decomposing the system according to echelon and installation and presented an iterative heuristic optimization algorithm. Recently, Bijvank and Vis (2011) provided a general review of lost sales inventory theory, they presented a classification scheme for the inventory policies most often used in literature and practice.

1.6.5 Guaranteed Service Approach for Multi–Echelon Inventory Systems

In this subsection, guaranteed service approach for multi-echelon inventory systems is presented. All previous works on the approach adopt base stock policies for the control of multi-echelon inventory systems without fixed order costs.

The guaranteed service approach originated from the work of Kimball (1955), which was later reprinted in 1988 (Kimball, 1988). In that paper, Kimball studied a single stock with random but bounded demand, controlled by a base-stock policy. He proved that the bound of the demand during a given service time of the stock can be used to set its base-stock level. Simpson (1958) extended Kimball's model to a serial inventory system and proved that the optimal inventory policy of the system is an "all or nothing" policy. Based on this so-called extreme point property, Graves (1988) noted that the optimization problem considered by Simpson can be solved by using a dynamic programming algorithm. In subsequent years, this approach has been extended to other network structures. Extensions to assembly and distribution systems, spanning trees or even general acyclic network structures can be found in Inderfurth (1991), Inderfurth and Minner (1998), Graves and Willems (1996, 2000), Minner (2000), Humair and Willems (2006), and Humair and Willems (2011).

Basically, all of the afore-mentioned contributions make use of dynamic programming as optimization technique. Minner (2001) studied the placement of strategic safety stocks in reverse supply chains under the GSA. Graves and Willems (2005) considered the safety stock optimization when a supply chain is configured for new products. For general acyclic networks, Lesnaia (2004) showed that the optimization problem is NP-hard, Humair and Willems (2011) imbed the dynamic program developed for spanning trees into an overall branch-and-bound algorithm. Minner (2000) presented several heuristic approaches for this network type. Humair and Willems (2006) studied the optimization of strategic safety stock placement in supply chains under with clusters of commonality. Magnanti et al. (2006) approximated the concave objective function with piecewise linear functions and make use of powerful Linear Programming solves.

Over the last two decades, the guaranteed service approach has been extended in several ways. Whereas the original guaranteed service model assumes a common re view period at all echelons, Bossert and Willems (2007) allow for an arbitrary, integer review period at echelon. Three different inventory control policies are analyzed, i.e., the constant base stock policy, constant base stock policy and adaptive base stock policy, and a solution to the inventory optimization problem is obtained by a modified version of the dynamic programming procedure of Graves and Willems (2000).

Jung et al. (2008) studied integrated safety stock management of multi-echelon supply chains under production capacity constraints and the GSA. Recently, Graves and Willems (2008) extended their previous work (1996, 2000) to supply chains with non-stationary demand, and Schoenmey and Graves (2009) extended the work to supply chains with evolving demand forecasts.

1.6.6 Comparison of Stochastic–Service Approach and Guaranteed–Service Approach

Only few papers in the literature can be found that compare the two approaches. One such comparison was presented in Graves and Willems (2003). They applied both approaches to an assembly system and a spanning tree network and found that the guaranteed service model outperforms the stochastic service model. Klosterhalfen and Minner (2010) provided a comparison of the two approaches on two-level distribution systems and showed that the superiority of any of the two approaches depends on their specific parameter settings and cannot be established in general. Moreover, they presented a method to derive appropriate internal service levels, which are used to define the operating flexibility costs in the guaranteed service model, Minner et al. (2003) gave some insights regarding the appropriate use of operating flexibility.

1.7 The Contributions of the Thesis

This thesis is motivated by the work of Graves and Willems (1996, 2000), they considered a general multi-echelon inventory system without fixed order costs and operating a base stock policy. In their work, they used the standard guaranteed service approach (GSA) to optimize the inventory policies and presented efficient dynamic programming algorithms for the optimization. We extend the GSA to multi-echelon inventory systems with fixed order costs at each stock (Li and Chen, 2011). Three inventory systems, serial, assembly and distribution systems, are successively in our study. We use the guaranteed service approach (GSA) to obtain the optimal (R, Q) inventory policies of the systems. In addition, we extend the standard GSA by considering also the operating flexibility costs for using extraordinary measures to fill excessive demand. In summary, this thesis brings the following four main contributions.

1) We extend the GSA to multi-echelon inventory systems with fixed order costs at each stock. Since all previous works on the GSA only deal with inventory systems without fixed order costs, this thesis is the first attempt to attack multi-echelon inventory systems with fixed order costs in the framework of the GSA (Li and Chen, 2013).

2) One open issue in the standard GSA is the consideration of the effect of the operating flexibility measures on the material flow and the total cost of a multi-echelon inventory system. We have addressed this issue by considering the effect on the material flow and including explicitly the operating flexibility costs in our inventory policy opti-

mization models. For each type of multi-echelon inventory systems considered, we establish a mathematical model for its inventory policy optimization problem with the objective function consisting of fixed order costs, on-hand inventory holding costs and operating flexibility costs. This model extends the standard GSA model.

3) The consideration of the operating flexibility effect makes the extended GSA model more complicated than the standard GSA model with an objective function depending on two service levels (α-service level and β-service level) of the system considered. We propose an iterative procedure to solve the model based on the estimation of β-service level and the calculation if its real value when the optimal inventory policy of the system is given.

4) The efficiency of the iterative procedure relies on the efficient resolution of the two sub-problems (sub-models) of the extended GSA model: One is to determine the optimal order size Q of each stock and the other is to determine the optimal reorder point R of each stock. For the first sub-problem, which is referred to as Q-problem, we develop an efficient dynamic programming (DP) algorithm. The second sub-problem, which is referred to as R-problem, is efficiently solved by using another DP algorithm we adopt from the literature.

5) For the Q-problem, we find two important properties to reduce the state space of its decision variables, this makes our DP algorithm for the problem much more efficient than a DP algorithm in the literature.

6) For the two-level distribution system we study, five different types of integer-ratio constraints that link the order size of the warehouse to the order sizes of the retailers are considered. For each type, we develop an efficient algorithm to solve the Q-problem. We compare these constraints in term of their cost-effectiveness, i.e., the cost of the system imposed by each type of integer-ratio constraints. In the literature, no such comparison was made.

7) All the algorithms developed in the thesis are evaluated and compared with numerical experiments on randomly instances. In addition, we conduct sensitivity analysis of the computation time of some algorithms with respect to the parameters of the multi-echelon inventory system considered in order to evaluate the impacts of the parame-

ters on the performance of the algorithms we have developed.

1.8 Conclusion

Guaranteed service approach (GSA) has attracted a lot of attention both in academic community and industrial practitioners in recent years because if its simplicity and generality. Previously, this approach was only used for optimal placement of safety stocks in multi-echelon inventory systems without fixed order costs. We apply this approach to inventory policy optimization of multi-echelon inventory systems with fixed order costs and extend the approach by considering operating flexibility costs. In Chapter 2, we will introduce some basic notions for multi-echelon inventory management and the guaranteed service approach and discuss its possible extension. In Chapter 3, Chapter 4, Chapter 5, we will present a series of mathematical models and solution approaches for inventory policy optimization of serial, assembly and two-level distribution systems. Conclusions and perspectives will be given in Chapter 6.

Chapter 2
Preliminaries

The goal of this chapter is to provide the reader with the basic terminology of multi-echelon inventory control theory as well as an understanding of an elementary inventory control model that forms the basis of the upcoming chapters. Section 2.1 outlines fundamentals that are required for a thorough understanding of the thesis. In Section 2.2, the basic inventory control terminology is introduced followed by a description of the batch ordering (R, Q) inventory policy and several performance measures for the evaluation of such policy. A major issue to be addressed in this thesis is how to use the guaranteed-service approach (GSA) to model the inventory control of different types of inventory systems. For this reason, we also describe the standard GSA in Section 2.3 and give some discussions about the operating flexibility and batch ordering (R, Q) policies under the framework of the GSA respectively in Section 2.4 and Section 2.5.

2.1 Fundamentals

2.1.1 Network Structures

If an inventory system involves multiple stocks, which are linked with each other through supply-demand relationships, it is called a multi-echelon inventory system. The system forms a supply network, which can be represented by a directed graph in which the nodes represent the stocks and the arcs represent the supply-demand relationships

(Zipkin, 2000). Each node or stock in the network corresponds to a processing stage or a stocking location in the system. If a node is connected to several upstream nodes, then the node corresponds to an assembly stock that requires inputs (components) from each of the upstream nodes (stocks). All nodes (stocks) in the network are locations for holding work-in-processing or final product inventories. We deal with multi-echelon inventory systems with different types of supply networks. For defining the basic network structures of multi-echelon inventory systems, we first introduce the following system parameters.

N = the number of nodes (stocks) in a system,

$s(i)$ = the set of the immediate successor of stock i, $i=1, \cdots, N$,

$SUC(i)$ = the set consisting of stock i and all its successors, $i=1, \cdots, N$,

$P(i)$ = the set of the immediate predecessors of stock i, $i=1, \cdots, N$,

$PRE(i)$ = the set consisting of stock i and all its predecessors, $i=1, \cdots, N$.

Serial Systems

A serial systemhas the simplest structure with links multiple stocks in a serial way. Such a system consists of multiple stocks where each stock supplies only one successor stock and each stock replenishes its inventory from only one predecessor stock. In addition, the most upstream stock is supplied by an external supplier and the most downstream stock faces external customer demand for a finished product. In a serial system, each stock has a single direct predecessor and successor. For the upcoming exposition it is useful to assign a level code to each stock (See Figure 2.1). Whereas this is less relevant in the serial system case, since there is only one stock at each level, it is of great importance for the description of other more complex systems. A practical example of this type of inventory system can be found in the mechanical industry, for instance, where a metal material passes through several processing operations such as cutting, drilling, grinding before it becomes a final product. From an academic point of view the

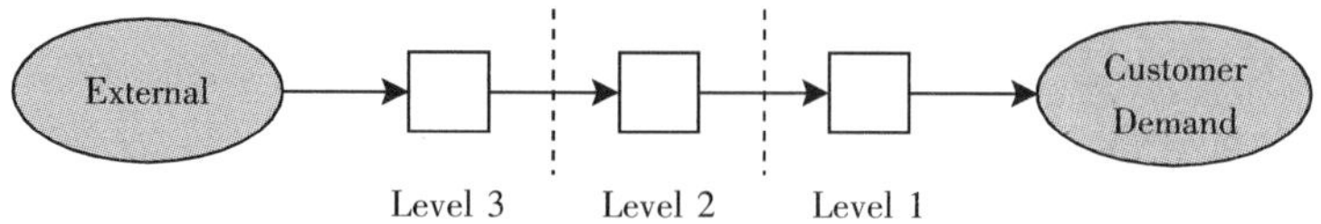

Figure 2.1　A serial inventory system

analysis of this simple system structure is a good starting point for investigating more complex ones.

Assembly Systems

In an assembly system a single finished product is assembled from several subassemblies. These subassemblies, in turn, may be assembled from several components or raw materials. Hence, an assembly system is characterized by the feature that each stock has at most one direct successor, but may have more than one direct predecessor. As in a serial system, all stocks on the most upstream level in an assembly system receive items from external suppliers and the stock on the most downstream level fills external customer demand (See Figure 2.2).

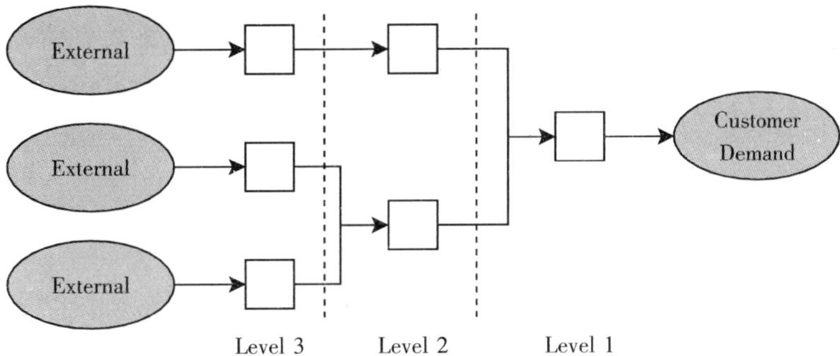

Figure 2.2 An assembly inventory system

Distribution Systems

Similar to a serial system, a distribution system has a single most upstream stock that receives external supply. However, now each stock in the system may supply multiple downstream stocks except for the most downstream stocks which fill external customer demands. The stocks in such a system can be interpreted as warehouses, e.g., a central warehouse supplies regional warehouses which, in turn, supply retail outlets (See Figure 2.3). In terms of production network, one can think of a raw material that is split (separated) and specialized into several products when it is moved through the system as in a refinery. The distinguishing feature of a distribution network is that each stock has only one direct predecessor, but can have multiple direct successors.

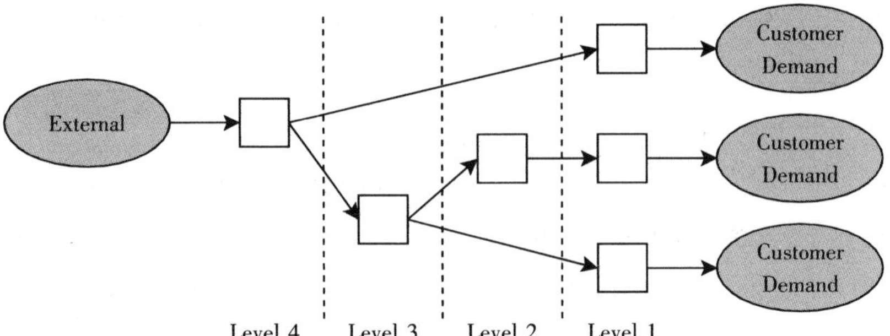

Figure 2.3 A distribution inventory system

In addition, a prototype network structure for most studies on distribution systems is a two-level distribution system whereby a central warehouse supplies a product to a group of retailers. This structure can be depicted as Figure 2.4.

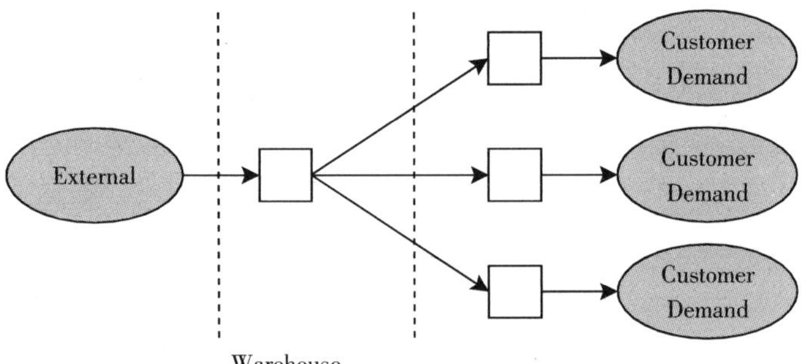

Figure 2.4 A two-level distribution system

2.1.2 Demand Processes

For industrial companies, except for uncertainties they face on the supply side resulting from possible raw material shortage or machine break downs, a major difficulty arises on the demand side, because future customer orders cannot be predicted exactly (Simchi-Levi et al., 2008).

In the literature, the most commonly used demand distribution in various inventory models may be the Poisson distribution in discrete case and the normal distribution in continuous case (Zipkin, 2000).

Poisson Distribution

The Poisson distribution is easy to specify, because it has only one parameter λ.

Further, in many situations the model is shown to be fairly accurate. Finally, its mathematical simplicity facilitates analytical calculations. The probability mass function is defined as

$$f(x) = \begin{cases} \dfrac{e^{-\lambda}\lambda^{x}}{x!}, & x = 0, 1, \cdots \\ 0, & otherwise \end{cases}$$

Since the ordered items are not received immediately, but after a lead time, during which further demands need to be satisfied, the demand distribution over the lead-time is relevant for inventory control. For a deterministic lead time L, the distribution is the L-fold convolution of the single period demand random variable, if the demand process is assumed to be stationary and the single period demands are identically and independently distributed (*i.i.d.*). Since the sum of i=1, 2, $\cdots$, m independent Poisson random variables with parameters λ_i is Poisson distributed with parameter $\lambda = \sum_{i=1}^{m} \lambda_i$. For the lead-time demand random variable it follows that, if period demands are identically and independently distributed according to a Poisson distribution with parameter λ_1, the lead-time random variable for a deterministic lead-time of L periods has a Poisson distribution with parameter $L \cdot \lambda_1$.

Normal Distribution

The normal distribution is characterized by two parameters, the demand expectation μ and standard deviation σ. The probability density function is given as

$$f(x) = \frac{1}{\sigma \cdot \sqrt{2\pi}} \cdot e^{-\frac{(x-\pi)^2}{2\sigma^2}}$$

Consequently, in case the single period demand has a normal distribution, the lead-time demand is also normally distributed with an expected value of μL and standard deviation $\sigma \cdot \sqrt{L}$. For the lead-time demand computation in case of stochastic lead times see, e.g., Tijms and Groenevelt (1984) and Eppen and Martin (1988).

2.2 Inventory Control

For an inventory system, its inventory control is to supervise the supply, the storage, and the accessibility of items in the system in order to ensure an adequate supply without excessive oversupply. The control requires an accounting procedure that determines the inventory system's state based on which the inventory replenishment decision of the system is made. Therefore, we first introduce basic notions of the inventory accounting in Section 2.2.1. These notions will be used in the description of the inventory policy considered in this thesis, i.e., batch ordering (R, Q) policy. The description of batch ordering (R, Q) policy and some performance measures for inventory control will be presented in Section 2.2.2 and Section 2.2.3, respectively.

2.2.1 Inventory Accounting

In multi-echelon inventory system setting, the following terms are used for conceptually classifying different inventories.

On-hand Inventory, *I*

This term describes the inventory quantity that is physically on the shelf and is available for directly satisfying customer demand. The on-hand inventory can never be negative. In connection with a time index t, $I(t)$ denotes the on-hand inventory at time t.

Backorders, *BO*

In case demand in a period exceeds the available inventory, a shortage occurs. Provided that customers are willing to wait for their products, the backorder represent the quantity of stocks that have already been requested, but are still to be delivered (backorder case). If customers do not wait, the shortage quantity is lost (lost-sales case). Similarly, $BO(t)$ refers to the backorders at time t.

Outstanding Orders, *OO*

The outstanding order denotes as the quantity of stocks, for which an order has already been placed, but has not yet been received. Together with the time index t, $OO(t)$

specifies the outstanding orders at time t, before any of these items arrive in stock at a location.

Inventory Level, *IL*

Inventory level is the net inventory quantity of a location, which is defined as the difference between the on-hand inventory and the backorders. Obviously, it can become negative. For a given time t, the inventory level at time t can be described as

$$IL(t) = I(t) - BO(t)$$

Inventory Position, *IP*

The inventory position comprises of the relevant information to trigger an order, because it also includes the inventory on order. The inventory position at a stock equals to its on-hand inventory minus all backorders of the stock locations at the lowest level, i.e., level 1. The inventory position at time t can be described as

$$IP(t) = I(t) + OO(t) - BO(t)$$

Echelon on–hand Inventory, I^e

This term describes the on-hand inventory of the location itself plus the physical inventories of all its downstream locations and in-transit physical inventory between these locations. $I^e(t)$ denotes the echelon on-hand inventory at time t.

Echelon Inventory Level, ILe

Echelon inventory level of a stock equals echelon on-hand inventory of the location minus all backorders of the stock locations at the lowest level, i.e., level 1. If a time index t is introduced, $IL^e(t)$ is the echelon inventory level at time t.

Echelon Inventory Position, IP^e

Echelon inventory position of a location equals outstanding orders of the location plus echelon on-hand inventory of the location minus all backorders of the stock locations at the lowest level, i.e., level 1. Echelon inventory position at time t ($IP^e(t)$) is calculated as follows:

$$IP^e(t) = I^e(t) + OO(t) - BO(t)$$

2.2.2 Batch Ordering (*R*, *Q*) Policy

An inventory control policy or system manages the inventory level of a stock by providing answers to the following three questions (Silver et al., 1998).

- How often should the inventory status be determined?
- When should a replenishment order be placed?
- How many units should the replenishment order orders?

In this thesis, we use (R, Q) policy as an inventory policy to control the inventories of the three different types of systems studied (serial, assembly and distribution systems). The motivation of choosing such a policy has been presented in the introduction. This policy can be used in a centralized or decentralized way, leading to echelon or installation (R, Q) policy. The installation (r, Q) policy is completely decentralized in the sense that ordering decision at each stock is exclusively based on its own inventory position. Such policy has the advantage that it does not require any information about the inventory situation at other stocks. However, the cost effectiveness of an installation (r, Q) policy is limited by the lack of information about the entire system. One way to take such information into account is to make order decisions based on the echelon inventory position of each stock instead of its installation inventory position. The echelon (R, Q) policy works exactly as an installation (r, Q) policy except that order decision at each stock is determined by its echelon inventory position. If a stock is controlled by an echelon (R, Q) policy, whenever its echelon inventory position is at or below the reorder point R, an order of Q units will be placed, where Q is the order size of the stock.

Axsater and Rosling (1993) compared the two types of inventory policies, and drew some important conclusions for serial and assembly systems. They first demonstrated that the two policies can be transformed each other under mild conditions. On the one hand, for any stock i in a system with N stocks, an installation (r_i, Q_i) policy can always be replaced by an equivalent echelon (R_i, Q_i) policy with the following relationship:

$$R_1 = r_1 \text{ and } R_i = R_{s(i)} + Q_{s(i)} + r_i \text{ for } i = 2, \cdots, N \tag{2-1}$$

On the other hand, an echelon (R_i, Q_i) policy can also be replaced by an equivalent installation (r_i, Q_i) policy (with the same relationship (2-1)) if the following initial condition (2-2) holds:

$$IP^e_i(0) - R_i = IP^e_{s(i)}(0) - R_{s(i)} + (k_i - 1)Q_{s(i)} \tag{2-2}$$

where $IP_i^e(0)$ is the initial echelon inventory position at stock i and k_i is a positive integer.

Moreover, Axsater and Rosling showed that echelon (R, Q) policy, in general, superior to installation (r, Q) policy for serial and assembly systems However, for general distribution systems, it is not clear under what conditions, one policy dominates the other. Axsater and Juntti (1996) analyzed a two-level distribution system by simulation studies, and demonstrated that echelon (R, Q) policies seem to dominate installation (r, Q) policies for systems with a long warehouse lead time, whereas the opposite domination is true for systems with a short warehouse leadtime, although the relative cost difference between the two types of policies is within 5%.

2.2.3 Performance Measures for Inventory Control

To optimize an inventory control system, some performance measures should be defined to evaluate its effectiveness. The performance of an inventory control system can be measured either in terms of cost or service. Under *a cost performance measure*, the objective is to find control parameters of the system that minimize its total cost which may include ordering costs, inventory holding costs, and stockout penalty/backorder costs. However, in many practical situations backorder costs are generally hard to quantify. To overcome this difficulty, *a service performance measuremay* be introduced under which the objective of the inventory control system is to achieve a predefined service level with minimal system costs. A detailed description of these cost and service measures are given in the following paragraphs.

2.2.3.1 Cost Performance Measures

For an inventory system, the major costs that will determine the structure and optimal parameters of its inventory policy mainly arise from the three costs related to ordering, inventory holding and shortage, respectively. By setting all these costs, the cost performance measure can be defined.

Fixed Order Costs, c

The fixed order cost only occurs when each order is placed. In practice, it may include the paper work cost for preparing the order and the costs for the inspection, packaging and delivery (transportation) of the order. Let c_i define a fixed order cost for placing an order by stock i to its supplier.

Inventory Holding Cost, *h*

This term is related directly to the maintenance cost of physical inventories. We define h^e or h as the echelon-or installation-inventory holding cost per unit of product per time unit. For stock i, note that the two types of holding costs can be transformed each other with the following relationship

$$h_i^e = h_i - \sum_{j \in P(i)} h_j \text{ and } h_{N+1} = 0$$

Backorder Costs, *b*

In SSA model, this cost incurred by a business when it is unable to fill an order and will be satisfied later. A backorder cost can be discrete, as in the cost to replace a specific piece of inventory, or intangible, such as the effects of poor customer service. Backorder costs are usually computed and displayed on a per-unit basis.

Flexibility Cost, *p*

Under the GSA model, it is assumed that, if lead time demand exceeds a prespecified level (maximum reasonable lead time demand level), additional countermeasures like overtime or expediting can be used to fill excessive demand beyond the level. This "operating flexibility" ensures the timely delivery of ordered items to its downstream stocks at a cost. Therefore, we define p as the cost of using such "operating flexibility" to fulfill each unit of excessive demand. In addition, since any stock except for the stock at the lowest level, i.e., level 1, never runs out of stock, the flexibility cost is only considered at stocks at level 1.

2.2.3.2 Service Performance Measures

The service performance measure of an inventory system can be defined in different ways. Since some customers may be interested in the percentage of the orders satisfied on-time among all orders and the others may be interested in the percentage of the demand satisfied on-time among the total demand, two different service levels, α-and β-service levels, are usually used to measure the service performance of an inventory system, which are defined in detail in the following.

α–service Level

In situations where only the occurrence of a stockout is important and not the quantity and duration of the shortage, the α-service level should be used. This service level is defined as the " probability of satisfying demand in an arbitrary period" (Klemm, 1973).

Under the GSA model, the safety stock is strongly related to the α-service level of the stock. In this thesis, we set a predefined α-service level as an input parameter, by specifying this service level to customer, each stock indicates implicitly its preference for what range of its demand is covered by the stock itself and what range is fulfilled by using extraordinary measures.

β–fill Rate

The β-fill rate is defined as the fraction of customer demand satisfied directly from stock. This service level can be written using the "expected units shortage" as follows:

$$\beta = 1 - \frac{\text{expected units shortage}}{\text{expected total demand}}$$

Different from α-service level, which represents the target probability of the extraordinary measures, the β-fill rate represents the quantity level need to be made available. In GSA model, it is assumed a predefined α-service level to express the maximum reasonable lead time demand level, so the optimization model and algorithm are described for the α-service level case only. Because of using (R, Q) policy, this thesis not only decide when should a replenishment order be placed (R), but also decide how large should the replenishment order be (Q). Therefore, β-fill rate is also a factor, need to consider in this thesis, we will give more detailed analysis of β-fill rate in the latter chapter.

2.3 Guaranteed Service Approach

The guaranteed service approach (GSA) was recently emerged as an alterative ap proach for optimally setting safety stocks in a supply chain. GSA provides inventory models different from those of SSA. In a GSA model, an inventory system is regarded as being more flexible than in the corresponding SSA model. The GSA assumes that further countermeasures besides safety stock exist to cope with demand variability. These additional measures are summarized by the term "operating flexibility" and comprise of measures such as overtime and expediting. With this operating flexibility, safety stock is only used to cover demand variability up to a certain level, the so-called maximum reasonable lead time demand level (Graves, 1998). If real lead time demand exceeds this level, the inventory system resorts to the operating flexibility in order to satisfy the whole demand on time. With this combination of safety stock and operating flexibility there will be no stochastic delay in demand fulfillment. Thus, each stock can always guarantee 100% on-time service to its customers (direct downstream stocks) with a promised service time. Here, the service time of a stock is the time from the placement of an order by a direct downstream stock to the receipt of the order by the downstream stock. In order to understand the basic ideas of the GSA, we briefly introduce the work of Graves and Willems (2000). In their work, a general multi-echelon inventory system with periodic review and normal distribution demand process is considered under the GSA. Only inventory holding costs are considered in the system, and each stock i (i=1, 2, $\cdots$, N) uses a base stock policy with base stock level BL_i to control its inventory. The base stock level of each stock is determined according to its maximum reasonable lead time demand. Neither operating flexibility costs nor the effects of the operating flexibil- ity on the material flows of the system are considered.

The demand in the system has two types, external demand and internal demand. The external demand is the demand of final customer, which occurs only at the stocks in the lowest echelon. Let us denote the set of external demand nodes (stocks) by F. For each stock i in F, let $d_i(t)$ denote its external demand at time (period) t, which comes from a stationary process. Let $d_i[t_1, t_2)$ denote the total external demand of the stock from time t_1 to time t_2 without including time t_2 for any $t_1 \leqslant t_2$. Any other stock $j \notin F$ has only internal demand generated from its successor stocks, the internal demand of stock j at time t, $d_j(t)$, can be calculated according to the orders placed by its immediate successor stocks.

For each stock i in F with normally distributed demand of mean μ_i and standard deviation σ_i, its maximum reasonable lead time demand level over lead time τ is defined as:

$$D_i(\tau_i) = \tau_i \cdot \mu + k_i \sigma \sqrt{\tau_i}, \quad i \in F \tag{2-3}$$

where k_i is a coefficient reflecting the percentage of time that the safety stock of stock i covers its demand variation. The choice of k_i indicates how frequently the manager of the stock is willing to resort to operating flexibility to cover demand variability.

For any other stock j ($j \notin F$), Graves and Willems (2000) also define its lead time demand bound by combining the lead time demand bounds of its downstream stocks while considering risk pooling effects.

In the GSA inventory model proposed by Graves and Willems (2000), there exist three types of service times, outbound service time (S), inbound service time (SI) and production time (T).

Outbound Service Times Under the GSA, each stock i guarantees a given service time S_i to its direct downstream stocks. This means that the demand arriving at stock i at time t must be filled at $t+S_i$.

For each stock i facing customer demand, i.e., $i \in F$, an upper bound simay be imposed on its outbound service time, i.e., $S_i \leqslant s_i$, where s_i is the maximum outbound service time for the stock. The maximum outbound service time is a parameter specified by the end customer. For example, if the end customer wants him/her to be served immediately, stock$i$ has to set s_i=0.

Inbound Service Times For each stock i, its inbound service time SI_i is defined as the time for stock i to get all of its inputs (ordered materials) from its direct upstream stocks ($P(i)$) and to commence production. We require that $SI_i \geqslant \max\{S_j \mid j \in P(i)\}$, since stock i cannot start production until all required inputs (materials) have been received.

Production Times Under the GSA, each stock i is assumed to have a deterministic production time T_i, which is the production lead time, given that all necessary components are available. T_i may be zero if stock i does not correspond to a production stage.

For the three types of service times, the production times are input parameters of a GSA model, whereas the outbound and inbound service times are decision variables of the model.

Net Lead Time

Consider an order process. At time t, stock i observes demand $d_i(t)$ from its immediate downstream stock(s) and starts replenishing inventory for the demand. It places an order with quantity $d_i(t)$ to the upstream stocks and fills the demand with this order at the time $t+SI_i+T_i$. According to the GSA, stock i guarantees to satisfy the demand at the time $t+S_i$. This implies that if $t+S_i \geqslant t+SI_i+T_i$, stock i can always satisfy the demand on time. Otherwise if $t+S_i < t+SI_i+T_i$, stock i has to store a certain amount of inventory to satisfy the demand occurred between time $t+S_i$ and time $t+SI_i+T_i$, the length $SI_i+T_i-S_i$ of the time interval $[t+S_i,\ t+SI_i+T_i]$ is thus called the net lead time of stock i.

The net lead times play an important role in the GSA, which can also be regarded as the decision variables in a GSA model. Since the maximum reasonable lead time demand level of each stock is usually defined as a function of its net lead time, it will be determined by an optimal solution of the model.

From the above analysis, for each stock i, if $t+S_i<t+SI_i+T_i$, stock i has to hold a safety stock to cover the demand over the time interval $(t+S_i,t+SI_i+T_i]$. Therefore, the demand has to be covered from the inventory or by subtracting the demand from the base stock level BL_i. Then, the on-hand inventory at each stock i (i=1, 2, ⋯, N) can be formulated as

$$I_i(t) = BL_i - d_i(t + S_i,\ t + SI_i + T_i,] \tag{2-4}$$

To provide 100% service level, $I_i(t)$ must be nonnegative. In order to satisfy this requirement, Grave and Willems (2000) set the base stock level BL_i to the maximum reasonable lead time demand level of stock i over its net lead time $SI_i + T_i - S_i$, namely $BL_i = D_i(SI_i + T_i - S_i)$. Hence, the expected on-hand inventory at stock i is

$$D_i(SI_i + T_i - S_i) - (SI_i + T_i - S_i)\mu_i \tag{2-5}$$

Consequently, instead of searching for the optimal base stock levels for the inventory system considered, the GSA model proposed by Graves and Willems (2000) attempts to find the optimal outbound and inbound service times or optimal net lead times for all stocks. This model can be formulated as follows:

$$\text{Min: } \sum_{i=1}^{N} h_i\{ D_i(SI_i+T_i-S_i)-(SI_i+T_i-S_i)\mu_i \}$$

Subject to:

$SI_i + T_i - S_i \geqslant 0$ for $i=1, 2, \cdots, N$

$SI_i - S_j \geqslant 0$, for $j \in P(i)$ and $i=1, 2, \cdots, N$

$S_i \leqslant s_i$ for $i \in F$

S_i, $SI_i \geqslant 0$ and integer for $i=1, 2, \cdots, N$

where h_i is unit inventory holding cost of stock i and P (i).

The objective of the model is to minimize the total inventory holding cost of the multi-echelon inventory system. The constraints ensure that the net lead time of each stock is nonnegative, each stock cannot start production until all required inputs (materials) have been received, and an upper bound is imposed on the outbound service time of each end stock (each stock facing customer demand). The decision variables are outbound service time (S_i) and inbound service time (SI_i) of each stock i. For this model, Graves and Willems (2000) developed an efficient dynamic programming algorithm to solve it when the network structure of the system is a spanning tree.

If the considered system is a serial inventory system and the outbound service time for the external customer is zero ($s_i=0$ for any $i \in F$), Simpson (1958) proved that there exist an "all or nothing" optimal solution for the model, such that each stock either has no safety stock ($S_i=0$) or has sufficient safety stock ($S_i=\max\{S_j, j \in P(i)\}+T_i$).

2.4 Operating Flexibility and GSA

The GSA optimization model presented in Sections 2.3 considers neither operating flexibility costs (i.e., the costs of using extraordinary measures to fill excessive demand) nor the effects of operating flexibility on the material flows of an inventory system. In order to incorporate operating flexibility costs in a GSA model, we should first know what kind of operating flexibility measures can be used in reality. There are several possibilities for using operating flexibility to achieve a guaranteed service, such as overtime, expediting or supplies from external/outside suppliers. By resorting to these oper ating flexibility measures, supply shortage is avoided since they can ensure that materials, which would not be available under normal conditions, are made available on time.

Minner (2000) and Klosterhalfen and Minner (2010) considered operating flexibility costs in their comparison of the GSA with the SSA. They assumed that the operating flexibility measure used is expediting. With this operating flexibility option, to appropriately incorporate operating flexibility costs into a GSA model requires the following information:

- The quantity of items that are expedited
- The timespan for which the expediting takes place.

In order to estimate the expediting timespan, Klosterhalfen and Minner (2010) conducted a simulation study on a two-level distribution system with one warehouse and two retailers. In their study, they tested various parameters settings, such as α-service level, the production time at the warehouse and coefficients of variation of customer demands. Specifically, the following parameter settings are considered for the system:

- the α-service level varies between 16.67% and 95%,
- the production time at the warehouse (T_0) is set to 2 or 6,
- the coefficient of variation of the customer demand (cv) is set to 0.2 or 0.4.

Each instance in the simulation study was randomly generated with the above parameter settings. Their experimental results on all randomly generated instances demonstrate that on average 98.53% of the items whose delivery is speeded up by using the operating flexibility measure are expedited by one period only. This means that the speeded-up items would have arrived in the second period. More specifically, all items are expedited by only one period when T_0 is 2, irrespective of the α-service level. In case of a longer T_0, i.e., T_0=6, only for the instances with low α-service level (16.67% or 33.33%) and large coefficient of variation, i.e., cv=0.4, some items may be expedited by two periods or three periods in very rare situations. Such rare situations occur only for at most 2% of all instances tested.

From this observation, instead of specifying operating flexibility costs depending on the expediting duration, we can approximately define the operating flexibility costs irrespective of the duration. This approximation is acceptable since on average 98.53% of the items expedited are expedited by one period only.

The difficulty of specifying operating flexibility costs is comparable to the specification of the backorder costs in an SSA inventory model. As we know, in most cases it is quite difficult to directly evaluate backorder costs. As an alternative, backorder costs are usually specified through a service level to customer. That is, for a single stock, if its expected service level is α and its inventory holding cost per unit of product per unit of time is h, then unit back order cost of the stock can be defined as $p/(h+p)=\alpha$. Greater the expected service level of the stock, bigger its unit backorder cost. Similarly, for the GSA, the unit operating flexibility cost of a stock, denoted also by p, can be defined according to its expected service level to customer.

The unit operating flexibility cost, p, must be larger than the unit inventory holding cost, h. Otherwise, it would be advisable to hold no stock at each stock by relying only on the operating flexibility option.

In this thesis, we will consider both operating flexibility costs and the effects of operating flexibility on the material flows of a multi-echelon inventory system. More detailed discussion about both of them will be given in the latter chapters.

2.5 Batch Ordering (*R, Q*) Policy and GSA

As we have mentioned, all previous works on the GSA only deal with inventory systems without fixed order costs, however, in practice, fixed order costs exist for most inventory systems when economics of scale in production and/or in distribution exist. In this thesis, we attempt to use the GSA to model and solve inventory policy optimization problem of multi-echelon inventory systems with fixed order costs. Because of the existence of fixed order costs at each stock in such systems, we choose batch ordering (*R, Q*) policies as inventory policies of the systems.

Because echelon (R, Q) policies are much easier to be handled than installation (r, Q) policies under the GSA framework, in this thesis we choose echelon (R, Q) policy as the inventory policy for a multi-echelon inventory system with order costs at each stock. In addition, for serial and assembly systems, we confine ourselves to echelon (R, Q) policy that can be transformed into equivalent installation (r, Q) policy with equation (2-1) when condition (2-2) holds, because with this transformation the echelon (R, Q) policy can be easily implemented in practice.

As most studies in the literature, we restrict our attention to echelon (R, Q) policies with integer-ratio relationships. For serial and assembly systems, integer-ratio constraints mean that the order size of each stock is a positive integer multiple of its immediate successor. For two-level distribution systems, such integer-ratio constraints also exist but have different forms. More detailed discussion about integer-ratio constraints in different systems will be given in latter chapters.

Echelon (R, Q) policies with integer-ratio constraints have been proved to be cost-effective for systems like serial and assembly systems. In practice, the coordination of order sizes among different stocks in a multi-echelon inventory system can facilitate quantity coordination among these stocks and can simplify packaging, transportation and stock count in the system.

For serial systems, under the GSA and the integer-ratio assumption, we have $r_i \geqslant -Q_{i-1}$. Because if $r_i \leqslant -Q_{i-1}-1$, then $r_i+Q_{i-1} \leqslant -1$. This implies that stocki will not place any replenishment order at its negative but reachable inventory position $IP_i=r_i+Q_{i-1}$, which is contradictory with the guaranteed service assumption of the GSA, because at the state, stock i is in shortage. Moreover, for any $r_i \in [-Q_{i-1}, -2]$, we can replace it by $r'_i=-1$ since this replacement will not change the timing of all replenishment orders of stock i, because: 1) $IP_i \leqslant r_i$ implies $IP_i \leqslant r'_i$, 2) if $IP_i \leqslant r'_i < 0$, from $IP_i \in \{r_i, r_i+Q_{i-1}, \cdots, r_i+m_{i-1}Q_{i-1}\}$ and $r_i+Q_{i-1} \geqslant 0$, we have $IP_i=r_i \leqslant r_i$. Similar results hold for assembly systems. So for these two types of systems, we assume $r_i \geqslant -1$ in the rest of this thesis.

In the next chapter, we will extend the standard GSA to optimize (R, Q) policies for serial systems with fixed order costs at each stock. The extended GSA will explicitly consider operating flexibility costs and the effects of operating flexibility on the material flows of the systems.

Chapter 3
Optimization of (*R*, *Q*) Policies for Serial Systems

After the description of multi-echelon inventory systems and the guaranteed service approach (GSA) in the last chapter, this chapter deals with the optimization of (*R*, *Q*) policies for serial inventory systems with Poisson demand under the GSA. Except for considering inventory holding costs as in standard GSA model, we also consider the fixed order costs and operating flexibility costs. Following a description of the main assumptions and notations in Section 3.1, a mathematical model for the optimization problem is formulated in Section 3.2. This model can be solved by an iterative procedure based on two dynamic programming (DP) algorithms. One DP algorithm is used to solve the order size decision sub-problem, and the other is used to solve the reorder point decision sub-problem of the model. The two algorithms will be described in detail in Section 3.3 and Section 3.4, respectively. The iterative procedure will be presented in Section 3.5. Numerical experiments for evaluating the performances of the procedure and the two DP algorithms will be reported in Section 3.6.

3.1 Problem Description

3.1.1 Serial System Studied

A continuous review serial inventory system with N (N>2) stocks is considered, where stock N orders from an external supplier with unlimited stock, stock N-1 orders from stock N, stock N-2 orders from stock N-1, and so on. Finally, at the lowest stock, stock 1, customer demand occurs. A stage may represent a production process, in which raw material is transformed into a product, or a distribution process, in which a product is moved from one location to another location. A serial inventory system with N stocks can be depicted as in Figure 3.1. No capacity constraints exist at any of the stocks. All stocks in the system operate echelon (R, Q) inventory policies. The customer demand is assumed to be stationary and independent Poisson distribution with the average demand rate λ.

We attempt to use the guaranteed service approach (GSA) to derive the optimal (R, Q) policy for the system, so as to minimize the total system costs while satisfying the customer service level. For the customer demand, the GSA sets a maximum reasonable lead time demand level $D(\tau)$ over τ periods, all excessive customer demand superior to this level will be treated by extraordinary measures.

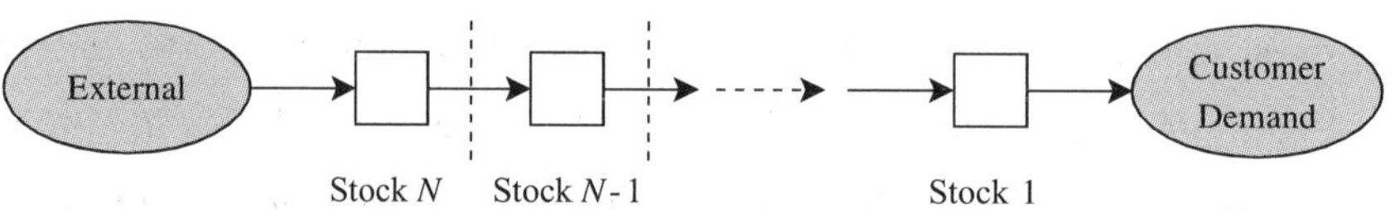

Figure 3.1 A serial inventory system with N stocks

Moreover, for echelon (R, Q) inventory policy considered, we restrict it to one satisfying the integer-ratio constraint, that is, the order size of each stock i is a multiple of the order size of its immediate successor, i.e., stock i-1. Specifically, Q_i is a multiple of Q_{i-1}, i.e., $Q_i=m_{i-1}Q_{i-1}$, where m_{i-1} is a positive integer for i=1, 2, ⋯, N. This assumption is natural since stock i-1 always places an order of Q_{i-1} units to stock i and each inventory replenishment order of stock i is used to fulfill the demands from stock i-1. Integer-ratio (R, Q) policies have been proved to be at least 98% cost-effective for systems like serial systems (Chen and Zheng, 1994). In practice, the coordination of order sizes among different stages in a multi-echelon inventory system can facilitate quantity coordination among these stocks and simplify packaging, transportation and stock count in the system.

3.1.2 Maximum Reasonable Lead Time Demand Level

One key assumption of the GSA is that a maximum reasonable lead time demand level is specified for lead time demand of the customer and excessive part of the lead time demand beyond the level is fulfilled by using operating flexibility. Here, the maximum level is not defined directly on the demand of each period (or a given period) but the lead time demand. Since the lead time is a decision variable in the GSA model, this level is usually defined as a function of the lead time.

Let us denote the lead time demand over τ units of time ($\tau \geqslant 0$) from time t-τ to time t (t-τ) by $d\ [t-\tau,\ t)$ and the maximum reasonable lead time demand level over the lead time demand by D (τ). The bounded lead time demand assumption can be described as follows:

$$D(\tau) \geqslant d\ [t \geqslant \tau,\ t) \tag{3-1}$$

Note that the bounded demand assumption and the GSA were adopted by Graves and Willems (1996, 2000) in the context of setting the safety stock in a supply chain. In their work, the base stock level of each stock is set to cover all realizations of its lead time demand that fall within an upper bound. If the lead time demand exceeds the upper bound, the stock might resort to extraordinary measures such as expediting and overtime to fulfill the excessive part of the demand. Following this logic, they set the bounds at the stock's average lead time demand plus safety stock. Since the base stock level (or safety stock) is strongly related to the service level of the stock, in this these, we set the lead time demand according to the event-oriented service level to final customer as described in the above. By specifying a service level to customer, each stock indicates implicitly its preference for what range of its demand is covered by the stock itself and what range is fulfilled by using extraordinary measures. Of course, the service level should be determined so that the total cost of the system is minimized, this will be discussed later.

In a serial system depicted in Figure 3.1, the customer demand only occurs at stock 1, that is, the maximum reasonable lead time demand level at stock 1 is defined as the minimum number $D(\tau)$ satisfying the following condition

$$p\{d[t-\tau,\ t) \leqslant D(\tau)\} \leqslant \alpha \tag{3-2}$$

Since the customer demand at stock 1 follows a Poisson process with average demand rate λ, $D(\tau)$ can be calculated by

$$\sum_{k=0}^{D(\tau)} \frac{[\lambda\tau]^k e^{-\lambda\tau}}{k!} \geqslant \alpha \tag{3-3}$$

We give a simple example, if λ=5 and α=0.9 according to the above inequality (3-3), the maximum reasonable lead time demand level $D(\tau)$ for different lead time $\tau \in [0, 10]$, can be derived as in Table 3.1, where $\Delta = D(\tau) - D(\tau - 1)$. From the table, we can see $D(\tau)$ is neither concave nor convex.

Table 3.1 Maximum reasonable lead time demand level

τ	0	1	2	3	4	5	6	7	8	9	10
$D(\tau)$	0	8	14	20	26	32	37	43	48	54	59
Δ		8	6	6	6	6	5	6	5	6	5

3.1.3 Cost Structure

For the serial inventory system considered, the total cost is assumed to consist of three costs: inventory holding cost, fixed order costs and operating flexibility costs for fulfilling excessive demand. Since we use an echelon (R, Q) inventory policy to control the system, the inventory holding costs will be evaluated based on the echelon on-hand inventory of each stock. The fixed order costs are evaluated based on the number of orders that each stock places to its supplier (immediate upstream stock). That is, the placement of each order incurs a fixed order cost. As for the third cost, they are assumed to depend linearly on the amount of demand fulfilled by using operating flexibility. Since any stock except for the stock 1 never runs out of stock under the GSA model, the costs for using operating flexibility is only accounted one time at stock 1. All parameters to be used in the formulation of the total cost are given as follows:

c_i: fixed cost for placing each order by stock i to its supplier, i.e., stock i+1,

h_i: installation holding cost per unit product per time unit for stock i,

h_i^e: echelon holding cost per unit of product per time unit for stock i, i=1, 2, ⋯, N,

p: cost for using operating flexibility to fulfill each unit of excessive customer demand.

After the description of basic assumptions about the optimization problem, a mathematical model will be formulated in the next section.

3.2 Mathematical Model Formulation

Before presenting the mathematical model, the definitions and notations used in it are first given in Section 3.2.1, and we also give the detailed description about the ob jective function. Finally, we will formulate a mathematical model for the optimization problem in Section 3.2.3.

3.2.1 Definitions and Notations

We first define the following notations that will be used later.

Indices

i: node index, i=1, ⋯, N, where N represents the number of stocks (levels) in the system,

t: time index, t=0, 1, ⋯, ∞ with continuous review.

Parameters

L_i: net lead time of stock i, i.e., $L_i=SI_i+T_i-S_i$, i=1, 2, ⋯, N,

λ: average demand rate of the customer demand at stock 1,

s_1: an upper bound of outbound service time at stock 1.

At any time t,

$I_i(t)$: on-hand inventory of stock i,

$I_i^e(t)$: echelon on-hand inventory of stock i,

$IL_i^e(t)$: echelon inventory level of stock i,

$IP_i^e(t)$: echelon inventory position of stock i,

$OO_i(t_1, t_2]$: the quantity of all orders placed by stock i from time t_1 to time t_2 (not including t_1), i=1, 2, ⋯, N.

$d\,[t-L_i, t)$: the lead time demand over L_i units of time of stock i, i=1, 2, ⋯, N,

$\hat{d}\,[t-L_i, t)$: the lead time demand over L_i units of time fulfilled normally by the considered system.

Decision Variables

β: fill rate of the system,

R_i: reorder point of stock i,

Q_i: order size of stock i,

S_i: outbound service time of stock i,

SI_i: inbound service time of stock i, i=1, 2, ⋯, N.

3.2.2 Objective Function

In this thesis, the objective is to minimize the average total costs of the system per time unit. To formulate the total cost, we have to formulate three types of costs mentioned in Section 3.1.3, inventory holding costs, fixed order costs and operating flexibility costs for each stock.

Inventory Holding Costs

The average inventory holding costs per unit of time for stock i can be formulated as $h_i^e \cdot E[I_i^e]$, i=1, 2, ⋯, N.

Fixed Order Costs

Since β represents the percentage of the quantity of customer demand fulfilled normally without operating flexibility, then, for each time unit the average number of units of customer demand fulfilled normally is $\lambda\beta$. Therefore, the average fixed order cost per unit of time for stock i can be formulated as $\frac{c_i \lambda\beta}{Q_i}$.

Operating Flexibility Cost

In order to formulate operating flexibility costs, we first need to know the average number of customer demand fulfilled by using operating flexibility, which can be for mulated as $\lambda(1-\beta)$. Then, the average cost of using operating flexibility to fulfill excessive customer demand per time unit is $p\lambda(1-\beta)$.

Therefore, the objective function for the optimization problem is the total system cost of each stock in the serial inventory system with N stocks. Therefore, the objective function is give as under

$$\sum_{i=1}^{N}\left(\frac{c_i\beta}{Q_i}+h_i^e\cdot E[I_i^e]\right)+p\lambda(1-\beta) \tag{3-4}$$

Note that for the system if all units of customer demand fulfilled by using operating flexibility are regarded as the units of demand not satisfied on-time under the SSA model, then β corresponds to the fill rate of the system.

3.2.3 Model Formulation

Under the GSA model, for stock i, if its immediate downstream stock, stock i-1, places an order to it at time t, this order must be filled by stock i at time t+S_i. In order to do so, stock i should replenish its inventory corresponding to the order form its supplier (stock i+1) at time t-(SI_i+T_i-S_i), because in this way the inventory replenishment of stock i can be used to fill the customer order at time t-(SI_i+T_i-S_i)+(SI_i+T_i)=t+S_i. The behavior of stock i *is* thus equivalent to the behavior of a stock with the same demand process, net lead time SI_i+T_i-S_i and zero outbound service time, i.e., this behavior can be modeled by that of the stock with inventory replenishment lead time SI_i+T_i-S_i under the assumption that any customer demand is filled (delivered) immediately without delay. With this equivalence, we can only consider net lead time at each stock and assume that each order placed by a downstream stock will be filled (delivered) immediately in analyzing the serial inventory system. For convenience, we replace SI_i+T_i-S_i by L_i in the following formulation process.

According to the definitions about $IP_i^e(t)$, we can derive the following equations for each stock i,

$$IP_i^e(t)=IP_i^e(0)+OO_i(0,\ t]-d[0,\ t)$$

$$IP_i^e(t-L_i)=IP_i^e(0)+OO_i(0,\ t-L_i]-d[0,\ t-L_i)$$

$$IP_i^e(t)-IP_i^e(t-L_i)=OO_i(t-L_i,\ t]-d[t-L_i,\ t) \tag{3-5}$$

At time t, stock i receives all its orders placed to its upstream stock i+1 in or before time t-L_i, but none of the orders placed after time t-L_i is received by stock i, then, we can derive

$$IL_i^e(t)=IP_i^e(t)-OO_i(t-L_i,\ t] \tag{3-6}$$

On the other hand, the following inventory balance equation is well-known:

$$IL_i^e(t)=IP_i^e(t-L_i)-d[t-L_i,\ t) \tag{3-7}$$

Under the GSA model, stock i has no backorder because of using operating flexibility, then,

$$IL_i^e(t)=I_i^e(t) \tag{3-8}$$

From equation (3-7), we can derive that

$$I_i^e(t)=IP_i^e(t-L_i)-d[t-L_i,\ t) \tag{3-9}$$

For stock i, in order to provide 100% guaranteed service, $I_i^e(t)\geqslant 0$ must be satisfied, then,

$$IP_i^e(t-L_i)\geqslant d[t-L_i,\ t) \tag{3-10}$$

Constraint (3-10) imposes a condition on IP_i^e. In addition, another constraint which ensures no stockout at each stock has to be considered. At stock i, no stockout means that on-hand inventory $I_i(t)$ is always nonnegative.

According to the definition above, $I_i(t)$ is given by

$$I_i(t)=I_i^e(t)-IP_{i-1}^e(t) \tag{3-11}$$

Under the condition $I_i(t)\geqslant 0$, we have

$$I_i^e(t)\geqslant IP_{i-1}^e(t) \tag{3-12}$$

According to equation (3-9), the following inequality can be derived

$$IP_i^e(t-L_i)\geqslant d[t-L_i,\ t)+IP_{i-1}^e(t) \tag{3-13}$$

Since the satisfaction of constraint (3-13) implies the satisfaction of constraint (3-10), only constraint (3-13) need to be considered in the following analysis.

Under an echelon (R, Q) inventory policy, at stock i, after order decision, but before demand occurrence, IP_i^e must be within the interval $[R_i+1,\ R_i+Q_i]$ for any stock i, such as

$$IP_i^e(t-L_i)\in[R_i+1,\ R_i+Q_i],\ \text{and}\ IP_{i-1}^e(t)\in[R_{i-1}+1,\ R_{i-1}+Q_{i-1}]$$

According to Hadley and Whitin (1961), IP_i^e is uniformly distributed over the interval $[R_i+1,\ R_i+Q_i]$, with the probability $\frac{1}{Q_i}$ of being at state R_i+j, $j=1, \cdots, Q_i$. This implies that there is $t \geqslant L_i$ such that $IP_i^e(t-L_i)=R_i+1$ and t can be taken as a time larger than any given number.

Two cases may happen for equation (3-13):

Case 1: $L_i \geqslant 0$. In this case, we have

1) $d[t-L_i,\ t)$ can take any positive integer value.

2) According to Zipkin (1986) or Simchi-Levi and Zhao (2007), as $t \to \infty$, the inventory position $IP_{i-1}^e(t)$ is statistically independent of the lead time demand $d[t-L_i,\ t)$.

3) $IP_{i-1}^e(t)$ is uniformly distributed over the interval $[R_{i-1}+1,\ R_{i-1}+Q_{i-1}]$.

The above three properties imply that starting from t-L_i with inventory position $IP_i^e(t-L_i)=R_i+1$, there exists a realization of the demand process from time $t-L_i$ to time t such that $d[t-L_i,\ t) \geqslant D(L_i)$ and $IP_{i-1}^e(t)=R_{i-1}+Q_{i-1}$.

In this case, in order to ensure that inequality (3-13) holds for any demand realization under the GSA (that is, the part $D(L_i)$ of the lead time demand $d[t-L_i,\ t)$ must be satisfied on time), we must have:

$$R_i+1 \geqslant D(L_i)+R_{i-1}+Q_{i-1} \text{ for } i=1, 2, \cdots, N \tag{3-14}$$

where R_0 and Q_0 are assumed to be 0.

Case 2: $L_i=0$. In this case, $D(L_i)=0$ and inequality (3-13) becomes $IP_i^e(t) \geqslant IP_{i-1}^e(t)$ for any time t. Since the echelon $(R_i,\ Q_i)$ policy we consider is transformed from an installation $(r_i,\ Q_i)$ policy according to equation (2-1), we have $R_i+1=R_{i-1}+Q_{i-1}+r_i+1$. Since $r_i \geqslant -1$ (See Section 2.3.3), we have $R_i+1 \geqslant R_{i-1}+Q_{i-1}$. This implies that inequality (3-14) also holds for this case.

Now, we can derive a lower bound for each R_i. After the replacement of L_i by the net lead time given above, we have,

$$R_i \geqslant \sum_{j=1}^{i} D(SI_j+T_j-S_j)+\sum_{j=0}^{i-1} Q_j-i \text{ for } i=1, 2, \cdots, N \tag{3-15}$$

Since the objective of the problem is to minimize the total cost, there exists an optimal solution with R_i, $i=1, 2, \cdots, N$ given by the following equations.

$$R_i=\sum_{j=1}^{i} D(SI_j+T_j-S_j)+\sum_{j=0}^{i-1} Q_j-i \text{ for } i=1, 2, \cdots, N \tag{3-16}$$

Since 100β% of the total demand is fulfilled normally and the demand rate is λ, we have

$$E[\hat{d}[t-L_i, t)]=\beta\lambda L_i \tag{3-17}$$

Assume that all excessive demands are satisfied without incurring inventory holding costs. This assumption is reasonable since the occurrence of excessive demand implies zero on-hand level in the considered system. With this assumption, we can ignore excessive demand in the calculation of expected inventory holding cost $E[I_i^e]$. That is, when calculate $E[I_i^e]$ according to equation (3-9), we must first replace $d[t-L_i, t)$ by $\hat{d}[t-L_i, t)$. After this replacement, $I_i^e(t)=IP_i^e(t-L_i)-\hat{d}[t-L_i, t)\geqslant 0$ is always true. Sinceis $IP_i^e(t)$ is uniformly distributed over the interval $[R_i+1, R_i+Q_i]$ in steady state, we have:

$$E[IP_i^e]=\frac{1}{Q}\sum_{j=1}^{Q_i}(R_i+j)=R_i+\frac{1+Q_i}{2} \tag{3-18}$$

So we can derive $E[I_i^e]$ as follows:

$$E[IP_i^e]=E[IP_i^e(t-L_i, t)-\hat{d}[t-L_i, t)]=R_i+\frac{1+Q_i}{2}-\lambda\beta L_i \tag{3-19}$$

By substituting R_i given by (3-16) into equation (3-19) and replacing L_i by $SI_i+T_i-S_i$, we can deriving the following equation:

$$E[I_i^e]=\sum_{j=1}^{i} D(SI_j+T_j-S_j)-\lambda\beta(SI_i+T_i-S_i)+\sum_{j=0}^{i-1} Q_j-\frac{1+Q_i}{2}-i \text{ for } i=1, 2, \cdots, N \tag{3-20}$$

With equation (3-4) and equation (3-20), the inventory policy optimization problem we study can be formulated as the following nonlinear programming problem:

P: Minimize

$$\sum_{i=1}^{N}\frac{c_i\lambda\beta}{Q_i}+\sum_{i=1}^{N}\{h_i^e\cdot[\sum_{j=1}^{i} D(SI_j+T_j-S_j)-\lambda\beta(SI_i+T_i-S_i)+\frac{1+Q_i}{2}-i]+\sum_{j=i}^{N} h_j^e\cdot Q_{i-1}\}+p\lambda(1-\beta)$$

Subject to:

$Q_{i+1}=m_iQ_i$ for $i=1, 2,\cdots, N-1$ (3-21)

$SI_i+T_i-S_i \geqslant 0$ for $i=1, 2,\cdots, N$ (3-22)

$SI_i \geqslant S_{i+1}$ for $i=1, 2,\cdots, N$ (3-23)

$0 \leqslant S_1 \leqslant s_1$ (3-24)

$Q_i \geqslant 0$ and integer for i=1, 2,$\cdots$, N (3-25)

SI_i, $S_i \geqslant 0$ and integer for i=1, 2,$\cdots$, N (3-26)

The objective function represents the average total costs of the system in the long run. Constraint (3-21) is the integer-ratio constraint between the order size of any two successive stocks, in which the order size of stock i+1 must be a positive integer multiple of the order size of its immediate successor, Q_i. Constraint (3-22) assures that the net lead time at each stock is nonnegative. Constraint (3-23) implies that each stock i can start production only when all the inputs are available, so the inbound service time of each stock i must equal to or greater than the outbound service time of its immediate upstream stock. Constraint (3-24) imposes an upper bound s_1 on the outbound service time of stock 1, where s_1 may be given by the required delivery lead time of final customer. Constraint (3-25) and Constraint (3-26) imply that all the decision variables must be integer.

When β is known, $p\lambda(1-\beta)$ in the objective function of model P becomes a constant which can be ignored and the model can be decomposed in two independent sub-models or sub-problems, one with decision variables Q_i and the other with decision variables SI_i and S_i. The two sub-problems are called order size decision sub-problem and reorder point decision sub-problem or Q-problem and R-problem for short, respectively hereafter. The Q-problem has a convex objective function composed of all Q-dependent cost terms and constraint (3-21) and constraint(3-25), whereas the R-problem has a nonlinear objective function composed of all R-dependent cost terms and linear Constraint (3-22), Constraint (3-23), Constraint (3-24) and Constraint (3-26).

***Q*-problem:**

Minimize: $\sum_{i=1}^{N}[\frac{c_i\lambda\beta}{Q_i}+h_i^e\cdot(\frac{1+Q_i}{2}-i)+\sum_{j=1}^{N}h_j^e\cdot Q_{i-1}]$

Subject to:

$Q_{i+1}=m_i Q_i$ for $i=1, 2, \cdots, N-1$

$Q_i \geqslant 0$ and integer for i=1, 2,⋯, N

***R*-problem:**

Minimize: $\sum_{i=1}^{N} h_i^e \cdot [\sum_{j=1}^{N} D(SI_j+T_j-S_j)-\lambda\beta(SI_i+T_i-S_i)]$

Subject to:

$SI_i+T_i-S_i \geqslant 0$ for i=1, 2, ⋯, N

$SI_i \geqslant S_{i+1}$ for i=1, 2, ⋯, N

$0 \leqslant S_1 \leqslant s_1$

SI_i, $S_i \geqslant$ 0 and integer for i=1, 2,⋯, N

Obviously, the objective function of Q-problem is convex with respect to Q_i, i=1, 2, ⋯, N, since it is a kind of EOQ cost function. However, we find the objective function of R-problem is neither convex nor concave through numerical analysis. The non-convex, non-concave nature of this function is due to the irregular nonlinearity of demand bound D（$SI_i+T_i-S_i$）. In the next two sections, we will use two efficient algorithms to solve the two sub-problems, respectively. As soon as the two sub-problems are solved, the optimal order size Q_i is given by the solution of the Q-problem, and the optimal reorder point R_i can be determined from $\{SI_j, T_j, S_j | 1 \leqslant j \leqslant i\}$ and $\{Q_j \mid 0 \leqslant j \leqslant i-1\}$ according to equation (3-16).

The above analysis assumes β is known. However β is not known, but it can be determined by the parameters and inventory policy of the system considered. In the following sections, we will first present two dynamic programming algorithms for solving the two sub-problems in Section 3.3 and Section 3.4, respectively when α and β are given, and then present an iterative procedure for solving the original inventory policy optimization problem in Section 3.5.

3.3 Dynamic Programming Algorithms for Q–problem

In this section, we propose a dynamic programming (DP) algorithm to solve Q-problem, which determine the optimal order size Q^* for echelon (R, Q) inventory policy used at each stock in the serial system studied. The basic principle of DP is first explained in Section 3.3.1, and how to use it to solve the Q-problem will be introduced in detail in Section 3.3.2.

3.3.1 Basic Principle of DP

Dynamic program is an optimization approach that transforms a complex problem into a sequence of simpler problems; its essential characteristic is the multistage nature of the optimization procedure. The three most important elements of DP are stage, state and recursive optimization.

Stages

The essential feature of a dynamic programming approach is the structuring of an optimization problem into a multi-stage decision problem in which the decisions at multiple stages are solved sequentially one stage at a time. Although each one-stage problem is solved as an ordinary optimization problem, its solution influences the characteristics of the next one-stage problem in the sequence. Often, the stages represent different time periods in the planning horizon of a problem or different subsystems of a system.

States

Associated with each stage of an optimization problem is the state of the underlying system or process. The state contains the information required to fully assess the consequences that the current decision has upon further actions. The specification of the state of the system is perhaps the most critical design parameter of a dynamic programming algorithm. Two general rules for defining the state are:

- The state of a system should convey enough information to make future decisions without regard to how the system reached the current state;

■ The number of state variables should be as small as possible, since the computational effort associated with a dynamic programming approach will be prohibitively expensive if there are more than two state variables involved in the dynamic programming algorithm.

Recursive Optimization

The final general characteristic of a dynamic programming approach is its recursive optimization procedure, which builds an optimal solution of a multi-stage decision problem by first solving a one-stage problem and sequentially including and considering one stage at a time until the optimal solution of the overall system has been found. This procedure can be derived based on a *backward induction process*, where the first one-stage problem to be considered is in the final stage of the problem and one-stage problems are solved moving back one stage at a time until all stages are considered. Alternatively, the recursive procedure can be derived based on a *forward induction process*, where the first one-stage problem to be solved is the initial stage of the problem and one-stage problems are solved moving forward one stage a time until all stages are considered. In certain problem settings, only one of the two induction processes can be applied.

The derivation of a recursive DP procedure for an optimization problem is based on the principle of optimality, which can be stated as the property of any optimal policy that, whatever the current state and decision, its remaining decisions must constitute an optimal (sub) policy with regard to the state resulting from the current decision.

3.3.2 Dynamic Programming Algorithm

In order to apply dynamic program to the Q-problem, we first formulate the problem as a multistage decision problem in a network whose nodes represent the states of the studied system as shown in Figure 3.2. The network has a single starting node (source node) 0, a single ending node (sink node) $N+1$, and intermediate nodes of N stages. Stage i corresponds to stock i, $i=1, 2, \cdots, N$. Each node at stage i in the network indicates a possible value of the order size Q_i for stock i, and there is a directed arc from a node at stage i to a node at stage i+1 if $Q_{i+1}=m_i Q_i$ for some integer m_i, where the decision variable m_i is associated with the arc. In the network, each path from the starting node to the ending node corresponds to a possible solution of the Q-problem.

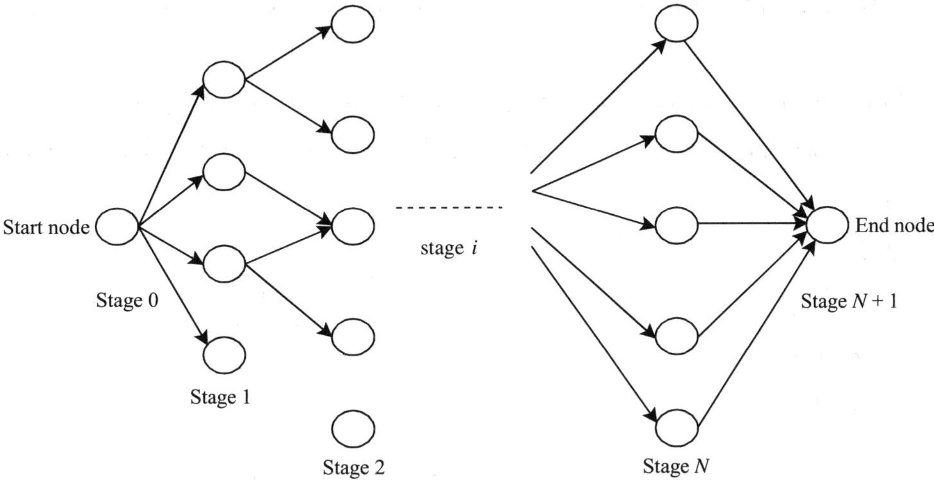

Figure 3.2 Dynamic programming network for Q–problem

If we associate each arc from a node at stage i-1 to a node at stage i with the length corresponding to the cost of stock i (i=1, 2, ⋯, N) and each arc from a node at stage N to the ending node with zero length (cost), the total cost of the system is given by the length of a path from the starting node to the ending node in the network since the total cost is the sum of the costs of all stocks. The minimization of the total cost is thus equivalent to finding the shortest path in the network.

The following notations will be used in the DP algorithm:

i: stage index, i=0, 1, ⋯, N+1, stage (stock) 0 and stage (stock) N+1are two additional stages (stocks) representing the starting state and ending state of the DP algorithm, respectively.

Q_i: state variable of stock i, which represents a possible order size of stock i, i=1, 2, ⋯, N,

W_i: the set of all possible values of Q_i, i=1, 2, ⋯, N,

m_{i-1}: decision variable of stock i, i=2, ⋯, N,

$M_{i-1}(Q_{i-1})$: the set of permissible values of m_{i-1} given the state Q_{i-1} of stock i-1, i=2, ⋯,

N,

$d_i(Q_{i-1}, m_{i-1})$: the cost of stock i when its decision is m_{i-1} and the state of stock i-1 is Q_{i-1},

$f_i(Q_i)$: the minimal total cost from stock 0 to stock i when the state of stock i is Q_i, i=1, 2, ⋯, N.

With the above notations and applying the dynamic programming optimality principle, the state transition functions and the recursion equations of the DP algorithm can be written as:

$$Q_i = m_{i-1} \cdot Q_{i-1}, \quad i=2, 3, \cdots, N,$$

$$\begin{cases} f_i(Q_i) = \min\limits_{m_{i-1} \in M_{i-1}(Q_{i-1})} \{ d_i(Q_{i-1}, m_{i-1}) + f_{i-1}(Q_{i-1}) \} \; i=1, 2, \cdots, N \\ f_0(Q_0) = 0 \end{cases}$$

where

$$\begin{cases} d_i(Q_{i-1}, m_{i-1}) = \dfrac{c_i \lambda \beta}{Q_i} + h_i^e\left(\dfrac{1+Q_i}{2} - i\right) + \sum\limits_{j=i}^{N} h_j^e \cdot Q_{i-1}, \; i=1, 2, \cdots, N \\ d_{N+1}(Q_N, m_N) = 0 \end{cases}$$

In order to apply the above recursion equations to calculate $f_i(Q_i)$ for each stock i, the state space W_1 of stock 1 and the permissible decision set $M_{i-1}(Q_{i-1})$ of stock i must be determined before the recursion process. The following two properties can be used to determine W_1 and $M_{i-1}(Q_{i-1})$ for i=2, 3, ⋯, N.

Property 1: For serial inventory system with N stocks, an upper bound of Q_1 is given by:

$$\overline{Q}_1 = \sqrt{\frac{2\lambda\beta(c_1 + c_2 + \cdots + c_N)}{h_1^e + 3h_2^e + \cdots + (2N-1)h_N^e}} = \sqrt{\frac{2\lambda\beta \sum\limits_{i=i}^{N} c_i}{\sum\limits_{i=1}^{N} (2i-1)h_1^e}}$$

Proof: Substitute $Q_i = \prod\limits_{j=1}^{i-1} m_j Q_1$ for i=2, ⋯, N into the objective function of the Q-problem, we have

$$\frac{c_1\lambda\beta}{Q_i}+h^e_1\left(\frac{1+Q_1}{2}-1\right)+\sum_{i=2}^{N}\left[\frac{c_i\lambda\beta}{\prod_{j=1}^{i-1}m_jQ_1}+h^e_i\left(\frac{1+\prod_{j=1}^{i-1}m_jQ_1}{2}-i\right)+\sum_{j=1}^{N}h^e_j\times\prod_{j=1}^{i-2}m_jQ_1\right]$$

If all m_i for i=1, 2, ⋯, N-1 are given, the above function contains only one variable Q_1. Because this function is convex with respect to Q_1, the optimalvalue of Q_1 can be derived at the point where the first derivative of the function with respect to Q_1 is equal to 0. After calculating the first derivative, we can get the following equation:

$$-\frac{\lambda\beta}{Q_1^2}\cdot G+H=0,$$

where $G=c_1+\frac{c_2}{m_1}+\frac{c_3}{m_1m_2}+\cdots+\frac{c_i}{\prod_{j=1}^{i-1}m_j}\cdots+\frac{c_N}{\prod_{j=1}^{N-1}m_j}$

$$H=\left(\frac{1}{2}h^e_1+h^e_2+\cdots+h^e_N\right)+\left(\frac{1}{2}h^e_2+h^e_3+\cdots+h^e_N\right)m_1+\cdots\left(\frac{1}{2}h^e_i+\sum_{j=i+1}^{N}h^e_j\right)\prod_{j=1}^{i-1}m_j+\cdots+\frac{1}{2}h^e_N\prod_{j=1}^{N-1}m_j$$

Then, $Q_1^2=\frac{2\lambda\beta}{\prod_{j=1}^{N-1}m_j}\cdot\frac{\prod_{i=1}^{N-1}c_i\prod_{j=1}^{N-1}m_j+c_N}{(h^e_1+2\sum_{j=2}^{N}h^e_j)+\sum_{i=2}^{N}(h^e_i+2\sum_{j=i+1}^{N}h^e_j)\prod_{j=1}^{i-1}m_j}$

From the above equation,it is obvious that the maximum value of Q_1 is attained when $m_1=m_2=\cdots=m_{N-1}=1$, then, we can derive,

$$\overline{Q}_1=\sqrt{\frac{2\lambda\beta(c_1+c_2+\cdots+c_N)}{h^e_1+3h^e_2+\cdots+(2N-1)h^e_N}}=\sqrt{\frac{2\lambda\beta\sum_{i=1}^{N}c_i}{\sum_{i=1}^{N}(2i-1)h^e_i}}$$

Since Q_1 must taken a positive integer value, W_1 for stock 1 can be taken as the integer set $\{1, 2, \cdots, \lceil\overline{Q}_1\rceil\}$, where $\lceil x\rceil=\min\{a\in Z|a\geqslant x\}$ and Z is the set of integers.

Property 2: For stock i (i=2, ⋯, N) of the serial inventory system, if the state of stock i-1 is Q_{i-1}, then an upper bound of m_{i-1} can be derived by:

$$m_{i-1}^{-}=\frac{1}{Q_{i-1}}\cdot\sqrt{\frac{2\lambda\beta\sum_{j=i}^{N}c_i}{\sum_{j=1}^{N-i+1}(2j-1)\cdot h_{i-1+j}^{e}}}$$

Proof: After substituting $Q_i=\prod_{j=1}^{i-1}m_jQ_1$, for $i=2$, $\cdots$, N into the objective function of the Q-problem, it can be rewritten as:

$$\frac{\lambda\beta}{Q_i}P\cdot\frac{1}{m_i}+R\cdot Q_i\cdot m_i+C$$

where $P=c_{i+1}+\frac{c_{i+2}}{m_{i+1}}+\frac{c_{i+3}}{m_{i+1}m_{i+2}}+\cdots+\frac{c_N}{m_{i+1}\cdots m_{N-1}}$

$$R=(\frac{1}{2}h_{i+1}^{e}+h_{i+2}^{e}+\cdots h_{N}^{e})+\sum_{j=i+2}^{N}[(\frac{1}{2}h_{j}^{e}+h_{j+1}^{e}+\cdots+h_{N}^{e})\prod_{k=i+1}^{j-1}m_k];$$

$$C=\frac{\lambda\beta}{Q_1}(c_1+\frac{c_2}{m_1}+\cdots+\frac{c_{\mathrm{i}}}{m_1m_2\cdots m_{i-1}})+(\frac{1}{2}h_{1}^{e}+h_{2}^{e}+\cdots+h_{N}^{e})+$$

$$\sum_{j=2}^{i}[(\frac{1}{2}h_{i}^{e}+h_{i+1}^{e}+\cdots+h_{N}^{e})\prod_{k=1}^{i-1}m_k]$$

The objective function is convex with respect to variable m_i, so the optimalvalue of m_i is attained at the point where the first partial derivative of the function withrespect to m_i is equal to 0, i.e.,

$$-\frac{\lambda\beta}{Q_i}P\cdot\frac{1}{m_i^2}+RQ_i=0 \text{ for } i=1, 2, \cdots, N-1$$

Then, $m_i=\frac{1}{Q_i}\sqrt{\lambda\beta\cdot\frac{P}{R}}$, for $i=1, 2, \cdots, N-1$

From the above equation, it is obvious that the maximum value of m_i is attained when $m_{i+1}=m_{i+2}=\cdots=m_{N-1}=1$, so we can derive that

$$m_{i-1}^{-}=\frac{1}{Q_{i-1}}\cdot\sqrt{\frac{2\lambda\beta\sum_{j=\mathrm{i}}^{N}c_i}{\sum_{j=i}^{N-i+1}(2j-1)\cdot h_{i-1+j}^{e}}}$$

Similarly, the permissible decision set $M_{i-1}(Q_{i-1})$can be taken as the integer set [1, 2, $\cdots$, $\lceil m_{i-1}^{-}\rceil$].

With the above two bounds, the main steps of our dynamic programming algorithm can be summarized in the following.

Step 1: Determine the set W_1 of possible values of Q_1 based on Property 1.

Step 2: Set i=1, calculate $f_1(Q_1)$ for each Q_1 in W_1, this gives the boundary condition of the DP algorithm.

For stage i=2, ⋯, N:

Step 3: Determine $M_{i-1}(Q_{i-1})$ based on Property 2, and according to the state transition function $Q_i=m_{i-1}\cdot Q_{i-1}$, calculate $f_i(Q_i)$.

Step 4: Set $i=N+1$, at the ending node, calculate $f_{N+1}(Q_{N+1})=\min\limits_{Q_N} f_N(Q_N)$. $f_{N+1}(Q_{N+1})$. is the minimal cost for the Q-problem.

Step 5: Backtrack from stock N+1 to stock N, stock N to stock N-1, ⋯, stock 1 to stock 0 to find the optimal Q_i^* for each stock i.

Note that Crowston and Wagner (1973) presented a dynamic programming algorithm to solve a lot size problem for assembly systems with deterministic demand. Their algorithm can also be used to solve our Q-problem. Their algorithm first calculates an upper bound and a lower bound of the optimal lost size for each stock, based on the lower bound and an upper bound of the optimal cost of the joint lot-sizing problem. The efficiency of the algorithm strongly depends on the second upper bound, which is obtained either by a heuristic or by a dynamic programming algorithm of the same type but with coarse grid.

We will compare our DP algorithm with Crowston and Wagner's algorithm in Section 3.6 for the purpose of evaluating the efficiency of the two algorithms for the Q-problem.

3.4 Dynamic Programming Algorithm for *R*–problem

In this section, we describe how to solve R-problem by dynamic programming when the underlying network for the supply chain is a spanning tree. This algorithm is developed by Graves and Willems (2000). Since the serial system we study also has a spanning tree structure and our R-problem is similar to their problem with the only difference on objective function, their dynamic programming algorithm can also be used to solve our problem. In the following, we briefly introduce their algorithm applied to our problem.

In the terminology of dynamic programming, the R-problem will be solved by decomposing it into N stages where there is a dynamic-programming stage for each node in the spanning tree. In a spanning tree, it is easy to show that there will always a node that is adjacent to at most one other node. The serial inventory system has a simple network structure, which already has this important characteristic. Therefore, for an N-stock serial system, we only label stock i as node i for i=1, 2, ⋯, N. And in order to show the characteristic of the spanning tree, we also define $p(i)$ to be the node with higher label that is adjacent to node i, for i=1, 2, ⋯, N-1, and $p(i)=i+1$ can be derived directly. The node N obviously has no adjacent node with higher label.

Next, we will numerate the nodes in a spanning tree so that there will be a single state variable. However, the state variable for the dynamic program will be either the inbound service time at a stock or its outbound service time, where the determination depends on the topology of the network.

In order to explain the dynamic programming recursion, we first define $N(i)$ as the subset nodes {1, 2, ⋯, i} that are connected to i on the sub-graph consisting of nodes {1, 2, ⋯, i}. And $N(i)$ can be determined by the following equations:

$$N(i)=\{i\}+N(i-1)$$

This implies that $N(i)$= {1, 2, ⋯, i}.

The dynamic programming algorithm evaluates a functional equation for all nodes (stocks), in the order of their labels. According to Graves and Willems (2000), generally the functional equation may have two different forms at each node (stock) i (i=1, 2, ⋯, N-1), depending on the location of the node (stock) with higher label that is adjacent to node (stock) i. However, for the serial system studied, each node (stock) i has only one upstream adjacent node (stock) with a higher label, i.e., node (stock) i+1, then the functional equation has the unique form. In order to formulate the equation, let us define:

$g_i(SI)$: the minimum inventory holding cost for the sub-system (of the original serial system) described by the sub-graph with node set $N(i)$, where the inbound service time of stock i is given by SI.

With this cost equation, the minimum inventory holding cost for the sub-system can also be defined as a function of both outbound service time and inbound service time of node (stock) i:

$$C_i(S, SI) = h_i^e \cdot [\sum_{j=1}^{i} D(SI_j + T_j - S_j) - \lambda\beta(SI_i + T_i - S_i)] + \min_{S \leqslant y \leqslant M_{i-1} - T_{i-1}} [g_{i-1}(y)]$$

The above function consists of two terms, the first term is the inventory holding cost of node (stock) i, which is a function of S and SI, and the second term corresponds to the nodes (stock) in $N(i)$ that are downstream of node (stock) i.

The functional equation for $g_i(SI)$ can be found by solving the following optimization problem.

$$g_i(SI) = \min_{S} (C_i(S, SI))$$

Subject to:

$$0 \leqslant S \leqslant SI + T_i$$

In the above model, SI is bounded by $M_i - T_i$. In addition, for the final stock, i.e., stock 1, S is also bounded by its maximum service time, i.e., $S_1 \leqslant s_1$.

In summary, the main steps of the dynamic programming algorithm are given in the following.

Step 1: For i:=1 to N, evaluate $g_i(SI)$ for SI=0, 1, $\cdots$, $M_i - T_i$;

Step 2: Minimize $g_i(SI)$ to derive the optimal cost value of the R-problem;

Step 3: Backtrack from node N to node N-1, $\cdots$, node 2 to node 1 to get the optimal inbound service time (SI) and outbound service time (S) of each node (stock).

To summarize, at each stock of the dynamic program, we find the minimum inventory holding costs for the sub-network with node set $N(i)$, as a function of a state variable. The state variable depends upon the location of the node (stock) with higher label that is adjacent to the node (stock) i, i=1, 2, .., N. When the higher labeling node (sock) is upstream of node (stock) i, the state variable is the inbound service time (Step 1). At node (stock) N (Step 2), we determine the inventory costs for the entire network as a function of the inbound service time to node (stock) N. At step 3, we optimize over the inbound service time to find the optimal inventory cost.

3.5 Optimization Procedure

The original optimization problem, i.e., optimization of echelon (R, Q) policy for the serial system under the GSA, can be resolved in two loops: 1) determine the optimal service level α, and 2) for each given α, solve model P. Here, the first loop calls the second loop. Since only one decision variable α is to be optimized in the first loop, it can be determined by using a line search. We don't know whether the total cost function of the system is convex with respect to α. If it is, the line search can be carried out by using a method such as the golden section method. Otherwise, it can be done by discretizing possible values of α over the interval [0, 1]. In practice, the service level α may be determined by customer or determined by the managers of system according to their evaluation about the importance of the costs of using extraordinary measures to fulfill excessive demand with respect to other costs. In such a situation, loop 1 can be omitted. In the following, we will discuss how to solve model P for a given α.

3.5.1 The Calculation of the Fill Rate β

To solve model P, we need to know the fill rate β, which can be determined by the parameters and the inventory policy of the system considered. This section presented a method for calculating the fill rate β of the system when its inventory policy is given.

For the serial system considered, let us denote the lead time of stock 1 by L, which is its net lead time to be determined by solving the inventory policy optimization problem presented in Section 3.4. Every time after the stock places an order with its (R, Q) policy to replenish its inventory, its inventory position will be brought to i, $i \in \{R+1, R+2, \cdots, R+Q\}$. For simplicity, the subscript "1" which indicates stock 1 is omitted in L, R, and Q. The shipment for this order will arrive at the stock after its lead time. If the total customer demand during the lead time, denoted by k, exceeds the inventory position i, i.e., $k \geqslant i+1$, the excessive part, i.e., $k-i$, must be fulfilled by using extraordinary measures. Since the probability that the inventory position of the stock reaches i ($i \in \{R+1, R+2, \cdots, R+Q\}$) after order placement is $1/Q$ according to the uniform distribution of the position, the fill rate β can be calculated according to the following equation:

$$1-\beta=\frac{1}{Q}\sum_{i=R+1}^{R+Q}\sum_{k=i+1}^{\infty}\frac{(\lambda L)^k e^{-\lambda L}}{k!}\cdot\frac{k-i}{k}$$

$$=\underbrace{\frac{1}{Q}\sum_{i=R+1}^{R+Q}\sum_{k=i+1}^{\infty}\frac{(\lambda L)^k e^{-\lambda L}}{k!}}_{\text{part 1}}-\underbrace{\frac{1}{Q}\sum_{i=R+1}^{R+Q}\sum_{k=i+1}^{\infty}\frac{(\lambda L)^k e^{-\lambda L}}{k!}\cdot\frac{i}{k}}_{\text{part 2}};$$

Note that $1-\beta$ in the equation is the percentage of customer demand (in quantity) fulfilled by using extraordinary measures.

The part 1 in the equation can be rewritten simply as follows:

$$\frac{1}{Q}\sum_{i=R+1}^{R+Q}\sum_{k=i+1}^{\infty}\frac{(\lambda L)^k e^{-\lambda L}}{k!}=\frac{1}{Q}\sum_{i=R+1}^{R+Q}\sum_{k=1}^{\infty}\frac{(\lambda L)^k e^{-\lambda L}}{k!}-\frac{1}{Q}\sum_{i=R+1}^{R+Q}\sum_{k=1}^{i}\frac{(\lambda L)^k e^{-\lambda L}}{k!}$$

$$=\frac{1}{Q}\sum_{i=R+1}^{R+Q}\sum_{k=0}^{\infty}\frac{(\lambda L)^k e^{-\lambda L}}{k!}-\frac{(\lambda L)^0 e^{-\lambda L}}{0!}-\frac{1}{Q}\sum_{i=R+1}^{R+Q}\sum_{k=1}^{i}\frac{(\lambda L)^k e^{-\lambda L}}{k!}$$

$$=1+e^{-\lambda L}-\frac{1}{Q}\sum_{i=R+1}^{R+Q}\sum_{k=1}^{i}\frac{(\lambda L)^k e^{-\lambda L}}{k!}$$

For part 2, we can derive that

$$\frac{1}{Q}\sum_{i=R+1}^{R+Q}\sum_{k=i+1}^{\infty}\frac{(\lambda L)^k e^{-\lambda L}}{k!}\cdot\frac{i}{k}=\frac{1}{Q}\sum_{i=R+1}^{R+Q}i\sum_{k=i+1}^{\infty}\frac{(\lambda L)^k e^{-\lambda L}}{k!}\cdot\frac{1}{k}$$

$$=\frac{1}{Q}\sum_{i=R+1}^{R+Q}i\sum_{k=1}^{\infty}\frac{(\lambda L)^k e^{-\lambda L}}{k!}\cdot\frac{1}{k}-\frac{1}{Q}\sum_{i=R+1}^{R+Q}i\sum_{k=1}^{i}\frac{(\lambda L)^k e^{-\lambda L}}{k!}\cdot\frac{1}{k}$$

$$=\frac{e^{-\lambda L}}{Q}\left[\sum_{i=R+1}^{R+Q}i\sum_{k=1}^{\infty}\frac{(\lambda L)^k}{k!}\cdot\frac{1}{k}-\sum_{i=R+1}^{R+Q}i\sum_{k=1}^{i}\frac{(\lambda L)^k}{k!}\cdot\frac{1}{k}\right]$$

Note that the term $\sum_{k=1}^{\infty}\frac{(\lambda L)^k}{k!}\cdot\frac{1}{k}$ is an infinite sum which cannot be calculated directly. In order to efficiently calculate it in a finite time, let us define a function $f(x)$ as follows:

$$f(x)=\sum_{k=1}^{\infty}\frac{x^k}{k!}\cdot\frac{1}{k};$$

This function is well defined, has a finite value for any finite x, and is differentiable.Since the infinite series $\{\frac{x^k}{k!}\cdot\frac{1}{k}\}$ is convergent with a finite sum for any given x, we have

$$\frac{df(x)}{dx}=\sum_{k=1}^{\infty}\frac{kx^{k-1}}{k!}\cdot\frac{1}{k}=\sum_{k=1}^{\infty}\frac{x^{k-1}}{k!}=\frac{1}{x}(\sum_{k=0}^{\infty}\frac{x^k}{k!}-1)=\frac{e^x-1}{x}$$

Then,

$$f(\lambda L)=\int_0^{\lambda L}\frac{df(x)}{dx}+f(0)=\int_0^{\lambda L}\frac{e^x-1}{x}dx$$

Therefore, part 2 can be derived as follows:

$$\frac{1}{Q}\sum_{i=R+1}^{R+Q}\sum_{k=i+1}^{\infty}[\frac{(\lambda L)^k e^{-\lambda L}}{k!}\cdot\frac{i}{k}]=\frac{e^{-\lambda L}}{Q}f(\lambda L)\sum_{i=R+1}^{R+Q}i-\frac{1}{Q}\sum_{i=R+1}^{R+Q}i\sum_{k=1}^{i}[\frac{(\lambda L)^k e^{-\lambda L}}{k!}\cdot\frac{i}{k}]$$

With this expression, β can be calculated efficiently in a finite time.

3.5.2 Algorithm for Original Model *P*

However, the inventory policy, which is derived from the optimal solution of model P, depending also on β. Thus, β cannot be derived directly from α by solving P on time. In the following, we propose an iterative procedure to solve model P based on guessing the value of β in each iteration. Since β usually larger than α and close to β when α approaches 1, it is initially set to α in the procedure. As soon as the value of β does not change in two successive iterations, we have got the real β and the optimal echelon (R, Q) policy for the system can be obtained by solving model P at the last iteration of the procedure.

The main steps of the procedure are given as follows:

Procedure BETA:

Step 0: Set $\beta:=\alpha$;

Step 1: Solve the Q-problem and the R-problem to get the values (R_i, Q_i) for each stock i;

Step 2: Calculate the real fill rate β^* of the system for the given echelon (R, Q) policy by using the method proposed;

Step 3: If $\beta^*=\beta$, stop; Otherwise, set $\beta:=\beta^*$ and go to Step 1.

The numerical experiments to be presented in the next section show that the proce dure is always terminated after few iterations for all randomly generated instances.

Note that when the optimal echelon (*R*, *Q*) inventory policy found in the last iteration of the above procedure is transformed into an installation (*r*, *Q*) policy for the serial inventory system considered, the installation reorder point for stock *i* can be easily derived as $r_i=D\ (SI_i+T_i-S_i)-1$. Obviously, $r_i\geqslant-1$, this coincides with one assumption made in Section 3.2.

3.6 Experiments Results

In this section, we evaluate the performance of the two dynamic programming algorithms for the *Q*-problem and *R*-problem respectively and the performance of the procedure BETA proposed by computational experiments on randomly generated instances. In addition, the structure of the (*R*, *Q*) policy found by our GSA model proposed in Section 3.2 is analyzed by numerical experiments in order to provide some managerial insights about the policy. The algorithms and the procedure were implemented in C++ with Visual Studio 6.0 Compiler. All experiments were carried out on a workstation 7550-XEON with 2GHz processor and 2Go RAM, where multiple processes might be activated and run by multiple users at the same time.

3.6.1 Experiments for the Resolution of *Q*–problem

In order to evaluate our proposed dynamic programming algorithm for the *Q*-problem, we first compare it with Crowston and Wagner's algorithm (referred to as algorithm CW hereafter) on medium to large sized instances in Section 3.6.1.1, and then, we also give sensitivity analysis on small sized instances in Section 3.6.1.2, for the purpose of analyzing the impact of system parameters on the performance of the algorithm.

3.6.1.1 Efficiency Analysis on Large Sized Instances

We give the comparison between our algorithm and algorithm CW on three sets of medium to large sized instances with 10 stocks, 50 stocks and 100 stocks, respectively. Each instance of the Q-problem was randomly generated with the following parameter settings:

$h_i^e \in U[1,\ 5], c_i \in h_i^e \cdot U[10,\ 20], \lambda \in U[1,\ 10]$

Without loss of generality, we set $\beta=1$. Because if $\beta<1$, we can change λ to $\lambda\beta$ so that after this change, the original Q-problem is equivalent to the Q-problem with fill rate 1 and average demand rate $\lambda\beta$.

For each set, 10 instances were generated and tested. The maximum and the average computation time for the instances of each set for the two algorithms are given in Table 3.2.

Table 3.2 The results for the tested instances of Q–problem

Instance set	Max/average computation time in seconds	
	Our algorithm	Algorithm CW
10 stocks	0.0011/0.0007	1.1517/0.1775
50 stocks	0.0183/0.0076	8.1493/1.4605
100 stocks	0.6206/0.1705	12.0918/2.2669

From the table, we can observe that our dynamic programming algorithm for the Q-problem is much more efficient than algorithm CW in terms of computation time. The results show that our algorithm is very efficient in solving large instances, with the maximum computation time for an instance with 100 stages less than 1 seconds.

3.6.1.2 Sensitivity Analysis on Small Sized Instances

In this section, we tested three sets of small sized instances with 2 stocks, 3 stocks and 4 stocks, respectively. In this test, all instances of the Q-problemwere generated with the following parameter settings:

$h_i^e \in \{1, 3, 5\},\ c_i \in \{10, 50, 100\},\ \lambda \in \{1, 10, 100\}$

Note that the installation holding cost h_i can be derived from h_i^e and h_i is decreasing from stock 1 to stock N.

For each combination of possible values of the parameters, one instance was generated, so the total number of instances generated for the instance set with 2 stocks, 3 stocks, and 4 stocks is 243, 2187 and 19683, respectively. For each instance, we computed its optimal order size Q_i^* and its cost using the dynamic programming algorithm. After analyzing the numerical results, we obtain the following observations:

1) The computation time for each instance is very short, the average computation time is 0.00064 seconds for an instance with 2 stocks, 0.00065 seconds for an instance with 3 stocks and 0.00079 for an instance with 4 stocks. This further confirms the efficiency of our algorithm.

2) Q_i^* increases in c_i, and decreases in h_i. This observation is obvious and already explained in Shang and Zhou (2009). When c_i become larger, in order to reduce fixed order costs, stock$i$ tends to increase Q_i^*. Also, when h_i becomes smaller, stock i tends to stock more inventory to deal with demand variation by increasing Q_i^*.

3) Q^* increases in λ since the average demand impacts on order costs.

3.6.2 Experiments for the Resolution of R–problem

In this section, we perform the experiments to evaluate the efficiency of the algorithm proposed for R-problem. Similarly, six set of small, medium to large sized instances with 2, 3, 4, 10, 50 and 100 stocks respectively were tested. Each set contains 10 instances. All the instances for R-problem were generated with parameters h^e_i, T_i, s_1 and λ randomly generated according to the uniform distributions described in Table 3.3, with the service level α specified as 0.95. The computation results of the instances are given in Table 3.4.

Table 3.3 Parameter settings of the tested instances of R–problem

Parameter	Value
h^e_i	$h^e_i \in U[1,5]$
T_i	$T_i \in U[1,10]$
s_1	$s_1 \in U[1,3]$
λ	$\lambda \in U[1,10]$

Table 3.4 The results for the tested instances of R-problem

Instance set	Max/average computation time in seconds	
Small instances	2 stocks	0.00056/0.00041
	3 stocks	0.00055/0.00047
	4 stocks	0.00072/0.00064
Medium to large instances	10 stocks	0.0041/0.0024
	50 stocks	0.8311/0.4567
	100 stocks	28.0513/12.1841

From Table 3.4, we can observe that for small instances (N=2,3 and 4) the R-problemcan be solved almost instantaneously by using the dynamic programming algorithm of Graves and Willems, whereas for larger instances (N=10, 50 and 100), the computation time of the algorithm becomes longer but is still quite short. This demonstrates the suitability of this algorithm in solving the R-problem.

3.6.3 Experiments for the Resolution of Problem P with a Given Service Level

The performance of the procedure BETA presented in Section 3.5 for solving problem P depends on the two DP algorithms for solving Q-problem and the R-problem respectively. It also depends on the number of iterations of Step 1-Step 3 performed by the procedure before β^* converges to β. This performance is evaluated by computational experiments on the same sets of randomly generated instances with 10, 50 and 100 stocks respectively as presented in Section 3.3 and Section 3.4, but for each set of instances, four different α-service levels ranged from 0.8 to 0.98 were considered. For each instance set and each service level, 10 instances were generated randomly with the same parameters setting in Section 3.3 and Section 3.4.

The maximum/average computation time and the maximum/average number of iterations of the procedure for solving the instances in each set are given in Table 3.5.

Table 3.5 The results for the tested instances of problem *P*

Instant sets	α-service level	Max/average computation times in seconds	Max/average number of iterations
10 stocks	0.80	0.0121/0.0066	3/2.9
	0.90	0.0065/0.0046	3/2.1
	0.95	0.0098/0.0058	2/2
	0.98	0.0096/0.0062	2/2
50 stocks	0.80	2.6976/1.1846	3/2.5
	0.90	1.2623/0.7305	3/2.2
	0.95	1.3267/0.7861	2/2
	0.98	1.5806/0.7629	2/2
100 stocks	0.80	23.8142/12.6553	3/2.1
	0.90	28.108/13.576	3/2.1
	0.95	15.2308/7.5805	2/2
	0.98	10.8419/6.1872	2/2

From the table, we can see the maximum number of iterations for each instance is no more than 3 and the average number of iterations for each instance is between 2 and 3, the two numbers, which are very close, are neither sensitive to the number of stages in a serial system nor sensitive to its α-service level. In addition, we can observe the two numbers of iterations decrease when the α-service level increases, this may be cause when α approaches to one, β is closer to α. For all instances tested, their maxi mum computation time and average computation time of the procedure are short even for the largest instances with 100 stocks. There is no direct relationship between the ser vice level and the two computation times. These results show that the procedure BETA has a good convergence property and is computationally efficient for solving the inventory policy optimization problem with a given α-service level.

Note that we did not test the finding of the optimal α-service level for each in-stance when the unit operating flexibility cost p is given, because this can be simply done by a line search or by the discretization of possible values of α as mentioned in Section 3.5.

3.6.4 Structural Analysis of the (*R*, *Q*) Policy Found by the GSA

For the base stock policy found by the GSA in the safe stock placement of a serial system, it respects all-or-nothing rule if the service time to final customer is set to zero (s_1=0), i.e., $S_i=0$ or $SI_i+T_i-S_i=0$ for each stock. In order to analyze whether this rule is also valid for the (*R*, *Q*) policy found by our proposed GSA, we conducted additional numerical experiments on randomly generated instances of the serial system with 10 stages and $s_1=0$. We tested 24 sets of instances, each set corresponds to a different pair of (λ, α), where λ and α are the demand rate and the service level respectively. For each instance, h_i^e and T_i are randomly generated as in Table 3.3, i.e., $h_i^e \in U[1, 5]$, $T_i \in [1, 10]$. For each set, 1000 instances are randomly generated. For each instance, in case that its optimal (*R*, *Q*) policy obtained by our model does not respect the all-or-nothing rule, we also calculate its optimal all-or-nothing (*R*, *Q*) policy by imposing the rule (constraint) on our model. The results of this test are given by Table 3.6, in which five numbers are given for each pair of (λ, α). The first number is the percentage of instances whose (*R*, *Q*) policy found by the GSA does not respect the all-or-nothing rule at some stages, the second and the third give respectively the maximum number and the average number of stages that does not respect the rule, and the fourth and the fifth give respectively the maximum relative gap and the average relative gap of the total cost between the optimal (*R*, *Q*) policy found by our model and the optimal all-or-nothing (*R*, *Q*) policy.

Table 3.6 Analysis of the all-or-nothing rule for the (*R*, *Q*) policy found by the GSA

	α=0.5	α=0.6	α=0.7	α=0.9	α=0.95	α=0.98
λ=1	0%, 0, 0, 0, 0	0%, 0, 0, 0, 0	99.3%, 6, 3.457, 5.37%, 1.99%	66.7%, 4, 1.458, 3.08%, 0.66%	38.3%, 3, 1.1018, 1.808%, 0.354%	36.1%, 2, 1.0997, 1.217%, 0.221%
λ=3	0%, 0, 0, 0, 0	84.5%, 5, 1.7503, 2.705%, 0.7534%	69.9%, 4, 1.4764, 2.052%, 0.578%	27.7%, 2, 1.075, 0.756%, 0.1403%	13.8%, 2, 1.0579, 0.461%, 0.142%	9.3%, 1, 1, 0.589%, 0.123%
λ=5	0%, 0, 0, 0, 0	64.8%, 3, 1.345, 0.977%, 0.275%	47.8%, 3, 1.2406, 0.953%, 0.259%	8.5%, 2, 1.0123, 0.332%, 0.0721%	10.2%, 2, 1.049, 0.333%, 0.0719%	1.4%, 1, 1, 0.37%, 0.084%

续表

	α=0.5	α=0.6	α=0.7	α=0.9	α=0.95	α=0.98
λ=10	0%, 0, 0, 0, 0	26.3%, 2, 1.061, 0.471%, 0.117%	24.2%, 2, 1.0728, 0.378%, 0.092%	0%, 0, 0, 0, 0	0%, 0, 0, 0, 0	0%, 0, 0, 0, 0

From the table, we can observe: 1) for α=0.5, all five numbers are zero; 2) the number of instances not respecting the all-or-nothing rule will increase first and decrease then with the increase of α, with only one exception for the case of λ=5 and α=0.9; 3) this number if it is not zero will decrease as the increase of λ; 4) when the demand rate and the α-service level are sufficiently large ($\lambda \geqslant 10$ and $\alpha \geqslant 0.9$), all randomly generated instances validate the all-or-nothing rule; 5) for the instances not validating the rule, the relative cost derivation between the optimal (*R*, *Q*) policy found by our model and the optimal all-or-nothing (*R*, *Q*) policy is quite small.

After a close examination, we find that the invalidity of the all-or-nothing rule by some instances is because their lead time demand bound $D(\tau)$ is not concave as illustrated by an example in Section 2 (See Table 3.1). Our numerical experiments show that $D(\tau+1)$-$D(\tau)$ oscillates between λ+1 and λ after a certain value of λ for these instances because of the discrete nature of the Poisson demand. This oscillation makes $D(\tau)$ neither concave nor convex. If we modify $D(\tau)$ a little bit by setting it to λ after the value, then $D(\tau)$ will be concave and the obtained (*R*, *Q*) policy will be all-or-nothing policy. This modification of $D(\tau)$ by one unit at certain time points will neither sacrifice much the service level nor increase much the total cost of the system.

3.7 Conclusion

In this chapter, we have studied a continuous review serial inventory system with Poisson demand, fixed order costs, and controlled by an echelon (*R*, *Q*) inventory policy. We used the guaranteed service approach (GSA) to optimize the parameters of the policy under the assumption that excessive beyond a prespecified bound will be fulfilled by using extraordinary measures. Different from classical GSA approach, we also consider fixed order costs and the operating flexibility costs for fulfilling excessive demand. A deterministic mathematical programming model is established for the inventory policy optimization problem. The model is solved by an iterative procedure based on two dynamic programming (DP) algorithms for solving its two sub-models respectively. Experimental results demonstrate the efficiency of the two algorithms and the procedure.

Chapter 4

Optimization of (R, Q) Policies for Assembly Systems

In terms of network structure, serial inventory systems can be regarded as a special case of assembly inventory systems, in which each stock has only one downstream stock. As an extension, this chapter deals with the optimization of (R, Q) policy for an assembly inventory system with Poisson demand under the GSA. The optimization methodology used in this chapter is similar to that for serial inventory systems. However, different from the serial system which has only one immediate predecessor, the assembly system studied in this chapter may have a stock that has more than one immediate predecessor, this leads to a more complicated network structure. Therefore, the dy namic programming algorithm for the order size decision sub-problem (Q-problem) proposed in the last chapter cannot be directly used for assembly systems. In this chapter, we develop a new dynamic programming algorithm to solve Q-problem for assembly systems studied. The key idea of the algorithm is that the dynamic programming recursive procedure is used in both forward and backward directions. A forward procedure is applied first for the purpose of reducing the solution space of the problem. Based on the solution obtained by the forward procedure, a backward recursive procedure is used to identify the optimal decisions.

This chapter is organized as follows: The problem description and notation are first given in Section 4.1. Then, a mathematical model for the optimization of (R, Q) policies for assembly systems is formulated in Section 4.2. Two efficient dynamic programming algorithms for order size decision sub-problem and reorder point decision sub-problem are developed in Section 4.3 and Section 4.4 respectively. The original model is solved in Section 4.5 by an iterative procedure based on the solutions of the two sub-problems. In Section 4.6, we give some numerical experiments for evaluating the performances of the procedure and the two DP algorithms.

4.1 Problem Description

Since the GSA has been described in the last chapter, this section will only briefly introduce the assembly system studied and some special assumptions on the system.

Assembly System Studied Consider a continuous review assembly inventory system with multiple intermediate items (components and sub-assemblies) and a single end item. The network structure of the system is defined by its bill-of-material (BOM) which is a tree whose root node corresponds to the end item, as illustrated in Figure 4.1. All components at the highest level of the BOM are purchased from outside suppliers, these components are assembled into a finished product (end item) at the lowest level of the BOM. Hereafter, the stock of item i in the system is also called stock i, i=1, 2, .., N. It is assumed that the outside suppliers never run out of stock. Let N denote the number of items (stocks) in the system, N>3. These items (stocks) are numbered from 1 to N, where item (stock) 1 represents the end item (stock). Moreover, it is assumed that customer demand occurs only at the end item (stock) and follows a Poisson process with

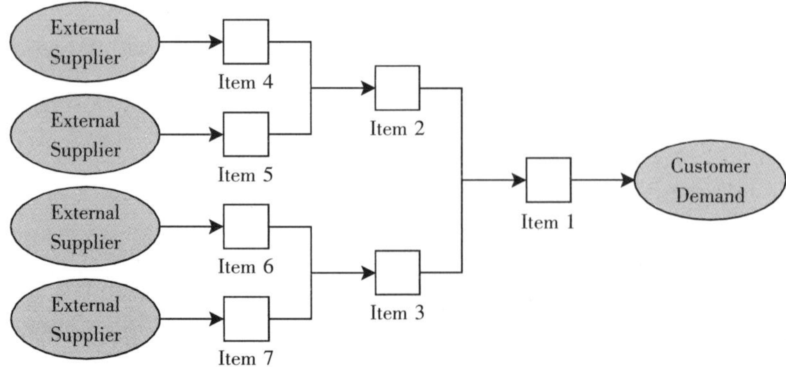

Figure 4.1 An assembly system with 7 items (stocks)

the average demand rate λ. For simplicity but without loss of generality, we assume the assembly of one unit of each intermediate or end item (stock) requires only one unit of each of its components.

For such a system, our objective is to derive its optimal (*R*, *Q*) policy by using the guaranteed service approach (GSA), so that the total cost of the system is minimized while satisfying a target service level to final customer. As mentioned in Chapter 3, the total system cost consists of three costs: Fixed order cost, inventory holding cost and operating flexibility cost (See Section 3.1.3).

Integer-ratio Constraint Under an (*R*, *Q*) policy, we assume an integer-ratio constraint between the order size of each stock *i* and its immediate successor *s*(*i*). Since each stock in the assembly system has more than one upstream stock, the integer-ratio constraints can be rewritten as:

$Q_i = m_{s(i)i} Q_{s(i)}$, for i=1, 2, ⋯, N

where $m_{s(i)i}$ is a positive integer and $m_{s(i)i}$ is assumed to be 1 when i=1.

Maximum Reasonable Lead Time Demand Level The key assumption in the GSA is that lead time demand of the customer is assumed to be bounded by a maximum reasonable lead time demand level and all excessive lead time demand superior to this level will be treated by extraordinary measures. Similar to serial systems, the assembly system has only a single end stock at which customer demand occurs. Therefore, under the assumption of Poisson customer demand with average demand rate λ and the predefined event-oriented service level α, the maximum reasonable lead time demand level $D(\tau)$ over any τ units of time can be determined by

$$\sum_{k=0}^{D(\tau)} \frac{(\lambda\tau)^k e^{-\lambda\tau}}{k!} \geqslant \alpha \tag{4-1}$$

4.2 Mathematical Model Formulation

Similar to serial systems, the total cost of the assembly system with *N* stocks and implemented with an (*R*, *Q*) policy can be formulated as equation (4-2).

$$\sum_{i=1}^{N}\left(\frac{c_i\lambda\beta}{Q_i}+h_i^e\cdot E[I_i^e]\right)+p\lambda(1-\beta) \tag{4-2}$$

In equation (4-2), the cost function has three terms, fixed order costs, inventory holding costs and the costs of using operating flexibility to fulfill excessive customer demand.

Next, we briefly introduce the formulation of cost term $E[I_i^e]$ for i=1, 2, ⋯, N.

At time t, the following balance equation is well-known:

$$IL_i^e(t)=IP_i^e(t-L_i)-d[t-L_i, t) \tag{4-3}$$

In the GSA, all customer demands inferior to the bounded demand can always be satisfied, so $IL_i^e(t)=I_i^e(t)$, we then have

$$I_i^e(t)=IP_i^e(t-L_i)-d[t-L_i, t) \tag{4-4}$$

For stock i, in order to provide 100% guaranteed service, $I_i^e(t)\geqslant 0$ must be satisfied, i.e.,

$$IP_i^e(t-L_i)\geqslant d[t-L_i, t) \tag{4-5}$$

In addition, for stock i, no stockout means that on-hand inventory $I_i(t)$ is always nonnegative. According to the definition above, $I_i(t)$ is given by

$$I_i(t)=I_i^e(t)-IP_{s(i)}^e(t) \tag{4-6}$$

Equation (4-6) is equivalent to the equation $IP_{s(i)}^e(t)=I_i^e(t)-I_i(t)$, which states that at time t the echelon inventory position of the downstream stock $s(i)$ of stock i is equal to the echelon on-hand inventory of stock i minus the on-hand inventory of stock i, i.e. $IP_{s(i)}^e(t)$ is equal to the inventories at or in transit to all i's downstream stocks at time t. This is true since no outstanding order placed by $s(i)$ is waiting for delivery at stock i (in the equivalence model), no backorder is at the lowest echelon of the system under GSA, and $IP_{s(i)}^e(t)$is defined as outstanding orders of $s(i)$ waiting for delivery at stock i plus the inventories at or in transit to all i's downstream stock minus backorders at the lowest echelon at time t. Note that for an assembly system, each stock has at most one immediate downstream stock.

From equation (4-4) and equation (4-6), we have

$$IP_i^e(t-L_i)\geqslant d[t-L_i, t)+IP_{s(i)}^e(t) \tag{4-7}$$

Since the satisfaction of constraint (4-7) implies the satisfaction of constraint (4-5), we only need to consider constraint (4-7).

Hadley and Whitin (1961) proved that IP_i^e is uniformly distributed over the interval $[R_i+1, R_i+Q_i]$, this means that there is $t \geqslant L_i$, such that $IP_i^e(t-L_i)=R_i+1$ and t can be taken as a time larger than any given number.

For equation (4-7), there may exist two cases, i.e., $L_i>0$ and $L_i=0$. According to the analysis in Chapter 3, we can derive the following two important results:

1) In the case of $L_i>0$, if starting from t-L_i with inventory position $IP_i^e(t-L_i)=R_i+1$, there exists a realization of the demand process from time t-L_i to time t such that $d[t-L_i, t) \geqslant D(L_i)$ and $IP_{s(i)}^e(t)=R_{s(i)}+Q_{s(i)}$.

In this case, in order to ensure that inequality (4-7) holds for any demand realization under the GSA, we must have

$$R_i+1 \geqslant D(L_i)+R_{s(i)}+Q_{s(i)} \text{ for } i=1, 2, \cdots, N \tag{4-8}$$

where $R_{s(i)}$ and $Q_{s(i)}$ are assumed to be 0.

2) In the case of $L_i=0$, $D(L_i)=0$ and inequality (4-7) becomes $IP_i^e(t) \geqslant IP_{s(i)}^e(t)$ for any time t. Since the echelon (R_i, Q_i) policy we consider is transformed from an installation (r_i, Q_i) policy according to equation (2-1), we have $R_i+1=R_{s(i)}+Q_{s(i)}+r_i+1$. Since $r_i \geqslant -1$(See Section 2.2.2), we have $R_i+1 \geqslant R_{s(i)}+Q_{s(i)}$, this implies that inequality (4-8) also holds for this case.

Since $L_i=SI_i+T_i-S_i$, we can derive

$$R_i \geqslant \sum_{j \in SUC(i)} D(SI_j+T_j-S_j)+\sum_{j \in SUC(i)} Q_j-Q_i-C_i \text{ for } i=1, 2, \cdots, N \tag{4-9}$$

Where C_i is the cardinality of SUC(i) for i=1, 2, ⋯, N.

Since the objective of the model is to minimize the total system costs in the long-run, there must be an optimal solution with R_i, i=1, 2, ⋯, N satisfying the following equations

$$R_i=\sum_{j \in SUC(i)} D(SI_j+T_j-S_j)+\sum_{j \in SUC(i)} Q_j-Q_i-C_i \text{ for } i=1, 2, \cdots, N \tag{4-10}$$

Assume that all excessive demands are satisfied without incurring inventory holding costs. With this assumption, we can ignore excessive demand in the calculation of expected inventory holding costs $E[I_i^e]$, that is,

$$E[d[t-SI_i-T_i+S_i,\ t)]=E[\hat{d}[t-SI_i-T_i+S_i,t)]=\lambda\beta(SI_i+T_i-S_i) \quad (4\text{-}11)$$

From equation (4-4), $E[I_i^e]$ for i=1, 2, ⋯, N can be derived as follows:

$$\begin{aligned}E[I_i^e] &= E[IP_i^e(t-SI_i-T_i+S_i)-d[t-SI_i-T_i+S_i,t)] \\ &= E[IP_i^e(t-SI_i-T_i+S_i)-\hat{d}[t-SI_i-T_i+S_i,t)] \\ &= R_i+\frac{1+Q_i}{2}-\lambda\beta(SI_i+T_i-S_i) \\ &= \sum_{j\in SUC(i)}D(SI_j+T_j-S_j)-\lambda\beta(SI_i+T_i-S_i)+\sum_{j\in SUC(i)}Q_j+\frac{1-Q_i}{2}-C_i \quad (4\text{-}12)\end{aligned}$$

With equation (4-2) and equation (4-12) and referring to the guaranteed service approach proposed in Graves and Willems (1996, 2000), we can formulate the inventory policy optimization problem as the following nonlinear programming problem:

P: Minimize

$$\sum_{i=1}^{N}\frac{c_i\lambda\beta}{Q_i}+\sum_{i=1}^{N}\{h_i^e\cdot[\sum_{j\in SUC(i)}D(SI_j+T_j-S_j)-\lambda\beta(SI_i+T_i-S_i)+\frac{1+Q_i}{2}-C_i]+ \sum_{j\in PRE(i)}h_j^e\cdot Q_{s(i)}\}+p\lambda(1-\beta)$$

Subject to:

$Q_i=m_{s(i)i}Q_{s(i)}$ for $i=1, 2, \cdots, N$ (4-13)

$SI_i+T_i-S_i\geqslant 0$ for $i=1, 2, \cdots, N$ (4-14)

$SI_i\geqslant \max\{S_{P(i)}\}$ for $i=1, 2, \cdots, N$ (4-15)

$0\leqslant S_1\leqslant s_1$ (4-16)

$Q_i\geqslant 0$ and integer for i=1, 2,⋯, N (4-17)

SI_i, $S_i\geqslant 0$ and integer for i=1, 2,⋯, N (4-18)

The objective function represents the average total costs of the system in the long run, which consists of average fixed order costs, average inventory holding costs and operating flexibility costs of using extraordinary measures. Constraint (4-13) is the integer-ratio constraint between the order sizes of any two successive stocks. Constraint (4-14) assures that the net lead time at each stock is nonnegative. Constraint (4-15) implies that each stock i can start production only when all the inputs are available. Constraint (4-16) imposes an upper bound s_1 on the outbound service time of stock 1. Constraint (4-17) and Constraint (4-18) imply that all the decision variables must be integer.

In the objective function, β is always unknown, this makes the optimization problem can not be solved easily. We first assume that β is given, then, the model P can be divided into two independent sub-problems, order size decision sub-problem (Q-problem) and reorder point decision sub-problem (R-problem). The Q-problem has a convex objection composed of all Q-dependent cost terms and Constraint (4-13) and Constraint (4-17), whereas the R-problem has a nonlinear objective function composed of all R-dependent cost terms and linear Constraint (4-14), Constraint (4-15), Constraint (4-16) and Constraint (4-18).

Note that when β is known, $p\lambda(1-\beta)$ becomes a constant which can be ignored, the constant term- $\sum_{i}^{N}(C_i h_i^e)+p\lambda(1-\beta)$ in the objective function of P can be omitted in the two sub-problems.

***Q*–problem:**

Minimize: $\sum_{i=1}^{N}\left[\frac{c_i\lambda\beta}{Q_i}+h_i^e\cdot\frac{1+Q_i}{2}+\sum_{j\in PRE(i)}h_j^e\cdot Q_{s(i)}\right]$

Subject to:

$Q_i=m_{s(i)i}Q_{s(i)}$ for $i=1, 2, \cdots, N$

$Q_i\geqslant 0$ and integer for $i=1, 2, \cdots, N$

***R*–problem:**

Minimize: $\sum_{i=1}^{N}h_i^e\cdot\left[\sum_{j\in SUC(i)}D(SI_j+T_j-S_j)-\lambda\beta(SI_i+T_i-S_i)\right]$

Subject to:

$SI_i+T_i-S_i\geqslant 0$ for $i=1, 2, \cdots, N$

$SI_i\geqslant\max\{S_{P(i)}\}$ for $i=1, 2, \cdots, N$

$0\leqslant S_1\leqslant s_1$

SI_i, $S_i>0$ and integer for $i=1, 2, \cdots, N$

Based on the analysis in Section 3.5, β is always unknown, but it can be determined by the inventory (R, Q) policy of the system. Therefore, in the next two sections, two efficient dynamic programming algorithms will be proposed to solve Q-problem and R-problem in Section 4.3 and Section 4.4 respectively when α and β are given. As soon as the two sub-problems are solved, the optimal order size Q_i and optimal reorder point R_i for each stock can be derived. Based on the optimal inventory (R, Q) policy, the fill rate β can also be calculated. Finally, the original optimization problem P can be solved by an iterative procedure based on deriving the optimal value of β in Section 4.5.

4.3 Dynamic Programming Algorithm for Q–problem

For a serial inventory system, we have proposed a dynamic programming algorithm to solve the Q-problem. In the algorithm, a recursive procedure is first used to identify the optimal decision at each stock depending on the state of its successor stock, and the optimal solution of the problem can then be derived by a simple backtrack process. Different from the serial systemwhich has only one immediate predecessor, the assembly system studied may have a stock that has more than one immediate predecessor, the dynamic programming algorithm cannot be directly applied to solve the Q-problem of the assembly system.

In this section, we develop a new dynamic program for solving the Q-problem of the assembly systems studied. The key idea of the algorithm is that the dynamic programming recursive procedure is applied in two directions, i.e., both forward direction and backward direction. In the forward procedure, the state of the system is extended forward from the end stock to the stocks purchased from external suppliers, whereas the state is extended in the reverse direction in the backward procedure. The forward procedure is applied first for the purpose of reducing the solution space of the problem. Based on the solutions obtained by the forward procedure, a backward recursive procedure is applied to identify the optimal decision at each stock and then obtain the optimal solution of the problem.

4.3.1 Assumptions and Notations

To present the new dynamic programming (DP) algorithm, the problem studied is first formulated as a multistep decision problem in a network whose nodes represent the states of the system. To facilitate the network modeling of the DP, we first label (number) the stocks of the assembly system with N stocks in a particular way based on its BOM as illustrated in Figure 4.1.

Labeling the Items (Stocks): let U denote the set of unlabeled stocks and u denote the label (number) assigned to the latest labeled stock. The labeling process starts from the end stock which is labeled as stock 1, in each step we choose from U a stock whose successor has been labeled, label (number) the stock as stock u+1, and remove it from U. This process is repeated until U becomes empty.

In the following, the stock corresponding to node i is called stock i, $i = 1, 2, \cdots, N$. Before presenting the state space reduction technique and the DP algorithm, we first introduce the following notations which will be used later.

i: stock index, i=0, 1, $\cdots$, N+1, stock 0 and stock N+1 are two dummy items (stocks) correspond to the starting state and ending state of the network model for DP, respectively;

Q_i: state variable of stock i, which represents a possible order size of stock i, and the set of all possible values of Q_i is denoted by W_i, i=1, 2, $\cdots$, N;

$m_{s(i)i}$ decision variable of stock i, which links Q_i with $Q_{s(i)}$, i.e., $Q_i = m_{s(i)i} Q_{s(i)}$, i= 2, $\cdots$, N;

$M_{s(i)i}(Q_{s(i)})$: the set of permissible values of $m_{s(i)i}$ given the state $Q_{s(i)}$ of stock i, i= 2, $\cdots$, N,

$d_i(Q_i)$: the cost of stock i when the current state is Q_i, i=1, 2, .., N.

4.3.2 State Space of Q_i

By analysis of the objective function of the Q-problem and its integer-ratio constraints, i.e., Constraint (4-13), we can find the following two important properties regarding W_1 and $M_{s(i)i}$ $(Q_{s(i)})$ for stock i, i=2, 3, $\cdots$, N. Based on the properties, the state space of each stock i (i=1, 2, ⋯, N) can be determined.

Firstly, an upper bound of Q_1 is given by property 4.1.

Property 4.1: For an assembly inventory system with Nstocks and the integer-ratio constraints among Q_i given by (4-13) for i=2, 3, ⋯, N, an upper bound of Q_1 is given by

$$\overline{Q}_1=\sqrt{\frac{2\lambda\beta\sum_{i=1}^{N}c_i}{\sum_{i=1}^{N}h_i^e+2\sum_{i=2}^{N}\sum_{j\in PRE(i)}h_j^e}}$$

Proof: Substitute Q_i by $\prod_{j\in SUC(i)}m_{s(j)j}\cdot Q_1$ for i=1, 2, ⋯, N in the objective function of the Q-problem, we have

$$\sum_{i=1}^{N}[\frac{c_i\lambda\beta}{\prod_{j\in SUC(i)}m_{s(j)j}\cdot Q_1}+h_i^e\cdot\frac{1+\prod_{j\in SUC(i)}m_{s(j)j}\cdot Q_1}{2}+$$

$$\sum_{j\in PRE(i)}h_j^e\cdot\prod_{k=s(i),\ u\in SUC(k)}m_{s(u)u}\cdot Q_1]$$

If $m_{s(i)i}$ for i=1, 2, ⋯, N are fixed, the above function contains only one variable Q_1. Because the function is convex, its optimalvalue of Q_1 can be derived at the point where its first derivative with respect to Q_1 is equal to 0. After calculating the first derivative, we can get the following equation:

$$-\frac{\lambda\beta}{Q_1^2}\cdot G+H=0$$

where

$$G=\sum_{i=1}^{N}\frac{c_i}{\prod_{j\in SUC(i)}m_{s(j)j}}$$

$$H=\sum_{i=1}^{N}[\frac{1}{2}h_i^e\cdot\prod_{j\in SUC(i)}m_{s(j)j}+\sum_{j\in PRE(i)}h_j^e\cdot\prod_{k=s(i),\ u\in SUC(k)}m_{s(u)u}]$$

Then

$$Q_1^2=(\sum_{i=1}^{N}\frac{c_i}{\prod_{j\in SUC(i)}m_{s(j)j}})$$

$$\frac{2\lambda\beta}{\sum_{i=1}^{N}[(h_i^e \cdot \prod_{j\in SUC(i)} m_{s(j)j}) + 2\sum_{j\in PRE(i)} h_j^e \cdot \prod_{k=s(i),\ u\in SUC(k)} m_{s(u)u}]}$$

By analyzing the above equation, the maximum value of Q_1 is attained when $m_{s(i)i}$=1 for i=1, 2, ⋯, N, then

$$\overline{Q}_1 = \sqrt{\frac{2\lambda\beta\sum_{i=1}^{N} c_i}{\sum_{i=1}^{N} h_i^e + 2\sum_{i=2}^{N}\sum_{j\in PRE(i)} h_j^e}}$$

Let $U_i(Q_{s(i)})$ denote the set of all possible values of Q_i when $Q_{s(i)}$ is given. Then, an upper bound of $m_{s(i)i}$ for each item i, i=2, 3, ⋯, N is given by Property 4.2 as a function of the state $Q_{s(i)}$ of item $s(i)$.

Property 4.2: For an assembly inventory system with Nstocks and integer-ratio constraints given by (4-13), if the order size of the immediate successor of stock i is $Q_{s(i)}$ (i=2,⋯, N), then an upper bound of $m_{s(i)i}$ can be derived by

$$m^{-}_{s(i)i} = \frac{1}{Q_{s(i)}} \cdot \sqrt{\frac{2\lambda\beta\sum_{j\in PRE(i)} c_i}{3\sum_{j\in PRE(i)} h_j^e - 2h_i^e}}$$

Proof: We first define $V(i)$ as the set consisting of all the predecessors of stock i, and $X(i)$ as the set consisting of all successors of stock i.

If we substitute Q_i by $\prod_{j\in SUC(i)} m_{s(j)j} \cdot Q_1$ for i=2, ⋯, N in the objective function of the Q-problem, the objective function, denoted by T, can be rewritten as:

$$T = \frac{\lambda\beta}{Q_{s(i)}} \cdot \frac{1}{m_{s(i)i}} P + Q_{s(i)} \cdot m_{s(i)i} \cdot R + M$$

where

$$P = \sum_{j\in PRE(i)} \frac{c_j \prod_{u\in SUC(i)} m_{s(u)u}}{\prod_{k\in SUC(j)} m_{s(k)k}}$$

$$R = \sum_{j\in PRE(i)} \frac{h_j^e}{2} \cdot \frac{\prod_{u\in SUC(i)} m_{s(u)u}}{\prod_{k\in SUC(j)} m_{s(k)k}} + \sum_{l\in V(i)} h_l^e$$

$$M=\sum_{j\in X(i)}\left[\frac{c_i\lambda}{Q_j}+h_j^e\left(\frac{1+Q_j}{2}\right)+\sum_{j\in PRE(i)}h_j^e\cdot Q_{s(i)}\right]+\frac{1}{2}\sum_{j\in PRE(i)}h_j^e$$

The objective function T is convex with respect to $m_{s(i)i}$, so the optimalvalue of $m_{s(i)i}$ can be derived at the point where the first partial derivative of the function withrespect to $m_{s(i)i}$ is equal to 0, so,

$$\frac{\partial T}{\partial m_{s(i)i}}=-\frac{\lambda}{Q_{s(i)}}P*\frac{1}{m_{s(i)i}^2}+RQ_{s(i)}=0 \text{ for } i=1, 2, \cdots, N$$

Then,

$$m_{s(i)i}=\frac{1}{Q_{s(i)}}\sqrt{\lambda\beta\cdot\frac{P}{R}} \text{ for } i=2, 3, \cdots, N$$

The maximum value of $m_{s(i)i}$ is attained when $m_{s(j)j}=1$ for $j\in V(i)$, so

$$m_{s(i)i}^{-}=\frac{1}{Q_{s(i)}}\sqrt{\frac{2\lambda\sum_{j\in PRE(i)}c_j}{3\sum_{j\in PRE(i)}h_j^e-2h_i^e}}$$

According to the integer-ratio Constraint (4-13), $U_i(Q_{s(i)})$ can be then be written as

$U_i(Q_{s(i)})=\{k|k=Q_{s(i)}\cdot j(j\in M_{s(i)i}(Q_{s(i)}))\}$, $i=1, 2, \cdots, N$

$U_i(Q_{s(i)})$ can be calculated by $m_{s(i)i}^{-}$ and $Q_{s(i)}$.

Then, the set of all possible value of Q_i can be described as

$W_i=\{U_i(k_1)\cup U_i(k_2)\cdots\cup U_i(k_n)$, where$\{k_1, k_2, \cdots, k_n\in W_{s(i)}\}\}$, $i=2, 3, \cdots, N$

Therefore, the state space of each stock i (i=1, 2, ⋯, N) can be derive as follows:

$$W_i=\begin{cases}\{1, 2, \cdots, \overline{Q}_1\}, i=1\\ \{U_i(k_1)\cup U_i(k_2)\cdots\cup U_i(k_n), \text{where}\{k_1, k_2, \cdots, k_n\in W_{s(i)}\}\}, i=2, \cdots, N\end{cases}$$

Under the two important Properties, the state space on each stock can be determined. And the state space of each stock only depends on the order size of its immediate successor.

4.3.3 State Space Reduction

From the above analysis, we have got all possible values of Q_i and its relationship with the order size of its successor $Q_{s(i)}$. However, the correspondence between Q_i and $Q_{s(i)}$ is not one-to-one, that is, for each value of Q_i ($Q_i\in W_i$), there may exist more than one possible values of $Q_{s(i)}$. In this subsection, we propose a forward DP recursive procedure to determine the unique $Q_{s(i)}$ for any given Q_i in the optimal solution of the Q-problem. This can help us to reduce the state space of the problem when we apply a backward DP recursive procedure to identify its optimal solution.

Observe that the objective function of the Q-problem is additive with respect to the order size of each stock and the integer-ratio constraints of the problem only relate the order size Q_i to the order size $Q_{s(i)}$ of its immediate successor stock $s(i)$, so the order size decision of each stock only depends on the order size of its immediate successor, not on the order sizes of other stocks.

Based on this observation, we can develop the forward recursive procedure, which starts from the end stock (stock 1) and extends the current stock to its immediate predecessors in each step until stock N.

Let $f_i(Q_i)$ as the minimal total cost of stock i and its successors (SUC(i)) when the order size of stock i is given by Q_i, i=0, 1, 2, ⋯, N. The state transition function and the recursion equations can then be formulated as:

State transition functions:

$$Q_i = m_{s(i)i} \cdot Q_{s(i)},\ i = 1, 2, \cdots, N$$

Recursion equations:

$$\begin{cases} f_i(Q_i) = \min\limits_{m_{s(i)i} \in M_{s(i)i}(Q_{s(i)})} \{ d_i(Q_{s(i)i}, m_{s(i)i}) + f_{s(i)}(Q_{s(i)}) \} i = 1, 2, \cdots, N+1,\ Q_i \in W_i \\ f_0(0) = 0 \end{cases}$$

where

$$\begin{cases} d_i(Q_{s(i)}, m_{s(i)i}) = \dfrac{c_i \lambda \beta}{Q_i} + h_i^e \cdot \dfrac{1+Q_i}{2} + \sum_{j \in PRE(i)} h_j^e \cdot Q_{s(i)},\ \mathrm{i} = 1, 2, \cdots, N,\ Q_i \in W_i \\ d_{N+1}(Q_N, m_N) = 0 \end{cases}$$

With the equations, for each stock i (i=0, 1, ⋯, N+1), we can calculate $f_i(Q_i)$ for each possible order size $Q_i \in W_i$ and the corresponding integer ratio $m_{s(i)i}$ that minimizes the right hand term in the recursion equations.

For each stock i, let us define $suc(i, Q_i)=(s(i),\ Q_{s(i)})$, where $Q_{s(i)}$ is the unique order sizeof stock $s(i)$ obtained by the forward recursion procedure when the order size of stock i is Q_i, for any $Q_i \in W_i$, i=1, 2, ···, N+1. The outputs of this procedure include a set of possible values of triple $(Q_i, f_i(Q_i), suc(i, Q_i))$. Table 4.1 gives an example of the outputs obtained by the procedure for stock 5 of the assembly system in Figure 4.1.

Table 4.1 The outputs of the forward procedure

Outputs		
Q_5	$f_5(Q_5)$	$suc(5, Q_5)$
1	131	(3, 1)
2	78.5	(3, 2)
5	69.33	(3, 1)

From Table 4.1, we can see that for stock 5, there are three possible values of $(Q_5, f_5(Q_5), suc(5, Q_5))$ with Q_5=1, 2, and 5, respectively. The outputs given in Table 4.1 show that Q_3=1 if Q_5=1 or 5, and Q_3=2 if Q_5=2.

After the forward recursive procedure, for each stock i and possible value of Q_i ($Q_i \in W_i$), there exists the unique possible value of $Q_{s(i)}$ given by suc (i, Q_i), and this one-to-one correspondence can help us to reduce the state space in which the optimal solution of the Q-problem is located.

4.3.4 Dynamic Programme Algorithm

The backward DP recursive procedure for the Q-problem of the assembly system studied can be formulated in the decreasing order of the labels of its stocks as described in the above, i.e., from stock N to stock 1. This is, an assembly system with N stock can be regarded as "a serial system" with N stages as depicted in Figure 4.2 (in this figure, N=7), where stage N+1 and stage 0 are two dummy stages correspond to the starting state and ending state for the DP procedure, respectively, stage i ($N \geqslant i \geqslant 1$) corresponds to stock i, and the state of stock i is given by a possible value of batch size Q_i. Since one-to-one correspondence between item i and its immediate successor $s(i)$, i.e., $suc(i, Q_i)$, is already given by the forward DP procedure, the backward DP procedure can operate as the DP procedure for the Q-problem of the serial system presented in the last chapter, except that the outputs of the forward DP procedure $(Q_i, f_i(Q_i), suc(i, Q_i))$ for each stock i (i=1, 2, ⋯, N) will be used in the backward DP procedure.

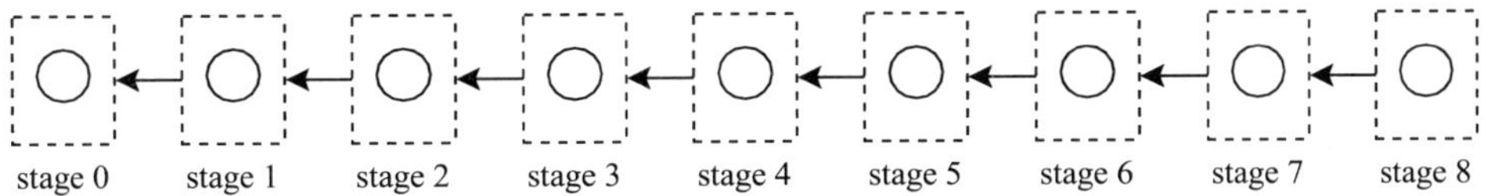

Figure 4.2 The stages of an assembly system

Let $g_i(Q_i)$ denote the minimal total cost of stock i and its all predecessor stocks of PRE(i) when the order size of stock i is given by $Q_i \in W_i$, i=N+1, N, ⋯, 1.

In the forward procedure, we already get all possible values of order size Q_i for each stock i and their corresponding values of suc (i, Q_i) for the order size $Q_{s(i)}$ of its immediate successor stock $s(i)$, i=0, 1, 2, ⋯, N+1. These values are used as the possible values of the state variables of stock i and stocks(i) in the backward search, for i=N+1, N, ⋯, 0.

Formally, the recursion equations of the backward DP procedure can be written as:

Recursion Equations:

$$\begin{cases} g_{N+1}(0)=0 \\ g_i(Q_i)=\min\limits_{(j,Q_j)\in\{(j,Q_{j'})|suc(j',Q_{j'})=(i,Q_i)\}} \sum_{j\in P(i)} g_j(Q_j)+d_i(Q_{s(i)}, m_{s(i)i}),\ i=N, N\text{-}1, \cdots, 1, Q_i\in W_i \\ g_0(0)=\min\limits_{Q_1} g_1(Q_1),\ Q_1\in W_1 \end{cases}$$

For item $j \in P(i)$, if there is no Q_j satisfying suc(j, Q_j) = (i, Q_i), then $g_i(Q_i)=\infty$.

After the execution of the backward recursive procedure, for each stock i, i=0, 1, 2, ⋯, N+1, we calculate $g_i(Q_i)$ for each $Q_i \in W_i$, where $g_0(0)$ is the optimal cost value of the Q-problem ofthe assembly system studied.

In summary, the main step of the dynamic programming algorithm is presented in the following.

Step 1: Set i=0, $f_0(0)$=0 as the boundary condition of the forward DP procedure.

Forward Recursion:

Step 2: i=1, calculate the set W_1 of possible values of Q_1 using Property 4.1. Then, calculate suc(1, Q_1) for each Q_1 in W_1.

For i=2, 3, ⋯, N;

Step 3: Calculate $M_{s(i)i}$ $(Q_{s(i)})$ based on Property 4.2, according to the state transition function $Q_i=m_{s(i)i} \cdot Q_{s(i)}$ and the forward recursion equations,calculate suc(i, Q_i) for each Q_i.

Backward Recursion:

For i=N+1, N, ⋯, 1;

Step 4: Based on $suc(i, Q_i)$, calculate $g_i(Q_i)$ for each Q_i.

Step 5: Calculate $g_0(Q_0)$, the minimal total cost of the Q-problem.

Step 6: Backtrack from stock 0 to stock 1, stock 1 to stock 2, ⋯, stock N-1 to stock N to find the optimal order size Q_i^* for each stocki, i=1, 2, ⋯, N.

4.4 Dynamic Programming Algorithm for *R*–problem

Under the GSA, Graves and Willems (2000) presented an efficient dynamic programming algorithm for finding the optimal service time of a multi-echelon inventory system with a spanning tree structure. In assembly inventory system, there is no apparent order of the items (nodes) in which the algorithm would proceed. However, Graves and Willems (1996, 2000) label (number) the nodes in a spanning tree so that only one state variable, either the inbound service time or outbound service time at each stock is required for the dynamic programming recursion. In this section, we use their dynamic programming algorithm to solve the R-problem. In the following, we will briefly introduce the algorithm applied to the R-problem.

We first label the nodes (stocks) in the assembly system and then describe the recursion equation of the dynamic programming algorithm for the R-problem.

Labeling the Nodes: Let U denote the set of unlabelled stocks and u denote the label (number) assigned to the latest labeled stock. The node labeling process starts from a node at the highest level of the BOM of the assembly system. In each step, we take a node $i \in U$ which is adjacent to at most one other node in U in the BOM, label it as node (stock) u+1, and remove it from U. This process is repeated until U becomes empty.

Similar to serial system optimization problem, we also denote $N(i)$ as the subset of nodes that are connected to node i in the sub-graph consisting of nodes $\{1, 2, .., i\}$ of the BOM. $N(i)$ can be determined recursively by the following equation:

$$N(i)=\{i\}+\sum_{j\in P(i)} N(j)$$

The dynamic programming algorithm recursively evaluates a functional equation for each node (stock), in the order of nodes give by the node labeling. Let us define $f_i(S)$ as the minimum holding cost of the nodes (stocks) in $N(i)$, when the outbound service time for item i is set of S in the assembly system. Since each node (stock) i has only one downstream adjacent node (stock) with a higher label, i.e., $s(i)$, in the assembly system, according to Graves and Willems (1996, 2000), the functional equation for each node (stock) i can be formulated as:

$$C_i(S, SI)=h_i^e\cdot[\sum_{j\in SUC(i)} D(SI_j+T_j-S_j)-\lambda\beta(SI_i+T_i-S_i)]+\sum_{j\in P(i)} \min_{0\leqslant S\leqslant \min\{SI, M_j\}}$$

$$[f_i(SI)]$$

where $C_i(S, SI)$ is a function of the outbound service time and the inbound service time of node (stock) i.

In the equation, the first term is the holding cost of node (stock) i as a function of S and SI, and the second term is the holding cost of the node in $N(i)$ that are upstream nodes of node (stock) i.

With this function, the minimum holding cost $f_i(S)$ can be obtained by solving the following optimization problem:

$$f_i(S)=\min_{SI}\{C_i(S, SI)\}$$

Subject to:

$$\max(0, S-T_i)\leqslant SI\leqslant M_i-T_i$$

Here, we can bind S by its maximum service time M_i, and if stock i is the end stock, we constrain S by its maximum service time as $S_1\leqslant s_1$.

The dynamic programming algorithm can be summarized in the following.

Step 1: For i: =1 to N, evaluated $f_i(S)$ for S=0, 1, $\cdots$, M_i;

Step 2: Minimize $f_N(S)$ to derive the optimal objective function value of the *R*-problem;

Step 3: Backtrack from node (stock) N to node (stock) N-1, ⋯, node (stock) 2 to node (stock) 1 to get the optimal inbound service time and outbound service time of each node (stock).

4.5 Optimization Procedure

After the introduction of two DP algorithms for the two sub-problems (Q-problem and R-problem), in this section we propose an iterative optimization procedure to solve the original optimization problem (model P). As mentioned in Section 3.5, for a given service level α, the original optimization problem can be solved by an iterative procedure based on guessing the value of β in each iteration. The procedure has two main steps in each iteration:

- For an estimated value of β, solve model P
- Calculate the real fill rate β of the considered system;

To solve model P, we first need to know the fill rate β, which can be determined by the (R, Q) inventory policy of the system considered. A method is developed for calculating the fill rate β in Section 3.5 when its inventory policy is given. Since the fill rate β only depends on the reorder point R and the order size Q of the end stock which is unique for the assembly system, its fill rate β can be calculated similarly by

$$\beta = 1 - \frac{1}{Q}\sum_{i=R+1}^{R+Q}\sum_{k=i+1}^{\infty}\frac{(\lambda L)^k e^{-\lambda L}}{k!}\cdot\frac{k-i}{k}$$
$$= 1 - \frac{1}{Q}\sum_{i=R+1}^{R+Q}\sum_{k=i+1}^{\infty}\frac{(\lambda L)^k e^{-\lambda L}}{k!} + \frac{1}{Q}\sum_{i=R+1}^{R+Q}\sum_{k=i+1}^{\infty}\frac{(\lambda L)^k e^{-\lambda L}}{k!}\cdot\frac{i}{k}$$

Note that in the above formula the subscript “1” which indicates stock 1 is omitted in L, R and Q, where L is the net lead time to be determined by solving the inventory policy optimization problem.

With the formula for calculating β, we can propose an iterative procedure similar to that of the serial system to solve model P. The procedure starts from setting α as an initial value of β. In each iteration, for an estimated β, the optimal echelon (R, Q) policy for the considered system is obtained by solving model P, and the real fill rate β of the system with the policy is then calculated. If the two values of β are identical, i.e., the value of β does not change in two successive iterations, the procedure stops. The main steps of the procedure are similar to that of serial systems (See Section 3.5).

When the optimal echelon (R, Q) inventory policy found in the last iteration, its corresponding installation (r, Q) policy can be derived by a simple transformation as $r_i = D(SI_i + T_i - S_i) - 1$ for $i=1, 2, \cdots, N$.

4.6 Experiments Results

In this section, we perform computational experiments to evaluate the performance of the two dynamic programming algorithms for the Q-problem and R-problem respectively and the performance of the procedure BETA proposed. In addition, we also conduct a sensitively analysis to examine the impacts of different system parameters on the performance of the algorithm.

4.6.1 Experiments for the Resolution of Q–problem

We first compared our algorithm with Crowston and Wagner's algorithm (referred to as algorithm CW hereafter) on three sets of medium to large sized instances (with 7 stocks and 3 levels, 15 stocks and 4 levels, 63 stocks and 6 levels, respectively). For each instance, each stock has only two immediate predecessors and one immediate successor, except for the components at the highest levels of the BOM with no predecessor and for the end stock at the lowest level with no successor. Each instance of the Q-problem was randomly generated with the following parameter settings:

$h_i^e \in U[1, 5]$, $c_i \in h_i^e \cdot U[10, 20]$, $\lambda \in U[1, 10]$

As mentioned above, Crowston and Wagner (1973) proposed two methods to calculate the upper bound of the total cost: A heuristic algorithm and a dynamic programming algorithm with coarse grid, leading to two versions of algorithm CW. We compared our algorithm with the two versions. Since both our dynamic programming algorithm and the algorithm CW are exact algorithms which can find the optimal solution of the *Q*-problem, we only compare their computation times.

For each set, 10 instances were randomly generated and tested. The average and the maximum computation time for all instances of each set are given in Table 4.2.

Table 4.2 The results for the instances of *Q*–problem

Instance set	Average/max computation time		
	Our algorithm	Algorithm CW (heuristic UB)	Algorithm CW (dynamic programming UB)
7 stocks, 3 levels	0.0008/0.0011	2.779/5.712	0.095/0.376
15 stocks, 4 levels	0.002/0.0028	13.958/38.005	4.35/24.17
63 stocks, 6 levels	0.0049/0.0068	100.34/278.96	10.35/24.62

From the table, we can observe that our dynamic programming algorithm for the Q-problem is more efficient than algorithm CW in both versions. The results in this table also demonstrate that our algorithm is very efficient in solving large instances, with the maximum computation time for an instance with 63 stocks less than 0.0068 seconds. In addition, if we examine the difference between the maximum computation time and the average computation time of each set of instances, we can find that the dif ference is quite small for our algorithm, whereas the difference is much larger for both versions of algorithm CW. This means that in terms of computation time, our algorithm is much less sensitive to the instance data than their algorithm.

To identify the reason behind the sensitiveness of algorithm in computation time, we extracted more detailed results of 5 instances from the instance set of 15 stocks. These results are given in Table 4.3, which include the lower bound *LB* and the upper bound UB of the optimal cost, the optimal cost (*OPT*) and the computation time obtained by algorithm CW. Note that *UB* for each instance in this table was obtained by using the dynamic programming algorithm with coarse grid.

From Table 4.3, we can observe large differences of the computation time among 5 instances, with the minimum computation time 0.018 seconds for No.1 instance and the maximum computation time 24.1729 seconds for No.5 instance. The results also show that when the *UB* of an instance is very close to its *OPT*, the computation time of

Table 4.3 The sensitiveness of the algorithm CW in computation time

No.	*LB*	*UB*	*OPT*	*Time*
1	1270.26	1280.5	1280.5	0.0018
2	2123.99	2138.69	2138.69	0.0047
3	2342.77	3939.03	2374.33	0.7322
4	3447.69	12619.5	3483.06	8.3726
5	2614.04	13455.9	2661.97	24.1729

algorithm CW is quite short, as in the case of instance 1 and 2. In contrast, if the *UB* of an instance is quite poor and far away from its *OPT*, the computation time will be much longer, as in the case of instance 3, 4 and 5. The bigger the gap between *OPT* and *UB*, the longer computation time of the algorithm. However, neither the heuristic nor the dynamic algorithm with coarse grid can guarantee to obtain a good *UB*. In some cases, the *UB* obtained by either of them is very poor. That's why the computation time of algorithm CW is very sensitive to the data of the instance considered.

Similar to algorithm CW, our algorithm also first get an upper bound and a lower bound of Q_i for each stock i, but the upper bound obtained by our algorithm is much tighter than that obtained by their algorithm. That's why our algorithm is much more efficient than algorithm CW for the Q-problem. For example, for an instance of 7 stocks with bill-of-materials given in Figure 4.1 and the following parameters:

$h_i^e = \{4, 3, 4, 3, 5, 5, 5\}$, $c_i = \{54, 50, 50, 51, 44, 39, 60\}$, $\lambda = 10$

Table 4.4 gives the upper bound Q_i^U and the lower bound Q_i^L of Q_i for each stock i obtained by our algorithm and algorithm CW, respectively.

Table 4.4 The bounds of Q_i by the two algorithms

7 stock, 3 level system	Our algorithm	Algorithm CW
stock 1	$Q_1^L=1$, $Q_1^U=8$	$Q_1^L=1$, $Q_1^U=41$
stock 2	$Q_2^L=1$, $Q_2^U=16$	$Q_2^L=1$, $Q_2^U=107$
stock 3	$Q_3^L=1$, $Q_3^U=16$	$Q_3^L=1$, $Q_3^U=86$
stock 4	$Q_4^L=1$, $Q_4^U=32$	$Q_4^L=1$, $Q_4^U=625$
stock 5	$Q_5^L=1$, $Q_5^U=24$	$Q_5^L=1$, $Q_5^U=379$
stock 6	$Q_6^L=1$, $Q_6^U=24$	$Q_6^L=1$, $Q_6^U=378$
stock 7	$Q_7^L=1$, $Q_7^U=28$	$Q_7^L=1$, $Q_7^U=384$

The results in Table 4.4 show that for this instance the upper bound of Q_i derived by our algorithm is much tighter than that obtained by algorithm CW.

4.6.2 Experiments for the Resolution of *R*-problem

Similarly, three sets of instances with 7 stocks, 15 stocks and 63 stocks respectively were considered. All the instances for the *R*-problem were created with parameters h_i^e, T_i, s_1 and λ randomly generated according to uniform distributions described in Table 4.5 and with the service level α given as 0.95.

Table 4.5 Parameter settings of the tested instances of *R*-problem

Parameter	Value
h_i^e	$h_i^e \in U[1, 5]$
T_i	$T_i \in U[1, 10]$
s_1	$s_1 \in U[1, 3]$
λ	$\lambda \in U[1, 10]$

The computation results of the instances are given in Table 4.6.

Table 4.6 The results for the instances of the *R*-problem

Instance set	Average/max computation time
7 stocks（3 levels）	0.0014/0.0029
15 stocks (4 levels)	0.0073/0.0152
63 stocks (6 levels)	0.1495/0.2303

For table 4.6, we can observe that the computation time of the dynamic programming algorithm for the *R*-problem is quite short for all three sets of instances with 7, 15 and 63 stocks, respectively, demonstrating the efficiency of the algorithm.

4.6.3 Experiments for the Sensitivity Analysis for the Two Algorithms

In order to analyze the impacts of key parameters h_i^e, c_i and λ of an assembly system on the performances of the two algorithms we developed, we conducted a sensitivity analysis of the computation times of the algorithms with respect to the parameters. The assembly system with 15 stocks was considered, and the values of its three parameters were varied according to the three sets respectively as follows:

$h_i^e=\{1, 2, 3, 4, 5\}$, $c_i=\{15, 25, 35, 45, 55\}$, $\lambda=\{1, 10, 20, 50, 80, 100\}$

For each combination of possible values of the parameters, one instance was generated.

4.6.3.1 Sensitivity Analysis for Q-problem

In terms of the objective function of Q-problem, the computation time for Q-problem are closely related to three parameters, h_i^e, c_i and λ. Then, the total number of instances tested is 150. For each possible value of the parameter, we calculate the average computation time of the instances when the other parameters changes. The main results are given in Figure 4.3, Figure 4.4 and Figure 4.5.

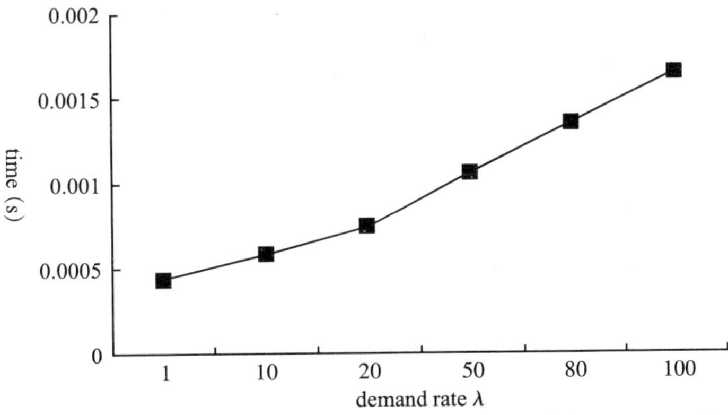

Figure 4.3 Computation time for Q-problem with respect to λ

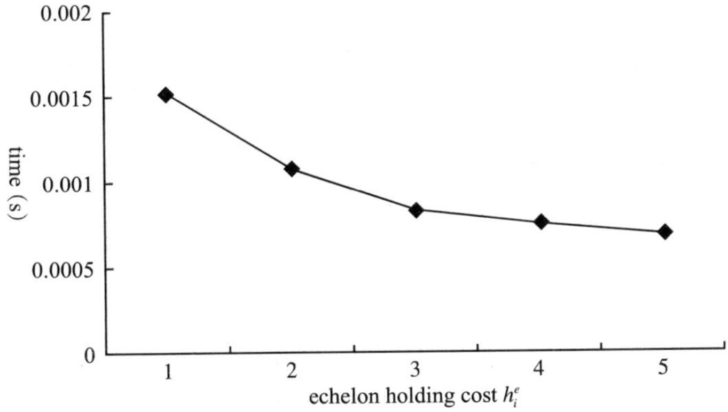

Figure 4.4 Computation time for Q-problem with respect to h_i^e

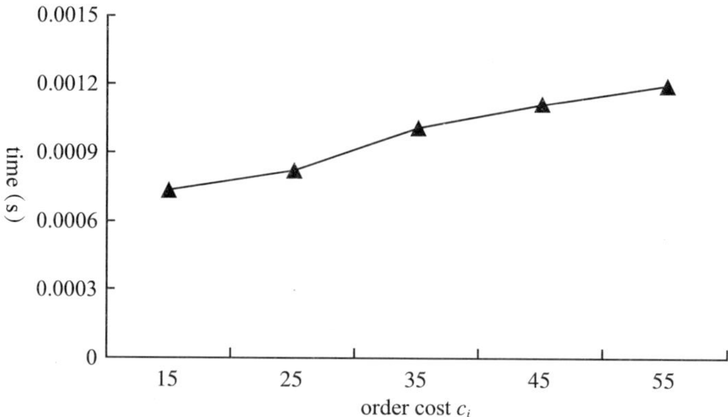

Figure 4.5 Computation time for Q-problem with respect to c_i

From the three figures, we can observe that the average computation time decreases in h_i^e, c_i, and increase in λ. That mainly because the state space of the order size at each stock i decreases in h_i^e, c_i, and increase in λ, larger state space of the order size will take more computation time to solve. Therefore, the results demonstrate that the param eters as h_i^e, c_i and λ has major influence on the computation time of the algorithm we developed for Q-problem.

4.6.3.2 Sensitivity Analysis for R-problem

Similar to Q-problem, the computation time for R-problem are related parameters as h_i^e and λ, so the total number of instances tested is 30. The results are given in Figure 4.6, Figure 4.7.

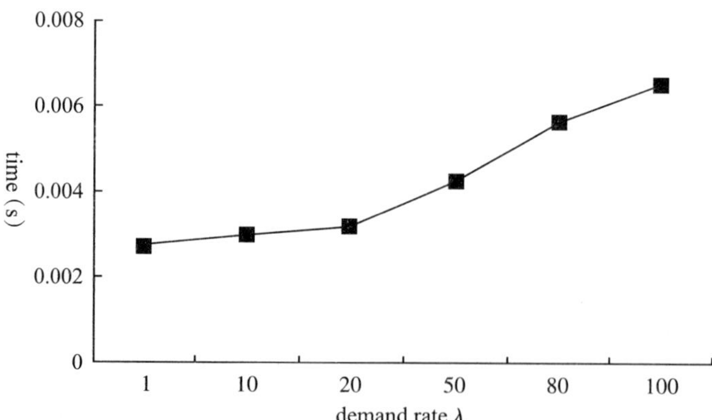

Figure 4.6 Computation time for R-problem with respect to λ

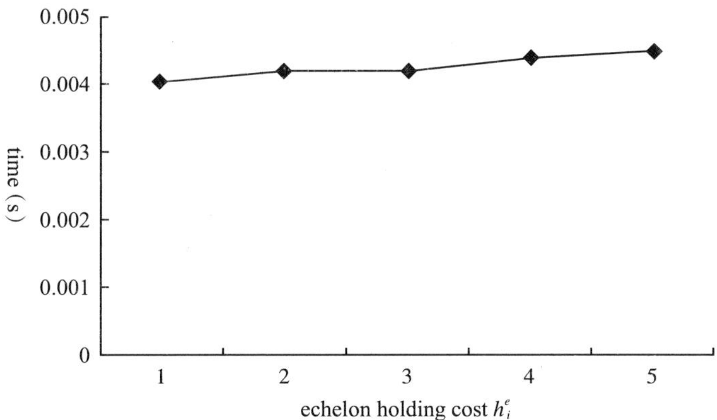

Figure 4.7 Computation time for *R*–problem with respect to h_i^e

The result in Figure 4.6 shows that the computation time increases obviously in λ, and from Figure 4.7, we can see that the computation time nearly increases in h_i^e, but the increments are very little. From the results, we can demonstrate that the parameter of λ has major influence in computation time of the algorithm of R-problem, relatively, the parameter of h_i^e has only little influence. Through analysis the results, we can find that the increase of λ will take larger bounded demand ($D(\lambda)$), and the computation time will also increase.

It should be noted that the computation time increase of decrease is not significant as the values of one or more these parameters change.

4.6.4 Experiments for the Resolution of Problem P with a Given Service Level

As we know, the performance of BETA mainly depends on two factors: The DP algorithms for solving Q-problem and R-problem respectively, and the number of iteration of Step 1-Step 3 by the procedure proposed in Section 4.5. This section will evaluate the performance of BETA from the above two factors by numerical experiments on the same sets of randomly generated instances with 7 stocks, 15 stocks and 63 stocks respectively as presented in Section 4.6.1 and Section 4.6.2, but for each set of instances, four different α-service level ranged from 0.8 to 0.98 were considered. For each instance set, 10 instances were generated randomly. We calculate the maximum/average computation time and the maximum/average number of iterations of the procedure for the instances, and the results are given in Table 4.7.

Table 4.7 The results for the tested instances of problem *P*

	α -service level	Max/average computation times in seconds	Max/average number of iterations
7 stocks and 3 levels	0.80	0.0021/0.0014	2/2
	0.90	0.0031/0.0017	2/2
	0.95	0.0036/0.0019	2/2
	0.98	0.0036/0/0018	2/2
15 stocks and 4 levels	0.80	0.0048/0.0036	2/2
	0.90	0.0055/0/0032	2/2
	0.95	0.0071/0.0044	2/2
	0.98	0.0074/0.004	2/2
63 stocks and 6 levels	0.80	0.1071/0.0198	2/2
	0.90	0.015/0.0109	2/2
	0.95	0.0201/0/0137	2/2
	0.98	0.0174/0.0139	2/2

From the table, we can see that the number of iterations for each instance is always 2, this indicates that the number of iterations is neither sensitive to the number of items in an assembly system nor sensitive to its α-service level. Moreover, the maximum computation time and average computation time of the procedure are short for all instances; this demonstrates the efficiency of the procedure BETA and its good convergence property.

4.7 Conclusions

As an extension, this chapter deals with the optimization of (R, Q) policy for a continuous review assembly system with Poisson demand under the GSA. Since each stock in the assembly system has more than one predecessor, the dynamic programming algorithm for the Q-problem proposed in the last chapter cannot be directly used. For this reason, we develop a new dynamic programming algorithm for the order size decision problem. The new feature of the algorithm is that the DP recursive procedure is used in both forward direction and backward direction. The numerical experiments demonstrate the efficiency of the dynamic programming algorithm and the iterative procedure used for solving the inventory policy optimization problem of the assembly system studied.

Chapter 5

Optimization of (R, Q) Policies for Two–Level Distribution Systems

In the inventory management literature, a lot of research papers have been dedicated to the study of two-level distribution systems in which a central warehouse supplies a product to a set of retailers. The most distinguishing feature of the distribution systems is that each stock has only one direct predecessor, but has multiple direct successors. This makes the analysis and optimization of such systems more difficult than serial and assembly systems. Because under the stochastic service approach (SSA), except for considering the inventory policy at each stock, we must also consider the warehouse's allocation policy which determines how the available on-hand inventory of the warehouse is allocated to the demands of the retailers when these demands cannot be totally satisfied. In this chapter, we try to optimize the (R, Q) policy of a two-level distribution system with fixed order costs at each stock under the GSA. Different from serial and assembly systems in which all items (stocks) have the same maximum reasonable lead time demand level as presented in Chapter 3 and Chapter 4, for the distribution system, we assume a maximum reasonable lead time demand level for each stock no matter it is the stock of a retailer or the stock of the warehouse, These bounds may be different. For each stock, its excessive lead time demand beyond the corresponding bound will be fulfilled by using extraordinary measures at operating flexibility costs. In addition, we assume a randomized initial condition for the system. This condition is introduced for simplifying the formulation of the (R, Q) policy optimization problem of the system. Because for distribution systems, echelon (R, Q) policies and installation (r, Q) policies cannot be transformed each other, this makes the formulation of the optimization prob lem more complicated. With these assumptions, we can first establish a mathematical model for the optimization problem and then propose an optimization procedureto solve the model based on the decomposition of the model into two sub-problems which are solved by using dynamical programming algorithms or EOQ-based methods. More par ticularly, we consider five different types of integer-ratio constraints possibly imposed on the order sizes of the stocks of the system, and compare their effectiveness by numerical experiments.

This chapter is organized as follows: The problem definition and the model formulation are given in Section 5.1 and Section 5.2 respectively. The two sub-problems (order size decision sub-problem with five types of integer-ratio constraints, and reorder point decision sub-problem) are solved by efficient dynamic programming algorithms in Section 5.3 and Section 5.4. In Section 5.5, we propose an optimization procedure for solving the original optimization problem for the two-level distribution system studied. Finally, in Section 5.6, numerical experiments for evaluating the performances of the algorithms are presented.

5.1 Problem Description

This section describes the two-level distribution inventory system studied as well as the assumptions made on the system for parameter optimization of its (R, Q) policy.

Two-level Distribution System Considera two-level distribution inventory system with a central warehouse and N retailers as illustrated in Figure 5.1. We refer to the warehouse as stock 0 and the retailer i as stock i, for i=1, 2, ···, N. The retailers order from the warehouse, which in turn orders from an outside supplier with unlimited stock. All customer demands (final demands) take place only at the retailers, and we assume that retailer i faces a Poisson demand with average demand rate $\lambda_i(i=1, 2, \cdots, N)$ and these N demand processes are independent. The internal demand occurring at the warehouse (stock 0) is generated by all retailers.

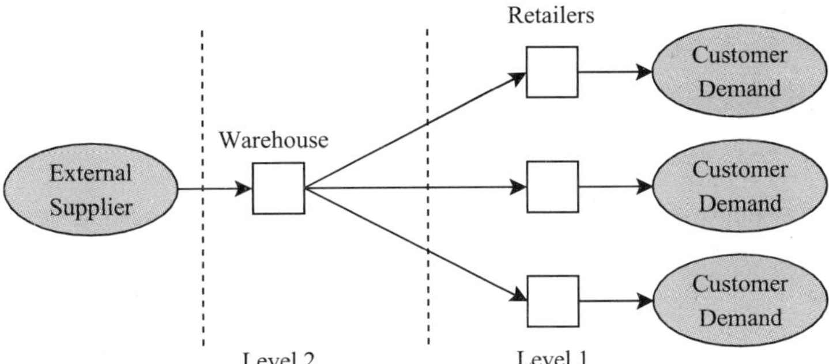

Figure 5.1 A two–level distribution system studied

The following assumptions are made on the system:

■ The demand of each retailer follows a Poisson process and the retailers have in dependent demands;

■ Under the GSA, except that each retailer uses extraordinary measures to fulfill its excessive demand, the warehouse may also use extraordinary measures to fulfill its excessive demand; In this case, operating flexibility costs are considered at both the retailers and the warehouse.

■ Under the GSA, backorder at the warehouse is not allowed if we exclude the part of any demand fulfilled by using extraordinary measures.

■ The total cost of the system consists of fixed order costs and inventory holding costs at all stocks, and operating flexibility costs at the retailers;

■ Echelon (R, Q) policy is used to control the system;

■ The initial echelon inventory position of each stock i can randomly take any integer value in the interval $[R_i+1, R_i+Q_i]$, this is referred to as randomized initial condition hereafter.

Maximum Reasonable Lead Time Demand Levels Denote by $d_i(t)$ the customer demand of stock i at time t, and by $d_i[t_1, t_2)$ the total demand of stock i from time t_1 to time t_2 without including t_2 for any $t_1 \leqslant t_2$. The total demand of the retailers at time t, $d_0(t)$, and their total lead time demand over the time period $[t_1, t_2)$, $d_0[t_1, t_2)$, can be defined as follows:

$$d_0(t)=\sum_{i=1}^{N} d_i(t),\ d_0[t_1, t_2)=\sum_{i=1}^{N} d_i[t_1, t_2)$$

Since $d_i(t)$, i=1, 2, ⋯, N are N independent Poisson processes, their sum $d_0(t)$ is also a Poisson process with average demand rate $\lambda_0=\sum_{i=1}^{N}\lambda_i$.

For each retailer i, suppose that it want to assurer a (event-oriented) service level α_i to its customers, its maximum reasonable lead time demand level $D_i(\tau)$ over τ units of time can then be determined according to the service level. That is, $D_i(\tau)$ can be de termined as the minimum number satisfying the following condition:

$$p\{d_i[t-\tau, t)\leqslant D_i(\tau)\}\geqslant\alpha_i,\ i=1, 2, \cdots, N \tag{5-1}$$

Note that $D_i(\tau)$ does not depend on time t because the customer demand of retailer i is stationary.

Since the customer demand of each retailer i follows a Poisson process with average demand rate λ_i, we have

$$\sum_{k=0}^{D_i(\tau)}\frac{[\lambda_i\tau]^k e^{-\lambda_i\tau}}{k!}\geqslant\alpha_i,\ i=1, 2, \cdots, N \tag{5-2}$$

The integer demand bound $D_i(\tau)$ can then be computed according to inequality (5-2).

In serial and assembly systems, the maximum reasonable lead time demand level is only defined for the end item (stock) and all other items (stocks) have the same lead time demand as that of the end item (stock). However, for the distribution system, since the demand of the warehouse is the sum of the demands of all retailers in the long run, its maximum reasonable lead time demand level should be different from these of the retailers, so we must also define a maximum reasonable lead time demand level for the warehouse. Let $D_o(\tau)$ denote the maximum reasonable lead time demand level of the warehouse over τunits of time. One way is to define $D_0(\tau)$ as $\sum_{i=1}^{N}D_i(\tau)$, but this definition does not take ac count of inventory risk pooling at the retail level, leading to an overestimation of $D_0(\tau)$ as pointed out in Graves and Willems (2000). As an alternative, we define $D_0(\tau)$ according to the service level that the warehouse want to assure for final customers, that is, $D_0(\tau)$ is defined as the minimum number satisfying the following condition:

$$p\{d_0[t-\tau, t)\leqslant D_0(\tau)\}\geqslant\alpha_0 \tag{5-1a}$$

where α_0 is the warehouse's service level to final customers and d_0 $[t-\tau, t)$ is the lead time demand of all retailers, i.e., total final customer demand from time $t-\tau$ to time t (not including time t). Since $d_0(t)$ is a Poisson process with average demand rate λ_0, we have:

$$\sum_{k=0}^{D_0(\tau)}\frac{[\lambda_0\tau]^k e^{-\lambda_0\tau}}{k!}\geqslant\alpha_0 \tag{5-2a}$$

Since the warehouse is controlled by an echelon inventory policy and D_0 (τ) is de fined based on the final customer demands rather than the orders placed by the retailers, we interpret D_0 (τ) in an "echelon" way. That is, the warehouse assures that no echelon stock out occurs if the total final customer demand over lead time τ does not exceed D_0 (τ), otherwise excessive part of the demand will be fulfilled by using extraordinary measures whose costs are in charge of the warehouse.

The remain thing is to specify the external service level α_0 of the warehouse. One way is to determine α_0 according to the inventory holding costs and the operating flexibility costs at the warehouse. If the second costs are high, the warehouse should choose a high service level α_0, otherwise it should choose a lower α_0. Another way is to determine α_0 according to the service levels and demand processes of all retailers, that is, we set $\alpha_0=\sum_{i=1}^{N}\lambda_i\alpha_i/\sum_{i=1}^{N}\lambda_i$. This α_0 can be regarded as the global service level of all the retailers, or the global service level of the system. The weight λ_i assigned to α_i in the definition takes account of the demand level of each retailer. When N=1, the distribution system becomes a serial system and $\alpha_0=\alpha_1$. This coincides with our definition of maximum reasonable lead time demand levels for serial systems.

5.2 Mathematical Model Formulation

In this section, a mathematical model for the optimization of (R, Q) policy for the distribution system considered will be described.

Since for the distribution system, the warehouse may also use extraordinary measures to fulfill its excessive demand, we should also consider operating flexibility costs at the warehouse level. Let us denote by p_i and β_i the unit operating flexibility cost and the fill rate of stock i (i=0, 1, $\cdots$, N), respectively, where stock 0 denotes the warehouse and stock i ($1 \leqslant i \leqslant N$) denotes retailer i. Here, the fill rate β_i is defined as the total demand normally fulfilled by stock i (in quantity) divided by its total demand in the long run under the GSA. For each retailer i, β_i is the same as its fill rate under the SSA if we consider all units of its demand fulfilled by using extraordinary measures are regarded as the units of the demand not satisfied on-time, so the calculation of β_i can be done in a similar way as we have done for the calculation of β in the cases of serial and assembly systems. For the warehouse, since it is controlled by an echelon (R, Q) policy and its maximum reasonable lead time demand level D_0 (τ) is interpreted in an echelon way (See Section 5.1), its fill rate β_0 can be calculated as if it is a single stock with demand $d_0(t)=\sum_{i=1}^{N} d_i(t)$.

Since the inventory replenishment of each stock i (i=0, 1, $\cdots$, N), in the distribution system is used to satisfy its normal demand (the part of the lead time demand not exceeding its prespeified maximum reasonable level D_i (τ)), the average order size of the warehouse per unit of time is given by $\lambda_i\beta_i$. Furthermore, as mentioned in Section 5.1, the operating flexibility costs are now charged at both the retailers and the warehouse, so the cost function of the optimization problem can be formulated as,

$$\sum_{i=0}^{N}\left(\frac{c_i\lambda_i\beta_i}{Q_i}+h_i^e\cdot E[I_i^e]\right)+\sum_{i=0}^{N}p_i\lambda_i(1-\beta_i) \tag{5-3}$$

Next, we formulate $E[I_i^e]$ for each stock i, i=0, 1, $\cdots$, N.

At time t, the following well-known inventory balance equation can be derived for each stock i, i = 0, 1, $\cdots$, N.

$$IL_i^e(t)=IP_i^e(t-L_i)-d_i[t-L_i,\ t) \tag{5-4}$$

Under the GSA, any lead time demand of retailer i inferior to its maximum reasonable levelcan always be satisfied, so $IL_i^e(t)=I_i^e(t)$, then,

$$I_i^e(t) = IP_i^e(t - L_i) - d_i[t - L_i, t) \tag{5-5}$$

For stock i, i=0, 1, ⋯, N, in order to provide 100% guaranteed service, $I_i^e(t) \geqslant 0$ must be satisfied, then,

$$IP_i^e(t - L_i) \geqslant d_i[t - L_i, t) \tag{5-6}$$

In addition, for each stock i, i=0, 1, ⋯, N, no stockout means that its installation on-hand inventory $I_i(t)$ is always nonnegative.

On the one hand, for each retailer i (stock i, i=1, 2, ⋯, N), since its installation on-hand inventory, $I_i(t)$, is equal to its echelon on-hand inventory $I_i^e(t)$, the nonnegative requirement of $I_i(t)$ is implied by constraint (5-6).

On the other hand, for the warehouse (stock 0), its installation on-hand inventory $I_0(t)$ can be formulated as

$$I_0(t) = I_0^e(t) - \sum_{i=1}^{N} IP_i^e(t) \tag{5-7}$$

Because $I_0(t) \geqslant 0$, we have

$$I^e{}_0(t) \geqslant \sum_{i=1}^{N} IP_i^e(t) \tag{5-8}$$

From (5-5), we have $I_0^e(t) = IP^e{}_0(t - \mathrm{L}_0) - d_0[t - L_0, t)$. This equation together with (5-8) implies that:

$$IP_0^e(t - L_0) \geqslant \sum_{i=1}^{N} IP_i^e(t) + d_0[t - L_0, t) \tag{5-9}$$

For the warehouse, Constraint (5-6) and Constraint (5-9) must be both satisfied. Since for i=0 the satisfaction of Constraint (5-9) implies the satisfaction of Constraint (5-6), we only need to consider Constraint (5-9) for the warehouse.

For each retailer i, in order to ensure inequality (5-6) holds for any demand realization, the following inequality must hold:

$$R_i + 1 \geqslant D_i(L_i) \tag{5-10}$$

Since $L_i = SI_i + T_i - S_i$, we can derive

$$R_i \geqslant D_i(SI_i + T_i - S_i) - 1 \text{ for } i=1, 2, \cdots, N \tag{5-11}$$

For the warehouse, under an echelon (R, Q) inventory policy, after order decision, its echelon inventory position $\overline{IP}_0^e$ will be within the interval $[R_0+1, R_0+Q_0]$. The echelon inventory position $\overline{IP}_0^e$ and the (echelon) inventory positions $\overline{IP}_i^e$ (i=1, 2, ⋯, N) of the retailers may be dependent, because they are driven by common demand processes (Simchi-Levi and Zhao, 2012). However, according to Simchi-Levi and Zhao (2012), if we assume randomized initial condition for the system, then $\overline{IP}^e=(\overline{IP}_i^e, i \in \{0, 1, \cdots, N\})$ is uniformly distributed in S^e, where $S^e=\{(s_i, i \in \{0, 1, \cdots, N\})| s_i \in \{R_i+1, R_i+2, \cdots, R_i+Q_i\}\}$ is the state space of $\overline{IP}^e$. With this jointly uniform distribution result and the independence between lead time demand $d_0[t-L_0, t)$ and inventory position IP_i^e(t) (i=1, 2, ⋯, N), the following inequality must hold:

$$R_0+1 \geqslant \sum_{i=1}^{N}(R_i+Q_i)+D_0(L_0) \tag{5-12}$$

Then,

$$R_0 \geqslant \sum_{i=1}^{N}(R_i+Q_i)+D_0(SI_0+T_0-S_0)-1 \tag{5-13}$$

In summary, the above conditions can be described as follows:

$$\begin{cases} R_i \geqslant D_i(SI_i+T_i-S_i)-1, \text{ for retailer } i, i=1, 2, \cdots, N \\ R_0 \geqslant \sum_{i=1}^{N}(R_i+Q_i)+D_0(SI_0+T_0-S_0)-1, \text{ for the warehouse} \end{cases} \tag{5-14}$$

Since our objective is to minimize the total cost of the system in the long-run, its optimal batching ordering (R, Q) policy must satisfy the following equations:

$$\begin{cases} R_i = D_i(SI_i+T_i-S_i)-1, \text{ for retailer } i, i=1, 2, \cdots, N \\ R_0 = \sum_{i=1}^{N}(R_i+Q_i)+D_0(SI_0+T_0-S_0)-1, \text{ for the warehouse} \end{cases} \tag{5-15}$$

Note we use the relationship between IP_i^e and I_i^e (i=0, 1, ⋯, N) described above to find the expected echelon on-hand inventory $E[I_i^e]$. Hadely and Whitin (1961) show that IP_i^e is uniformly distributed over the interval $[R_i+1, R_i+Q_i]$, then the probability of being at state R_i+j, $j=1, \cdots, Q_i$ is given by

$$E[IP_i^e]=\frac{1}{Q_i}\sum_{j=1}^{Q_i}(R_i+j)=R_i+\frac{1+Q_i}{2} \tag{5-16}$$

From the definition of $\hat{d}_i[t-L_i, t)$ and β_i, we have:

$$E[\hat{d}_i[t-L_i, t)]=\lambda_i\beta_i L_i \tag{5-17}$$

Similarly, we assume that all excessive demands are satisfied by using extraordinary measures without incurring inventory holding costs. With this assumption, we can ignore excessive demand in the calculation of expected inventory holding cost $E[I_i^e]$. That is, when calculate $E[I_i^e]$ according to equation (5-5), we first replace $d_i[t-L_i, t)$ by $\hat{d}_i[t-L_i, t)$. So we can derive $E[I_i^e]$ as

$$E[I_i^e]=E[IP_i^e]-E[\hat{d}_i[t-L_i, t)]=R_i+\frac{1+Q_i}{2}-\lambda_i\beta_i L_i \tag{5-18}$$

By substituting R_i given by equation (5-15) into equation (5-18), we can derive

$$E[I_i^e]=\begin{cases} D_i(SI_i+T_i-S_i)-\lambda_i\beta_i(SI_i+T_i-S_i)+\dfrac{Q_i-1}{2}, \text{ for } i=1, 2, \cdots, N \\ \sum\limits_{i=0}^{N}[D_i(SI_i+T_i-S_i)]-\lambda_0\beta_0(SI_0+T_0-S_0)+\dfrac{Q_0-1}{2}+\sum\limits_{i=1}^{N}Q_i-N, \text{ for } i=0 \end{cases} \tag{5-19}$$

With equation (5-3) and equation (5-19), the inventory optimization problem studied can be formulated as the following nonlinear programming problem:

P: Minimize

$$\sum_{i=0}^{N}\frac{c_i\lambda_i\beta_i}{Q_i}+h_i^e\cdot[(D(SI_i+T_i-S_i))-\lambda_i\beta_i(SI_i+T_i-S_i)+\frac{Q_i-1}{2}]+ h_0^e[\sum_{i=1}^{N}D(SI_i+T_i-S_i)+\sum_{i=1}^{N}Q_i-N]+\sum_{i=0}^{N}p_i\lambda_i(1-\beta_i)$$

Subject to:

$$SI_i+T_i-S_i\geqslant 0 \text{ for } i=1, 2, \cdots, N \tag{5-20}$$

$$SI_i\geqslant S_0 \text{ for } i=1, 2, \cdots, N \tag{5-21}$$

$$0\leqslant S_i\leqslant s_i, i=1, 2, \cdots, N \tag{5-22}$$

$$Q_i\geqslant 0 \text{ and integer for } i=1, 2, \cdots, N \tag{5-23}$$

$$SI_i,\ S_i\geqslant 0 \text{ and integer for } i=1, 2, \cdots, N \tag{5-24}$$

In the above model, the objective function represents the average total costs of the two-level distribution system in the long-run. Constraint (5-20) assures that the net lead time of each stock is nonnegative. Constraint (5-21) implies that the inbound service time of each retailer is no less than the outbound service time of the warehouse. Constraint (5-22) imposes an upper bound s_i on the outbound service time of the stock of each retailer i, i=1, 2, ⋯, N. Constraint (5-23), Constraint (5-24) implies that all decision variables must be nonnegative. Note that additional integer-ratio constraint on order size Q_i(i=0,1, ⋯, N) may be added to be the model because of practical requirements, this will be discussed in Section 5.3.

When all β_i are known, both the objective function and the constraints of model P can be separated into two sub-problems, order size sub-problem and reorder point sub-problem. The two sub-problems, which are referred to as Q-problem and R-problem respectively hereafter, have decision variables Q_i and $\{SI_i, S_i\}$, respectively.

Note that the constant term-$(\frac{1}{2}\sum_{i=0}^{N} h_i^e + h_0^e N) + \sum_{i=0}^{N} p_i\lambda_i(1-\beta_i)$ in the objective function of P can be omitted in the two sub-problems.

***Q*–problem:**

Minimize: $\sum_{i=0}^{N}[(\frac{c_i\lambda_i\beta_i}{Q_i} + h_i^e \cdot \frac{Q_i}{2}) + h_0^e \cdot \sum_{i=1}^{N} Q_i]$

Subject to:

$Q_i \geqslant 0$ and integer for i=1, 2, ⋯, N

***R*–problem:**

Minimize: $\sum_{i=0}^{N} h_i^e \cdot [(D(SI_i+T_i-S_i)) - \lambda_i\beta_i(SI_i+T_i-S_i) + h_0^e \cdot \sum_{i=1}^{N} D(SI_i+T_i-S_i)]$

Subject to:

$SI_i+T_i-S_i \geqslant 0$ for $i=1, 2, \cdots, N$

$SI_i \geqslant S_0$ for $i=1, 2, \cdots, N$

$0 \leqslant S_i \leqslant s_i$, $i=1, 2, \cdots, N$

SI_i, $S_i \geqslant 0$ and integer for i=1, 2,⋯, N

In the next two sections, we will develop efficient algorithms to solve the two sub-problems for the given α_i and β_i. Moreover, for the Q-problem, five different types of integer-ratio constraints are considered, and we present an efficient algorithm to solve the Q-problem with each type of integer-ratio constraints.

All the above analysis assumes that all β_i are known. However, β_i are unknown, but they can be determined by the inventory policies of the system. Based on the solutions of the two sub-problems, we will introduce a method for calculating β_i, and the original optimization problem (model P) can be resolved by an optimization procedure.

5.3 Dynamic Programming Algorithm for Q–problem

In practice, integer-ratio constraints may be imposed on the order size of the warehouse (Q_0) and the order sizes of the retailers (Q_i, i=1, 2, ···, N). That is, the order size of a stock may be required to be a multiple of the order size of another stock. Such constraints can facilitate order/shipment quantity coordination between two supply/demand facilities and simplify their order packaging, transportation and inventory accounting. Many companies have recognized these managerial benefits of having such integer-ratio constraints in multi-echelon inventory management (Cheng and Zheng, 1997).

For the two-level distribution system studied, researchers have considered different types of integer-ratio constraints, but no comparison among them was made in terms of the effectiveness. In Section 5.3.1, we will introduce five different types of integer-ratio constraints possibly imposed on the system, and the Q-problem with each type of integer-ratio constraints will be solved by a dynamic programming algorithm or an EOQ-based algorithm in Section 5.3.2. Numerical experiment results on the evaluation of the effectiveness of the five different types of integer-ratio constraints and their impacts on the optimal order sizes of the system will be given in Section 5.6.

5.3.1 Integer–ratio Constraints for Q–problem

Five different types of integer-ratio constraints corresponding to five cases respectively are described as follows.

Case 1: without integer-ratio constraint

In this case, no relationship exists between the order size of the warehouse (Q_0) and the order size of any retailer (Q_i, i=1, 2, ···, N). This corresponds to the situation when the warehouse and the retailers have no intention to coordinate their order/shipment quantities. In this case, the Q-problem has a simple structure, which can be divided into N-independent sub-problems and solved as the classical EOQ model.

Case 2: $Q_i=m_i \cdot Q_N$, for some integers m_i, i=1, 2, ···, $N-1$

This kind of integer-ratio constraints was considered by Chen and Zheng (1997) in their model of a two-level distribution system with one warehouse and multiple retailers, where retailer N is taken as the reference retailer and its order size Q_N is taken as the base-lot of all other retailers in the system. Here, retailer N can be replaced by any other retailer ($i \neq N$)and the choice of the reference retailer and its order size depends on the average demand rate of each retailer. Under the assumption that initial on-hand inventory at the warehouse is also an integer multiple of the base-lot, they showed that such a restriction is not too costly.

Case 3: $Q_i=m_i \cdot q$, for some integers m_i, i=0, 1, 2, ···, N

Similarly, this case also assumes a base-lot for the distribution system, in which the order size of each stock (Q_i, i=0, 1, ···, N) is an integer multiple of the base-lot denoted by q. Here, q can also be regarded as the common factor of Q_0, Q_1, ···, Q_N. In practice, q may correspond to the capacity of a pallet for delivery. The capacity is the number of units of a product that the pallet can carry for order shipment.

Case 4: $Q_0=m_i \cdot Q_i$, for some integers m_i, i=1, 2, ···, N

This case assumes that the order size at the warehouse (Q_0) is always an integer multiple of the order size of each retailer (Q_i, i=1, 2, ···, N). This assumption, which is commonly adopted in the inventory management literature, is quite natural if the inventory replenishment policy of the warehouse is to satisfy all or nothing of each retailer's order (Axsater, 1996). This coordination strategy sets a strict restriction between the order size of the warehouse and the order size of each retailer, it may bring extra coordination costs to the system.

Case 5: $Q_0=m_0 \cdot q_0$, $Q_i=m_i \cdot q_1$, $1 \leq i \leq N$, $q_0=k_0 \cdot q_1$, **for some integers** m_i, $i=1, 2, \cdots, N$, k_0

In Case 2 and Case 3, a base-lot is assumed for both the warehouse and the retailers in the distribution system. However, since the warehouse and the retailers belong to different levels in a supply chain, this order size coordination strategy may be difficult to implement. Based on this observation, we propose the case 5 of integer-ratio constraints. This case assumes there exist a base-lot for each level in the system, i.e., q_0 for the warehouse level (level 0) and q_1 for the retailer level (level 1). That is, the order sizes of all the stocks at the same level have a common base-lot and the base-lot at a high level (level 0) is an integer multiple of the base-lot at a lower level (level 1), i.e., the base-lot at the warehouse (q_0) is an integer multiple of that at the retailers (q_1).

In the next section, we will develop efficient algorithms to solve the Q-problem with the integer-ratio constraints in five cases.

5.3.2 Dynamic Programming for Q–problem

According to the characteristic of the cases for the Q-problem, we present efficient algorithms to solve for deriving the optimal Q^* at each stock.

Before introducing the algorithms, we first transform the objective function of the Q-problem as the following expression.

$$\sum_{i=0}^{N} \frac{c_i \lambda_i \beta_i}{Q_i} + \frac{H_i}{2} \cdot Q_i$$

where $H_i = \begin{cases} h^e_0 \\ h^e_i + 2h^e_0,\ i=1, 2, \cdots, N \end{cases}$

The new expression of the objective function will be used later for describing the procedure of the algorithms.

5.3.2.1 EOQ Model for Q–problem with Case 1

For the Q-problem without integer-ratio constraints, the problem can be divided into N-independent sub-problems, and each sub-problem will be solved as EOQ model.

Therefore, the optimal Q^* at each stock i (i=0, 1, $\cdots$, N) can be divided as follows:

$$Q^*_i = \sqrt{\frac{2c_i \lambda_i \beta_i}{H_i}},\ i=0, 1, \cdots, N$$

5.3.2.2 The Algorithm for Q–problem with Case 2

We develop a simple algorithm to solve the Q-problem respect to Case 2, the key idea of the algorithm is that we first use two important properties we have found to reduce the state space of the problem. After the state space reduction, a simple algorithm working on the reduced state space is used to identify the optimal solution.

The following notations are first introduced as follows:

Q_i: state variable of stock i, which represents a possible order size of stock i, i=0, 1, ⋯, N and the set of all possible values of Q_i is denoted by W_i,

W_N: the set of all possible values of the base-lot Q_N,

m_i: decision variable of stock i, i=0, 1, ⋯, N-1,

$M_i(Q_N)$: the set of permissible values of m_i given the state of the base-lot Q_N,

$d_i(Q_i)$: the cost of stock i when its state of stock i is Q_i,

C: the minimum total cost for the system.

State Space Reduction

By analysis of the objective function of the Q-problem and its integer-ratio constraints, i.e., Case 2, we can find the following two important properties regarding W_N and $M_i(Q_N)$ for stock i, i=0, 1, ⋯, N-1. Based on the properties, the state space of each stock i, i=0, 1, ⋯, N can be derived.

Firstly, an upper bound of the base-lot Q_N is given by Property 5.1.

Property 5.1: For a two-level distribution system with one-warehouse, N-retailers and the integer-ratio constraints among Q_i given by Case 2, an upper bound of the base-lot Q_N is given by

$$\overline{Q}_N=\sqrt{\frac{\sum_{i=0}^{N}2c_i\lambda_i\beta_i}{\sum_{i=0}^{N}H_i}}$$

Since Q_N is an integer, with the property, W_N can be taken as the integer set of $\{1, 2, \cdots, \lceil\overline{Q}_N\rceil\}$, where $\lceil x\rceil=\min\{a\in Z|a\geqslant x\}$ and Z is the set of integers.

Let $U_i(Q_N)$ denote the set of all possible values of Q_i when Q_N is given. Then, an upper bound of $\mathrm{m_i}$ for each stock i, i=0, 1, ⋯, N-1 is given by Property 5.2 as a function of the state Q_N.

Property 5.2: For a two-level distribution system with N retailers and the integer-ratio constraints of Case 2, if the order size of the base-lot is Q_N, then an upper bound of mi is given by

$$\overline{m}_i = \frac{1}{Q_i} \cdot \sqrt{\frac{2c_i\lambda_i\beta_i}{H_i}} \quad \text{for } i=0, 1, \cdots, N-1$$

From this property, if Q_N is given, the permissible decision set $M_i(Q_N)$ can be taken as the set $\{1, 2, \cdots, \lceil \overline{m}_i \rceil\}$. According to the integer-ratio constraints given by Case 2, $U_i(Q_N)$ can then be written as

$$U_i(Q_N) = \{Q \mid Q = Q_N \cdot m,\ m \in M_i(Q_N)\},\ i=0, 1, 2, \cdots, N-1$$

$U_i(Q_N)$ can be calculated from $\overline{m}_i$ and Q_N.

The Procedure of the Algorithm

Since the objective function of the Q-problem is additive with respect to the order size of each stock and the integer-ratio constraint with Case 2 of the problem only relate the order size Q_i to the order size of the base-lot Q_N, so the order size decision of each stock only depends on the order size of the base-lot Q_N. Therefore, we develop a simple algorithm based on the base-lot given by $Q_N \in W_N$ for solving the problem.

Let $g_i(Q_N)$ denote the minimal cost of stock i for i=0, 1, .., N-1 when the base-lot is Q_N.

$$g_i(Q_N) = \min_{j \in U_i(Q_N)} d_i(j),\ Q_N \in W_N$$

Therefore, the minimal total cost C of the Q-problem with Case 2 can be derived by

$$C = \min_{Q_N} d_N(Q_N) + \sum_{l=0}^{N-1} g_l(Q_N),\ Q_N \in W_N$$

where $d_i(Q_i) = \dfrac{c_i\lambda_i\beta_i}{Q_i} + \dfrac{H_i}{2} \cdot Q_i,\ i=0, 1, \cdots, N.$

In summary, the main step of the algorithm is presented in the following.

Step 1: Calculate the upper bound of the base-lot W_N and the set of $U_i(Q_N)$ for i=0, 1, .., N-1 using the two properties;

Step 2: For i=0, 1, $\cdots$, N-1, calculate $g_i(Q_N)$ for $Q_N \in W_N$;

Step 3: Calculate C, the minimal total cost of the Q-problem;

Step 4: Backtrack from stock N to stock i, i=0, 1, ⋯, N-1 to get the optimal batch size Q_i^* for each stock i, i=0, 1, 2, ⋯, N.

5.3.2.3 The Algorithm for Q-problem with Case 3

Similar with Case 2, the integer-ratio constraint in this part also set a base-lot for the Q-problem; therefore, we can use the algorithm in Section 5.2 to solve the problem in this case.

There also exist two similar important properties to reduce the state space for the problem, here, let W_q as the upper bound of the base-lot Q, then, based on the two properties, we can calculate W_q and $M_i(q)$ for i=0, 1, ⋯, N as follows:

$$\bar{q}=\sqrt{\frac{\sum_{i=0}^{N}2c_i\lambda_i\beta_i}{h_0^e+\sum_{i=1}^{N}H_i}},\ \bar{m}_i=\frac{1}{q}\sqrt{\frac{2c_i\lambda_i\beta_i}{H_i}},\ i=0,1,\cdots,N$$

Since q and m_i are integers, then, W_q and $M_i(q)$ can be taken as the integer set of $\{1, 2, \cdots, \lceil\bar{q}\rceil\}$ and $\{1, 2, \cdots, \lceil\bar{m}_i\rceil\}$ for i=0, 1, ⋯, N, respectively.

According to the integer-ratio constraints given by Case 3, $U_i(q)$ can be written as

$$U_i(q)=\{Q\,|\,Q=q\cdot m,\ m\in M_i(q)\},\ i=0,1,2,\cdots,N$$

Next, the minimal cost of each stock i when the base-lot is q, i.e., $g_i(q)$ (i=0, 1, ⋯, N) can be calculate by

$$g_i(q)=\min_{j\in U_i(q)}d_i(j),\ q\in W$$

Thus, minimal total cost of the Q-problem with Case 3 can be derived by

$$C=\min_{q}\sum_{l=0}^{N}g_l(q),\ \mathrm{q}\in \mathrm{W}$$

And the optimal Q^* for each stock i, i=0, 1, ⋯, N can be derived by a simple backtrack process.

5.3.2.4 Crowston–Wagner's Algorithm for Q-problem with Case 4

Crowston and Wagner (1973) presented a dynamic programming algorithm (referred to algorithm CW) to solve a lot size problem for assembly systems with deterministic demand. Their algorithm can also be used to solve our Q-problem with Case 4 since it has the same structure. Their algorithm first calculates an upper bound and a lower bound of the optimal lot sizefor each stock, based on a lower bound and an upper bound of the optimal cost of the joint lot-sizing problem. Next, we give the following procedures for solving such a problem by algorithm CW.

Firstly, the objective function can be written as:

$$f_i(Q_i)=\frac{c_i\lambda_i\beta_i}{Q_i}+\frac{H_i}{2}\cdot Q_i,\quad \begin{cases} H_0=h_0^e \\ H_i=h_i^e+2h_0^e,\ i=1,2,\cdots,N \end{cases}$$

Next, the upper and lower bounds of order size Q_i for each stock i (i=0, 1, ⋯, N) can be calculate by the following procedures:

Step1: take $Q_i=\sqrt{\frac{2c_i\lambda_i\beta_i}{H_i}}$, $i=0, 1, 2, \cdots, N$ into $f_i(Q_i)$, i=0, 1, 2, ⋯, N, then,

$$z_i=\frac{c_i\lambda_i\beta_i}{\sqrt{\frac{2c_i\lambda_i}{H_i}}}+\frac{H_i}{2}\cdot\sqrt{\frac{2c_i\lambda_i\beta_i}{H_i}},\quad i=0, 1, 2, \cdots, N$$

Step 2: get the lower bound of the total cost $L=\sum_{i=0}^{N} z_i$;

Step 3: an upper bound of the total cost, U, can be derived from a feasible heuristic solution.

Step 4: with the upper bound U and the lower bound L, the cost of each stock i (f_i (Q_i)) for i=0, 1, 2, ⋯, N may be determined: U-(L-Z_i), that is

$$\frac{c_i\lambda_i\beta_i}{Q_i}+\frac{H_i}{2}\cdot Q_i=Z_i+U-L$$

Then, we can solve directly for upper and lower bounds of each stock i, Q_i^U, Q_i^L.

In addition, better bounds on the optimal Q_i, such that $Q_i^{\min}\leqslant Q_i^*\leqslant Q_i^{\max}$ can be obtained as follows:

$$Q_i^{\min}=\max\ (Q_i^L;\ Q_m^L),\ m\in s(i),\ Q_i^{\max}=\min\ (Q_i^U;\ Q_m^U),\quad m\in P(i)$$

Let W_i denote the state space of each stock i, i=0, 1, 2, ⋯, N, then, W_i can be derived by

$$W_i=[Q_i^{\min},\ Q_i^{\max}]$$

Since the order size at the warehouse must be an integer multiple of each retailer, i.e., $Q_0=m_iQ_i$, i=1, 2, ⋯, N, we assume $V_i(Q_0)$ (i=1, 2, ⋯, N) as the set of all possible value of Q_i of stock i (retailer i) when the order size of stock 0 (the warehouse) is given by $Q_0 \in W_0$.

Let $g_i(Q_i)$ present the minimal cost at stock i and all its successors when Q_i is given by $Q_i \in W_i$. The state transition function and the recursion equations of the DP algorithm can then be formulated as:

State transition function:

$$Q_0 = m_i \cdot Q_i,\ i=1, 2, \cdots, N$$

Recursion equations:

$$\begin{cases} g_i(Q_i) = d_i(Q_i),\ Q_i \in W_i,\ i=1, 2, \cdots, N \\ g_0(Q_0) = d_0(Q_0) + \sum_{j \in s(0)} \min\limits_{k \in V_j(Q_0)} g_i(k),\ Q_0 \in W_0 \\ g_{-1}(0) = \min\limits_{Q_0} g_0(Q_0),\ Q_0 \in W_0 \end{cases}$$

where

$$d_i(Q_i) = \frac{c_i \lambda_i \beta_i}{Q_i} + \frac{H_i}{2} \cdot Q_i,\ i=0, 1, \cdots, N$$

Then, the problem can be solved by the dynamic recursive procedure, and the optimal Q^* for each stock can be derived by a backtrack procedure.

5.3.2.5 The Algorithm for Q–problem with Case 5

In two-level distribution system studied, the key meaning of Case 5 is that for each level, there exists a base-lot, i.e., q_0 for the warehouse and q_1 for all retailers, and moreover, the base-lot q_0 must be an integer multiple of that of q_1, therefore, there exist the following constraint for the system:

$$Q_0 = m_0 q_0,\ Q_i = m_i q_1,\ i=1, 2, \cdots, N,\ q_0 = k_0 q_1$$

In this part, we may consider the two levels separately. First, for the lowest level (the level of all retailers), i.e., level 1, similar with the algorithm for Case 2, we calculate the upper bound of the base-lot q_1, denoted by W_1, and $M_i(q_1)$ for i=1, 2, $\cdots$, N.

$$\overline{q}_1 = \sqrt{\frac{\sum\limits_{i=0}^{N} 2c_i \lambda_i \beta_i}{\sum\limits_{i=1}^{N} H_i}},\ \overline{m}_i = \frac{1}{q_1}\sqrt{\frac{2c_i \lambda_i \beta_i}{H_i}},\ i=1, \cdots, N$$

Since q and m_i are integers, then, W_1 and $M_i(q)$ can be taken as the integer set of $\{1, 2, \cdots, \lceil \bar{q}_1 \rceil\}$ and $\{1, 2, \cdots, \lceil \bar{m}_i \rceil\}$ for i=1, ⋯, N, respectively.

Then, $U_i(q_1)$ for stock i, i=1, 2, ⋯ N at level 1 can be written as

$U_i(q_1)=\{Q \mid Q=q_1 \cdot m, m \in M_i(q_1)\}, i=1, 2, \cdots, N$

Secondly, for level 0, considering the above constraints, we can derive the following relationship between Q_0 and q_1.

$Q_0=k_0 m_0 q_1$

If we assume $r_0=k_0 m_0$, then, the upper bound of r_0, denoted by R_0, can be get by

$$\bar{r}_0=\frac{1}{q_1}\sqrt{\frac{2c_0\lambda_0\beta_0}{H_0}}$$

Then, R_0 can be taken as the integer set of $\{1, 2, \cdots, \lceil \bar{r}_0 \rceil\}$.

And $U_i(q_1)$ for stock 0 at level 0 can be written as:

$U_0(q_1)=\{Q \mid Q=q_1 \cdot r, r \in R_0\}$

After getting $U_i(q_1)$ for each stock i, i=0, 1, ⋯, N, next, the minimal cost of each stock i when the lowest base-lot q_1 is given by $q_1 \in W_1$, can be calculated by

$$g_i(\mathrm{q}_1)=\min_{j \in U_i(q_1)} d_i(j), q_1 \in W_1$$

Thus, minimal total cost of the Q-problem with Case 5 can be derived by

$$C=\min_{q_1} \sum_{l=0}^{N} g_1(q_1), q_1 \in W_1$$

And the optimal Q^* for each stock i, i=0, 1, ⋯, N can be derived by a simple back-track process.

5.4 Dynamic Programming Algorithm for *R*–problem

In this section, we also use an efficient dynamic programming algorithm (Graves and Willems, 1996) to solve the optimization problem for finding the optimal service times of a two-level distribution system with a spanning tree structure under the GSA. In the following, we briefly introduce their algorithm applied to the R-problem studied.

In the algorithm, a multi-echelon inventory system is described by a graph in which each node represents a stock in the system and two nodes are connected by a directed arc if the corresponding two stocks are connected (one stock is a supplier of the other stock). In the graph, let $N(i)$ denote the subset of nodes (stocks) $\{1, 2, \cdots, i\}$ that are connected to i on the sub-graph consisting of nodes $\{1, 2, \cdots, i\}$. $N(i)$ will be used to ex- plain the dynamic programming recursion. For the distribution system studied, $N(i)$ can be recursively determined by the following equation:

$N(i)=\{i\}+P(i)$

This implies that $N(0)= \{0\}$, $N(i)=\{0, i\}$, $i=1, 2, \cdots, N$.

The dynamic programming algorithm evaluates a functional equation for all nodes (stocks), in the order of their indexes (labels). According to Graves and Willems (1996), generally the functional equation may have two different forms at each node i ($i=1, 2, \cdots, N-1$), depending on the location of the node with higher index that is adjacent to node i. However, for the distribution system studied, each node i has only downstream adjacent nodes with a higher index, then the functional equation has the unique form. In order to formulate the equation, let us define:

$f_i(S)$: the minimum inventory holding cost for the sub-system (of the original distribution system) described by the sub-graph with node set $N(i)$, where the outbound service time of stage i is given by S.

With this cost function, the minimum inventory holding cost for the sub-system can also be defined as a function of both outbound service time and inbound service timeof node i (stock i):

$$C_i(S, SI)=h_i^e \cdot [\sum_{j=1}^{i} D(SI_j+T_j-S_j)]-\lambda_i\beta_i \cdot (SI_i+T_i-S_i)+\min_{0\leqslant y\leqslant SI_i}[f_{P(i)}(y)]$$

The first term is the inventory holding cost of node i (stock i), which is a function of S and SI. The second term corresponds to the nodes (stocks) in $N(i)$ that are upstream of node i (stock i).

The functional equation for $f_i(S)$ can be found by solving the following optimization problem.

$f_i(S)=\min_{SI}\{C_i(S, SI)\}$

Subject to:

$\max\{0, S-T_i\} \leqslant SI \leqslant M_i - T_i$ and SI integer.

In the above model, SI is bounded by M_i-T_i, where M_i is the maximum replenishment time of node i (stock i). In addition, if node i is the retailer, S is also bounded by its maximum service time, i.e., $S_i \leqslant s_i$ for i=1, 2, ⋯, N.

In summary, the main steps of the dynamic programming algorithm are given in the following.

Step 1: For i:=0 to N, evaluate $f_i(S)$ for S=0, 1, ⋯, M_i.

Step 2: Minimize $f_N(SI)$ to derive the optimal cost value of the R-problem.

Step 3: backtrack from node (stock)N to Node (stock)N-1, ⋯, Node (stock) 2 to Node (stock) 1 to get the optimal inbound service time and outbound service time of each node (stock).

5.5 Optimization Procedure

Similar to serial systems, the original optimization problem, i.e., optimization of echelon (R, Q) policy under the GSA for the distribution system can be resolved by an iterative procedure as presented in Section 3.5. The procedure has two main steps: Firstly, for an estimated fill rate of the system, the optimal order size Q and the optimal reorder point R for each stock are calculated by solving two sub-problems using two dynamic algorithms. Secondly, the real fill rate of each stock in the system is calculated given its inventory policy. When the real fill rate of each stock equals to its estimated fill rate, the optimal solution of the original problem is found.

For the serial and assembly systems considered in last two chapters, they have only one end stock, so there is only one fill rateβ for the entire system, i.e. the fill rate of stock i (i = 1, 2, ⋯, N) can be written as:

$\beta_1 = \beta_2 = \cdots = \beta_N = \beta$

However, for the two-level distribution system considered, the warehouse has multiple retailers (end stocks) and these retailers may have different fill rates. For each retailer i, if its reorder point and its order size of retailer i are given by R_i and Q_i, respectively, its fill rate β_i can be calculated in the following way:

$$\beta_i = 1 - \frac{1}{Q_i}\sum_{i=R_i+1}^{R_i+Q_i}\sum_{k=i+1}^{\infty}\frac{(\lambda_i L_i)^k e^{-\lambda_i L_i}}{k!}\cdot\frac{k-i}{k}$$

$$= 1 - \frac{1}{Q_i}\sum_{i=R_i+1}^{R_i+Q_i}\sum_{k=i+1}^{\infty}\frac{(\lambda_i L_i)^k e^{-\lambda_i L_i}}{k!} + \frac{1}{Q_i}\sum_{i=R_i+1}^{R_i+Q_i}\sum_{k=i+1}^{\infty}\frac{(\lambda_i L_i)^k e^{-\lambda_i L_i}}{k!}\cdot\frac{i}{k}$$

Similarly, with the echelon interpretation of $D_0(\tau)$, the fill rate β_0 of the warehouse can be calculated as:

$$\beta_0 = 1 - \frac{1}{Q_0}\sum_{i=R_0+1}^{R_0+Q_0}\sum_{k=i+1}^{\infty}\frac{(\lambda_0 L_0)^k e^{-\lambda_0 L_0}}{k!}\cdot\frac{k-i}{k}$$

$$= 1 - \frac{1}{Q_0}\sum_{i=R_0+1}^{R_0+Q_0}\sum_{k=i+1}^{\infty}\frac{(\lambda_0 L_0)^k e^{-\lambda_0 L_0}}{k!} + \frac{1}{Q_0}\sum_{i=R_0+1}^{R_0+Q_0}\sum_{k=i+1}^{\infty}\frac{(\lambda_0 L_0)^k e^{-\lambda_0 L_0}}{k!}\cdot\frac{i}{k}$$

From the above analysis, the fill rate of each stock in the distribution system can be calculated according to its inventory control parameters (R_i, Q_i) (i=0, 1, ⋯, N); however, the inventory (R, Q) policy is also derived from the optimal solution of model P, depending on β_i. Therefore, β_i cannot be derived directly from α_i by solving P on time. In the following, we use an iterative procedure to solve the original problem (model P) based on guessing the value of β_i at each iteration. When the real β_i equals to its estimated value, the optimal solution of the original problem can be resolved. The procedure has the following characteristics: 1) the initial value of β_i is set to α_i; 2) the procedure stops when the estimated value of β_i does not change in two successive iterations for each i (i = 0, 1, ⋯, N). The main steps of the procedure are given as follows:

Procedure BETA:

Step 0: For i=0, 1, ⋯, N, set $\beta_i = \alpha_i$;

Step 1: Solve the Q-problem and the R-problem to get the values (R_i, Q_i) for each stock i;

Step 2: Calculate the real fill rate β_i^*(i=0, 1, ⋯, N) of the system for the given (R, Q) policy by using the method proposed;

Step 3: If $\sum_{i=0}^{N}|\beta_i^* - \beta_i| \leq \varepsilon$ (ε is a very small positive number), stop; Otherwise, set

$\beta_i = \beta_i^*$ for i=1, 2, ⋯, N and go to Step 1.

In the next section, we will perform series of numerical experiments to evaluate the efficiency of the procedure proposed in this section.

5.6 Numerical Experiments

In this section, we evaluate the performance of the two algorithms for the Q-problem and R-problem respectively and the performance of the procedure BETA proposed for solving the inventory policy optimization problem P by computational experiments on randomly generated instances.

5.6.1 Experiments for the Resolution of Q–problem

In section 5.3, for the five different cases of integer-ratio constraints in Q-problem, we develop relevant algorithms to solve it, and furthermore, derive the optimal Q^* on the base of the characteristic of each case. In order to identify the sensitiveness of algorithms in the five different cases of Q-problem, we first give a set of small sized instance (N=4) for the purpose of analyzing more detailed information for the algorithms, and then, we will consider five sets of medium to large sized instances with N=10, 20, 50, 100, respectively, in an attempt to give further analysis in larger systems by using the algorithms proposed.

5.6.1.1 Small Sized Instances (N=4)

For this set of instance, 5 instances are generated and tested, and all parameters are given to be deterministic. For each instance, we will evaluate three index, optimal value (*OPT*), optimal order size (Q^*) and the computation time. The parameter setting and the results are given in Table 5.1.

From Table 5.1, after analyzing the numerical results, we can obtain the following observations:

1) For five integer-ratio constraints cases, we always developed efficient algorithms to solve, and the optimal order size Q^* for each stock can be derived;

Table 5.1 The results for the small sized instances of Q-problem with $N=4$

No.	Parameters	Cases	OPT	Q^*	time(s)
1	$h_i^e=\{1, 1, 1, 1, 1\}$, $\lambda_i=\{4, 1, 1, 1, 1\}$, $c_i=\{20, 20, 20, 20, 20\}$	Case 1	56.6538	13, 4, 4, 4, 4	0.00037
		Case 2	56.6667	12, 4, 4, 4, 4	0.00061
		Case 3	56.6538	13, 4, 4, 4, 4	0.000451
		Case 4	56.6667	12, 3, 3, 3, 3	0.000669
		Case 5	56.6538	13, 4, 4, 4, 4	0.000271
2	$h_i^e=\{1, 0.1, 1, 0.1, 1\}$, $\lambda_i=\{12, 3, 3, 3, 3\}$, $c_i=\{35, 35, 35, 35, 35\}$	Case 1	121.233	29, 10, 8, 10, 8	0.000371
		Case 2	121.622	27, 9, 9, 9, 9	0.000489
		Case 3	121.233	29, 10, 8, 10, 8	0.00046
		Case 4	121.622	27, 9, 9, 9, 9	0.008461
		Case 5	121.233	29, 10, 8, 10, 8	0.000294
3	$h_i^e=\{1, 0.1, 1, 0.1, 1\}$, $\lambda_i=\{10, 1, 2, 3, 4\}$, $c_i=\{25, 25, 25, 25, 25\}$	Case 1	92.222	22, 5, 6, 8, 8	0.000326
		Case 2	92.819	21, 7, 7, 7, 7	0.000705
		Case 3	92.222	22, 5, 6, 8, 8	0.000464
		Case 4	93.475	24, 4, 6, 8, 8	0.00041
		Case 5	92.222	22, 5, 6, 8, 8	0.000395
4	$h_i^e=\{0.1, 0.1, 0.1, 0.1, 0.1\}$, $\lambda_i=\{16, 1, 3, 5, 7\}$, $c_i=\{15, 15, 15, 15, 15\}$	Case 1	29.7729	69, 10, 17, 22, 26	0.000477
		Case 2	30.988	63, 21, 21, 21, 21	0.000161
		Case 3	29.7729	69, 10, 17, 22, 26	0.000586
		Case 4	29.85	72, 9, 18, 24, 24	0.000241
		Case 5	29.7729	69, 10, 17, 22, 26	0.00044
5	$h_i^e=\{0.1, 0.1, 0.1, 0.1, 0.1\}$, $\lambda_i=\{16, 1, 3, 5, 7\}$, $c_i=\{15, 15, 15, 15, 15\}$	Case 1	13.0278	40, 6, 8, 7, 9	0.000419
		Case 2	13.175	40, 8, 8, 8, 8	0.000971
		Case 3	13.0278	40, 6, 8, 7, 9	0.000562
		Case 4	13.075	40, 5, 8, 5, 10	0.000231
		Case 5	13.0278	40, 6, 8, 7, 9	0.000386

2) By observing the optimal value (*OPT*), we can see that the *OPT* are similar among the five different cases, only exiguous differences exists; this result demonstrate that the system-wide costs tend to be insensitive to the choice of order sizes in the system. And if we give further analysis about the results, the following rules about the *OPT* can be derived:

$$OPT_{Case1}=OPT_{Case3}=OPT_{Case5}<OPT_{Case4}\leqslant OPT_{Case2}$$

From the above observation, we can see that the *OPT* of Case 1, Case 3 and Case 5 are equal, this circumstance only occurs when the base-lot of Case 3 and Case 5 are equal to 1, in this situation, the Case 3 and Case 5 can be regarded as the case of without integer-ratio constraints, i.e., Case 1. And we can also see that the *OPT* of Case 4 are less than or equal to that of Case 2, this means that the integer-ratio constraint of Case 2 are tighter than that of Case 4 for the system studied.

From the table, the computation times of the five cases are quite short for all five cases, demonstrating the efficiency of the algorithms.

5.6.1.2 Large Sized Instances (*N*=10, 20, 50, 100)

For each set, 10 instances are generated and tested. Each instance of *Q*-problem was randomly generated with the following parameters settings:

$h_i^e \in U[1,5]$, $c_i \in h_i^e \cdot U[10,20]$, $\lambda \in U[1,10]$

The optimal value (*OPT*) and the computation time for the instances of each set are given in Table 5.2, Table 5.3, Table 5.4 and Table 5.5.

Table 5.2 The results for the instances of *Q*–problem with *N*=10

	OPT (optimal value)					Time (*s*)				
No.	Case 1	Case 2	Case 3	Case 4	Case 5	Case 1	Case 2	Case 3	Case 4	Case 5
1	409.57	417.66	409.57	411.63	409.57	0.0002	0.00088	0.00045	0.0045	0.00034
2	454.77	460.5	456.77	457	456.77	0.00023	0.00054	0.00042	0.0047	0.00033
3	607.14	612.83	607.14	610.5	607.14	0.00023	0.00085	0.00043	0.0041	0.00036
4	609.12	620	609.12	612.08	609.12	0.00024	0.00093	0.00042	0.0043	0.0004
5	515.67	518.67	515.67	517.5	515.67	0.00023	0.00092	0.00037	0.0046	0.00037
6	664.73	668.32	664.73	668.94	664.73	0.00021	0.00148	0.00047	0.0042	0.00038
7	356.89	367.7	356.89	358.25	356.89	0.00023	0.00095	0.00038	0.0041	0.00038
8	361.79	369.62	361.79	364.66	361.79	0.00022	0.00095	0.00065	0.0044	0.00035
9	379.14	384.66	379.14	380	379.14	0.00025	0.00117	0.00038	0.0039	0.00037
10	432.56	434.37	432.56	434.37	432.56	0.00022	0.0001	0.00037	0.0041	0.00032

Table 5.3 The results for the instances of *Q*–problem with *N*=20

	OPT (optimal value)					Time (*s*)				
No.	Case 1	Case 2	Case 3	Case 4	Case 5	Case 1	Case 2	Case 3	Case 4	Case 5
1	916.95	947.85	916.59	920.70	916.59	0.00026	0.0011	0.00053	0.0085	0.00048
2	747.49	769.2	747.49	749.95	747.49	0.00031	0.00067	0.00064	0.0085	0.00047
3	620.42	626.44	620.42	623.3	620.42	0.00025	0.00069	0.00068	0.0091	0.00042
4	1299.8	1309.9	1299.8	1301.5	1299.8	0.00028	0.00069	0.00058	0.0116	0.00041

续表

No.	*OPT* (optimal value)					Time (*s*)				
	Case 1	Case 2	Case 3	Case 4	Case 5	Case 1	Case 2	Case 3	Case 4	Case 5
5	939.04	960.9	939.04	943.55	939.04	0.00036	0.002	0.00078	0.0123	0.001
6	1415.5	1447.1	1415.5	1422.5	1415.5	0.00028	0.0016	0.00075	0.0116	0.00057
7	1002.9	1020.4	1002.9	1006.7	1002.9	0.0003	0.0014	0.00058	0.0078	0.00045
8	905.83	918.38	905.83	908.97	905.83	0.00028	0.0011	0.00055	0.0174	0.00065
9	1372.1	1387.6	1372.1	1381.0	1372.1	0.0003	0.0012	0.00051	0.0129	0.00045
10	804.66	807.25	804.66	807.3	804.66	0.00028	0.0011	0.00065	0.0173	0.00056

Table 5.4 The results for the instance of *Q*–problem with *N*=50

No.	*OPT* (optimal value)					Time (*s*)				
	Case 1	Case 2	Case 3	Case 4	Case 5	Case 1	Case 2	Case 3	Case 4	Case 5
1	3247.7	3294.7	3247.7	3257.6	3247.7	0.00038	0.0062	0.0012	0.0135	0.00079
2	2154.3	2162.3	2154.3	2159.4	2154.3	0.00032	0.0053	0.00098	0.0129	0.00072
3	2324.5	2361.0	2324.5	2329.8	2324.5	0.00031	0.0052	0.0013	0.0127	0.00074
4	1864.3	1903.5	1864.3	1868.8	1864.3	0.00033	0.0052	0.0013	0.0125	0.0014
5	2632.6	2668.7	2632.6	2643.8	2632.6	0.00043	0.0056	0.0011	0.0124	0.0013
6	2233.9	2273.4	2233.9	2240.1	2233.9	0.00034	0.0051	0.0012	0.0083	0.0012
7	3018.4	3064.6	3018.4	3028.3	3018.4	0.00041	0.0052	0.0012	0.0152	0.0015
8	2259.9	2285.4	2259.9	2267.3	2259.9	0.00034	0.0055	0.0011	0.0178	0.0013
9	2411.2	2434.2	2411.2	2419.8	2411.2	0.00036	0.0057	0.0013	0.0164	0.00074
10	2067.2	2078.1	2067.2	2073.6	2067.2	0.00037	0.0053	0.00096	0.0163	0.0011

Table 5.5 The results for the instances of *Q*–problem with *N*=100

No.	*OPT* (optimalvalue)					Time (*s*)				
	Case 1	Case 2	Case 3	Case 4	Case 5	Case 1	Case 2	Case 3	Case 4	Case 5
1	6233.3	6339.2	6233.3	6246.3	6233.3	0.00064	0.0061	0.0027	0.0139	0.0013
2	5505.2	5530.2	5505.2	5524.4	5505.2	0.00053	0.014	0.0023	0.013	0.0023
3	5463.1	5488.8	5463.1	5478.2	5463.1	0.00074	0.0075	0.0019	0.0198	0.0029
4	4598.9	4614.6	4598.9	4609.0	4598.9	0.00063	0.0102	0.0024	0.0324	0.0023
5	4049.8	4123.1	4049.8	4063.7	4049.8	0.00062	0.0101	0.0021	0.0224	0.0027

续表

	OPT (optimalvalue)					Time (*s*)				
No.	Case 1	Case 2	Case 3	Case 4	Case 5	Case 1	Case 2	Case 3	Case 4	Case 5
6	4687.0	4732.8	4687.0	4702.0	4687.0	0.00065	0.0073	0.0018	0.0208	0.0026
7	5445.5	5498.1	5445.5	5461.6	5445.1	0.00072	0.0066	0.0025	0.0148	0.0024
8	5800.9	5822.6	5800.9	5817.6	5800.9	0.00064	0.0061	0.0022	0.0271	0.0015
9	5317.2	5351.7	5317.2	5331.9	5317.2	0.00076	0.01	0.012	0.0431	0.0016
10	4955.5	5063.1	4955.5	4973.3	4955.5	0.00066	0.0086	0.015	0.0329	0.0015

From the four tables, we can observe that the computation time of the dynamic programming algorithmis very short for each instance in the four sets of instances; this demonstrates that, even for the large instances with 100 retailers, the *Q*-problem with different integer-ratio cases can be solved efficiently by using the algorithm. In addition, the observations about theoptimal costof the problem obtained for the small instancesin the last subsection are also valid for the large instances in this subsection.

5.6.2 Experiments for the Resolution of *R*–problem

Similarly, a set of small sized instances with N=4 and four sets of medium to large sized instances with N=10, 20, 50, 100, respectively were tested. Each set contains 10 instances. All the instances for *R*-problem were generated with parameters h_i^e, T_i, s_i and λ_i randomly generated according to the uniform distributions described in Table 5.6, with the service level (i=1, 2, ⋯, N) for all retailers specified as 0.95. The computation results of the instances are given in Table 5.7.

Table 5.6 Parameter settings of the tested instances of R–problem

Parameter	Value
h_i^e	$h_i^e \in U[1, 5]$
T_i^e	$T_i^e \in U[1, 10]$
s_i	$s_i \in U[1, 3]$
λ_i	$\lambda_i \in U[1, 10]$

Table 5.7 The results for the tested instances of *R*–problem

Instance set		Max/Average computation time (s)
Small instance	N=4	0.00299s/0.00167s
Medium to large instances	N=10	0.00313s/0.00202s
	N=20	0.00512s/0.00303s
	N=50	0.08188s/0.01688s
	N=100	0.06219s/0.0322s

From Table 5.7, we can observe that for small instance (N=4) the R-problemcan be solved almost instantaneously by using the dynamic programming algorithm of Grave and Willems, whereas for larger instances (N=10, 20, 50 and 100), the computation time of the algorithm becomes longer but is still quite short. This demonstrates the suitability of this algorithm in solving the R-problem.

5.6.3 Experiments for the Resolution of Problem p with a Given Service Level

In this section, we evaluate the performance of procedure BETA by numerical experiments on the same sets of randomly generated instances with N=10, 20, 50 and 100 respectively as presented in Section 5.6.1 and Section 5.6.2. For each instance set, four different α-service levels ranged from 0.8 to 0.98 were considered and 10 instances were generated randomly for each α. We calculated the maximum/average computation time and the maximum/average number of iterations of the procedure BETA for the instances, and the results are given in Table 5.8.

Table 5.8 The results for the tested instances of problem *P*

	α-service level	Max/average computation times in seconds	Max/average number of iterations
N=10	0.80	0.2799/0.1193	4/3.8
	0.90	0.2412/0.1113	4/3.2
	0.95	0.3167/0.1646	3/3
	0.98	0.1575/0.1165	3/3
N=20	0.80	1.4726/0.7084	4/4
	0.90	2.5285/0.8465	4/3.5
	0.95	0.8885/0.5517	3/3
	0.98	1.3599/0.5706	3/3

续表

	α-service level	Max/average computation times in seconds	Max/average number of iterations
N=50	0.80	2.1309/1.7164	4/4
	0.90	6.2981/2.4684	4/4
	0.95	4.4845/2.5109	4/3.2
	0.98	2.6383/1.4581	3/3
N=100	0.80	4.476/3.2181	4/4
	0.90	7.3628/4.1323	4/3.9
	0.95	4.285/2.6031	4/3.2
	0.98	5.3823/3.8045	3/3

From the table, we can observe that the maximum number of iterations for each in stance is no larger than 4, and is very close to its corresponding average number of iter ations. The two numbers of iterations decrease when the α-service level increases. This observation about the number of iterations of procedure BETA is similar to that in the last two chapters. It demonstrates that the number is neither sensitive to the number of retailers nor sensitive to the α-service level of the distribution system considered. In addition, the maximum computation time and the average computation time of the procedure are short even for the largest instances with N=100. These results show that the procedure BETA has a good convergence property and is very efficient in solving the inventory optimization problem of the distribution system with a given α-service level.

5.7 Conclusion

This chapter has studied a two-level distribution system with Poisson final demands and fixed order costs at each stock.As we know, for distribution systems, echelon (R, Q) policies and installation (r, Q) policies can not be transformed each other, this makes the inventory policy optimization problem of the considered system more complicated. To simplify the formulation of the problem, we have assumed randomized initial condition for the distribution system. With this assumption, we have proposed a mathematical model and an iterative procedure for optimizing the (R, Q) policyof the system under the GSA framework. The procedure is based on the resolution of the model's two sub-problems, *Q*-problem and *R*-problem, which are solved by using a dynamic programming algorithm or an EOQ-based method. Five different types of integer-ratio constraints are considered for the *Q*-problem and their cost-effectiveness are compared. Finally, the performances of the algorithms and the procedure are evaluated by numerical experiments.

Chapter 6
Conclusions and Perspectives

In this thesis, we have studied the inventory policy optimization of multi-echelon inventory systems with fixed order costs at each stock. Because of existing fixed order costs, this problem becomes very difficult for general multi-echelon inventory systems. In the literature, two competing approaches are used to solve inventory optimization problems, stochastic service approach (SSA) and guaranteed service approach (GSA). Compared with the SSA whose model usually has a very complicated structure, the GSA describes a multi-echelon inventory system in an approximate fashion and can provide a relatively simple mathematical programming model for the system. This simplified model allows a planner to make strategic and tactical decisions on the inventories of the system such as safety stock placement. The key assumption of the GSA is that excessive demand superior to a certain level is treated by operating flexibility. Based on this assumption, the GSA can formulate the inventory optimization problem as a deterministic mathematical programming problem. However, in most studies of the GSA, the costs of using operating flexibility were not considered in its optimization model. This has caused the criticism of this approach in the past. In addition, fixed order costs which often exist in industrial supply chains were ignored in the model. To the best of our knowledge, no previous work has used the GSA to optimize multi-echelon inventory systems with fixed order costs. Therefore, in this thesis we have focused on two major research topics: 1) Use the GSA to optimize multi-echelon inventory systems with fixed order costs at each stock. 2) Extend the GSA to consider operating flexibility costs in inventory policy optimization of the systems.

This thesis has considered three different types of multi-echelon inventory systems: Serial systems, assembly systems, and two-level distribution systems. For each system, we assume that its final customer demand is generated by a Poisson process, a fixed cost is charged at each stock when it places an order, and each stock is controlled by a (R, Q) policy. Our objective is to find optimal (R, Q) policy for the system so that the system's total cost which contains inventory holding costs, fixed order costs, and operating flexibility costs is minimized while satisfying a given service level to customer.

After a general introduction and literature review in Shapter 1 and some preparatory work in Chapter 2, Chapter 3 deals with the optimization of (R, Q) policies for a continuous-review serial inventory system with Poisson demand and fixed order costs. Under the GSA, we first establish a mathematical model for the problem, which is a nonlinear programming model. Since the objective function of the model depends on two service levels (α-service level and β-fill rate) of the system, we propose an iterative procedure to solve the model based on estimation of β-fill rate when α-service level is giv en. The iterative procedure relies on the resolution of two sub-problems of the model: order size decision sub-problem (Q-problem) and reorder point sub-problem (R-problem). We develop an efficient dynamic programming (DP) algorithm to solve the Q-problem, based on two important properties about the state space of its decision variables; this makes our DP algorithm much more efficient than a DP algorithm in the literature. The R-problem is solved by using another DP algorithm proposed by Graves and Willems. The numerical experiments demonstrate that the two DP algorithms are very efficient in solving the Q-problem and R-problem of large size with a short computation time. The numerical results also show that the iterative optimization procedure has a good convergence property and is computationally efficient in solving the inventory policy optimization problem.

Chapter 4 extends the model and the solution approach proposed in Chapter 3 to assembly systems. Since the assembly systems studied have a more complicated struc ture than serial systems, in which a stock may have more than one direct predecessor stocks, the DP algorithm of the Q-problem for serial systems cannot be directly used for assembly systems. Therefore, we develop a new DP algorithm to solve the Q-problem of the assembly systems, in which both forward recursive procedure and backward recursive procedure are used to identify the optimal solution of the problem. The numerical experiments demonstrate the efficiency of the DP algorithm.

Chapter 5 focuses on the optimization of (R, Q) policies for two-level distribution systems. The most distinguishing feature of a distribution system is that each stock may have multiple direct successor stocks; this network structure makes the analysis and optimization of the system more difficult. For the system, we also establish a mathematical model for its inventory policy optimization problem and present an optimization procedure to solve the model. More particularly, for the Q-problem, we consider five different types of integer-ratio constraints imposed on the order sizes of the warehouse and the retailers. For each type, we propose an efficient algorithm to solve the Q-problem. We compare the five types of integer-ratio constraints in terms of their cost-effectiveness by numerical experiments. The numerical experiments also demonstrate the efficiency of the optimization procedure in solving the inventory optimization problem of the distribution system studied.

This thesis has extended the application domain of the GSA from safety stock placement of multi-echelon inventory systems without order costs to the optimization of (R, Q) policies of multi-echelon inventory systems with fixed order costs at each stock. It has also extended the standard GSA by explicitly considering operating flexibility costs and effects in the GSA model of the optimization problem.

Although the work of this thesis has demonstrated advantages of the GSA in the optimization of multi-echelon inventory systems, much work remains to be done. There are some potential directions for future research. Firstly, the performance of the inventory policy found by the GSA should be compared with the performance of the inventory policy found by the SSA. In the literature, very few contributions that conduct such a comparison are available, especially, for multi-echelon inventory system with fixed order costs. This is mainly because the stochastic inventory model employed by the SSA usually has a very complicated structure if fixed orders are taken into consideration, and it is very difficult to derive an optimal inventory policy for such system, only heuristic algorithms were developed. Moreover, how to fairly compare the two approaches is still an open problem because they are based on two different settings: The SSA has backorder costs whereas the GSA has operating flexibility costs. For these reasons, we have not compared the two approaches in this thesis, but it is one of important topics for our future research.

Secondly, in this thesis, the customer demand process is assumed to be a Poisson process, but in reality, this demand may follow another stochastic process. In future, we will extend our work to multi-echelon inventory systems with other demand processes, such as normal distributed or compound Poisson processes.

Thirdly, this thesis only considers continuous-review inventory systems. In practice, the inventory position of each stock may be reviewed periodically. In this case, (R, Q) policy is generalized and replaced by (R, nQ) policy. Optimizing (R, nQ) policies for periodic review multi-echelon inventory systems under the GSA are also in the list of our future research topics.

Fourthly, in this thesis, when we consider inventory policy optimization of a two-level distribution system, we assume the system has randomized initial condition. It is worthy to study whether this condition can be relaxed for the distribution system. Moreover, extending our GSA approach to distribution systems with more than two levels is also a future research topic.

Finally, this thesis has considered individually three types of multi-echelon inventory systems, i.e., serial systems, assembly systems and two-level distribution systems. In practice, a supply chain may have both assembly structure and distribution structure. One of our future work is to study general multi-echelon inventory systems in which all possible links between stocks are permitted.

Résumé en Français

Introduction Générale

Une chaîne d'approvisionnementestun réseau d'entreprisesà travers lequelles produits sont fabriquéset livrésaux consommateurs finaux. La gestion de la chaîned'approvisionnement (SCM) vise à optimiser sa performance de manière globale par coordonnerles flux etles stockages desmarchandises desfournisseurs de matières premièresaux magasins passés parles fabricants. Au cours des dernièresannées, la mondialisationéconomique,la prolifération et l'innovationrapide des produitsont considérablementaccru la complexitéde cette gestion. Une question importantedans la gestionde la chaîne d'approvisionnement est la gestiondes stocks dansun tel réseau faceaux demandes clientèles incertaines. L'objectif de cettegestion est de réduireles coûts de stockagetout en assurantunhaut niveau de servicedonnéaux clients.

Traditionnellement, différentsstocks dansune chaîne d'approvisionnementont étégérés de manière indépendante, menant à un niveau élevé de certains stocks dans la chaîne. Les pressions compétitives accrueset la mondialisationdes marchés ontobligéles entreprises àfaire plus d'effortspour réduireleurs stocks tout en améliorantleservice à la clientèle. Cela a attiré de plus en plus d'attention des chercheurs académiqueset des praticiensindustrielsà la gestion des stocks multi-échelons quiprend en compte lesinteractions entre les différentsstocks dansla chaîne d'approvisionnement.

Une chaîne d'approvisionnementavec plusieursstocks peutêtre modélisée commeun système de stocks multi-échelons, où les stocksse trouvent enplusieursé chelonsou niveaux. La gestion des stocksmulti-échelons adopte une approche d'optimisation globale.Dans une telle approche, les optimisationsde tous les stockssont considéréessimultanément, avecun objectifde minimiserleur coût total tout en répondant auxexigences deservice clientèle. Par conséquent, la stratégie clé pour la gestion des stocksmulti-échelons estla coordinationefficace des approvisionnements de tous les stocks dansune chaîne d'approvisionnement.

Dans la littérature, il existe deux approches concurrentespour l'optimisation des systèmes de stocks multi-échelons: l'approche de servicestochastique (SSA) et l'approchedeservice garanti(GSA). Dans la SSA, la disposition d'un stock de sécurité pour chaque stock est le seul moyen pour protéger contrela variabilitéde la demande clientèle. En revanche, la GSAprésume que lestock de sécuritéest dimensionné pourcouvrirla variabilitéde la demandejusqu'àun certain niveau, i.e., le niveau maximum raisonnablede la demande. Si la réalisation de cette demande est supérieure àce niveau, la partie excessive delademandesera satisfaite par des mesures extraordinaires telles que les heures supplémentaires ou la sous-traitance. Par rapport à la SSA, la GSA modélise un système de stocks multi-échelons de manièreapproximative, maiselle permet à un planificateur du système de prendre ses décisions stratégiques ou tactiques sur la gestion de ces stocksbasées sur unmodèle simplifié.

Dans la littérature, la plupart des études sur les systèmesde stocksmulti-échelons ne considèrent pas le coût de passation de commandeàchaque stock.Cependant,dans la pratique,chaque stocka généralementun coût fixe pour passer une commande, qui peut correspondreau coûtdela livraisonde la commandeou à d'autres coûtsindépendants de la quantitéde la commande. Pourun système de stocksmulti-échelons, siun coûtde passation de commande se produit àchaque stock, la politique (R, Q) ou la politique(s, S) est généralement utilisée pourla gestion du système. En raison desa simplicité et sapopularitédans la pratique, nous choisissons la politique (R, Q) plutôt que la politique (s, S) pour la gestion d'un système de stocksmulti-échelons avec des coûts de passation de commandedans cette thèse.Nous étudionsl'optimisation de la politique (R, Q) pour les systèmesde stocksmulti-éche lons avec la demande clientèlesuivant un processus de Poissonet un coût de passation de commande à chaque stock.

L'existence d'un coût de passation de commande àchaque stockrendl'optimisation de lapolitique de stockage pour un système de stocksmulti-échelonstrès diffi cile.La SSA,comme une approcheclassique, a étégénéralement utilisé pourrésoudre un tel-problème d'optimisation. Toutefois, en raisonde la grande complexitéd'un tel système avec des coûtsde passation de commande, seuls les algo rithmesapproximatifs (heuristiques) ont été développéspour trouver despolitiquesde stockageproches de l'optimum dans le cadre de la SSA.

D'autre part, dans l'hypothèse que la demandeexcessivesupérieure àun certain niveausoit satisfaite par la flexibilité d'exploitation d'un système telle que les heures supplémentaires ou la sous-traitance, laGSAest capable demodéliser leproblèmed'optimisation de la politique de stockage du système comme un problèmede programmation mathématiquedéterministe, qui peut être résoluplus facilement. Dans la littérature, aucuns travaux antérieurs n'ontutilisé cette approche pouroptimiser un système destocks-multi-échelons avec des coûts de passation de commande àchaque stock. Par conséquent, dans cette thèse, nous utilisons la GSA pour modéliseret résoudre des problèmesd'optimisation de politique de stock age pour plusieurs systèmes de stocks multi-échelons avec des coûts de passation de commande. Différente de la GSA standard quiignore lescoûts de flexibilité d'exploitation engendrés lors que des mesures extraordinaires sont utilisées pour satisfaire la demandeexcessive, nous développons une nouvelle approche de type GSA qui considèreles coûts de flexibilité d'exploitationet les effets de cette flexibilité surlesflux physiques du système de stocksmulti-échelons dans cette thèse. Dans notre étude, le niveau maximum raisonnable de la demande d'un stock durant son délai d'approvisionnement est déterminéen fonction d'unniveau de serviceau clientfinal.

Les principalescontributions de cette thèsesont les suivantes:

1) Nous appliquons la GSA à l'optimisation des systèmes de stocksmulti-échelons avec des co ûts de passation de commandeàchaque stock. Puisque tous lestravaux antérieurs surla GSA ne considèrent que dessystèmes de stocksmulti-échelons sanscoûts

de passation de commande, le travail de cette thèse estle premier essaide l'optimisation des systèmesde stocksmulti-échelons avec des coûts de passation de commande dans le cadre dela GSA.

2) La GSA standard ignoreles effets de la flexibilité d'exploitation sur lesflux physiques etlecoût total d'unsystème de stocksmulti-échelons. Dans cette thèse, nous généralisons la GSA standarden tenant compte deces effets eten incluant les coûtsde flexibilité d'exploitationdans notre modèle d'optimisation despolitiquesde stockage d'un tel système. Dans ce modèle, le coût total du système inclut non seulementles coûts fixesde passation de commande, les coûts de possession des stocks, mais aussi les coûts de flexibilité d'exploitation.

3) Pour les systèmes en série, les systèmes d'assemblage, et les systèmes de distribution à deux niveaux, nousétablissons des modèlesde programmation mathématiquepourles problèmes d'optimisationde leurs politiquesde stockage (R, Q) dans le cadre dela GSA.

4) La prise en comptedes effets et des coûts de la flexibilitéd'exploitationrend notremodèle de la GSA plus compliqués que celui de la GSA standard. Ce premier modèle a une fonction objectifdépendante de deuxniveaux de service(niveau de service αet taux de remplissage β). Nousproposonsune procédure itérative pour résoudre lemodèle basé sur l'estimation du taux de remplissage.

5) Pourun niveau de service αet un taux de remplissage β donnés, le problème d'optimisation dela politiquede stockage pour un système de stocks multi-échelons peut être décomposéen deux sous-problèmes: le sous-problème de détermination de quantités de commande (Q-problème) et le sous-problème de détermination de points de recommande (R-problème). Nousdéveloppons des algorithmesde programmation dynamique (DP) pour résoudreefficacementlesdeux sous-problèmes.

6) Les efficacités desalgorithmesde DPet de laprocédure itérativesont évaluéespar des expériencesnumériques.

Le résumé français de cette thèsese compose de cinqchapitres. Dans le chapitre 1, un état de l'art est fait sur les études en gestion des stocks multi-échelons liées ànotre travail. Dans le chapitre 2, nous considérons les systèmesen sérieavecla demande clientèle suivant un processus de Poissonetcoûts de passation de commande à chaque-stock etdéveloppons un modèlede programmation mathématiqueet une approche de résolutionpour l'optimisation des politiques de stockage (R, Q) des systèmes dans le cadre de la GSA. Le modèle prend enconsidération à la foisles coûts de passation de commande et les coûtsde flexibilitéd'exploitationet l'approchede résolution est basée surdeux algorithmesde programmation dynamiqueque nous développonsou adoptonspourdeux sous-problèmesdu modèle. Les performances desalgorithmeset de l'approchede résolutionsont évaluées par desexpériences numériques. Chapitre 3généralise le modèleetl'approche de résolution développésdans le chapitre3 aux systèmesd'assemblageavecdes expériences numériquespourl'évaluation de performanceaussi. Dans le chapitre 4, nous considérons les systèmes de distributionà deux niveauxavecunentrepôtetplusieursdétaillants. L'analyseet l'optimisationde ces systèmessont plus difficiles que les systèmes ensérie et les systèmes d'assemblage. Nous développonségalementun modèle de programmationmathématiqueet une approche de résolutionpourl'optimisation dessystèmes de distributiondans le cadre de laGSA. Plus particulièrement, nous considérons cinq différents types decontraintesde ratio entier éventuellement imposées sur les quantités de commande des stocks du système étudié, et comparons leursefficacitéspar des expériencesnumériques. Enfin, le chapitre5 conclut le travail réalisé de cette thèse et présente des perspectives pour la recherche future.

Chapitre 1 Etat de l'art

Dans ce chapitre, nous faisons un état de l'art sur lesmodèles et les méthodespro posées dans la littératurepour l'analyseet l'optimisation dessystèmes de stocks multi-échelons, en particulier pour lessystèmes avec descoûts de passation de commande.

Nousdonnons d'abordune introduction généralesurles travaux dansla gestion des stocksmulti-échelons. Ensuite, nous nous concentrons surlesétudes actuelles surla gestion des stocksmulti-échelons en utilisant deuxapprochesd'optimisation: l'approche de servicestochastique (SSA)et l'approchedeservice garanti (GSA). Une comparaison entre les deuxapproches concurrentesest également abordée dansce chapitre.

Les études Généralesdela Gestion des Stocksmulti–échelons

L'étude dessystèmes de stocksmulti-échelons a été lancée paruntravail pionnier de ClarketScarf (1960). Dans ce travail,ils ont montréque la politique optimale de stockage pour un systèmeen série dans lequel le coûtde passation de commande est facturéqu'au-plus haut échelon est une politiqueéchelon. Pour un système de stocks multi-échelons avec un coût de passation de commande ὰ chaquestock, ils ont souligné quesa politique optimale, si elle existe, a une structure complexeet est difficile ὰ calculer.

Depuis 1960, beaucoup d'études ont été menées pour généraliser le tra vail de Clark et Scarf, comme Federgruen et Zipkin (1984), Chen et Zheng (1994), Zip kin (2000) et ainsi de suite. Récemment, Sinha et al. (2011) ont fourni une approche de calcul plus simple et unifiée pour le modèle Clark-Scarfavec un horizon temporal fini ou infini.Rosling (1989) a montré que la politique échelon de stockage est aussi optimale pour, les systèmes d'assemblage sansco ûtsde passation de commande. Pour les systèmes de distribution sans co ûtsde passation de commande, la politique échelonde stockage n'est pas optimal dans le cas général (Van Houtum, 2006). En raison de la complexité des systèmes de stocks multi-échelons avec un co ût de passation de commande ὰ chaque stock, la plupart d'études ont concentrésur l'optimisation et l'évaluation de la politique de point de commande, i.e., la politique (R, Q), pour ces systèmes.

Presque dans la même décennie, Simpson (1958) a proposé l'approche de service garanti (GSA) pour la modélisation et la gestion des stocks d'un système en série sans co ûtsde passation de commande. Dans ce système, chaque stock, qui a une demande aléatoire mais bornée, est gérépar une politique base-stock (une poli tique d'approvisionnement ὰ recomplètement périodique). Les résultats de Simpson ont montré que la politique optimale de stockage pour le système en série est une politique " tout ou rien", c'est ὰ dire, chaque stock soit ne possède d'aucun stock de sécurité soit possède d'un stock de sécurité suffisant pour lui découpler des stocks en aval et des stocks en amont. Différentes extensions du travail de Simpson pour les systèmes d'assemblage et de distribution ont été faites plus tard.

Sur la base des deux articles fondamentaux de Clark et Scarf (1960) et de Simpson (1958), deux approches concurrentes ont été développées au fil de temps.

Les étudesde l'approche de service stochastique pour les systèmes en série

Dans ce paragraphe, l'approche de service stochastique pour les systèmes en série estrevue, en particulier pour les systèmes avec des coûts de passation de commande et gérés par la politiquede stockage (*R*, *Q*).

Sur l'évaluation decoût, Axsater (1998) a considéré un système en série à deux niveauxgéré pardes politiques installations (*R*, *Q*) et a proposé une méthode pour évaluer exactement le coût de stockage et le coût de rupture de stock du système. Axsater et Rosling (1993) ont montré que les politiques échelons (*R*, *Q*) dominent les politiques installations (*R*, *Q*) pour les systèmesen série et les systèmes d'assemblage. Chen et Zheng (1994) ont développé une procédure pour l'évaluation exacte de la performance de la politique échelon (*R*, *nQ*) pour les systèmes en série. Dans leur procédure, un coût de passation de commande est facturé pour chaque approvisionnement plutôt que pour chaque commande.

Sur l'optimisation depolitiques de stockage, Chen (2000) a montré que si l'on ignore les coûts de passation de commande mais laquantité de chaque commande est donnée, une politique échelon (*R*, *Q*) est optimale pour les systèmes en série et les systèmes d'assemblage. Shang et Song (2007) ont considéré deux modèles stochastiques des systèmes en série en supposant que soit la quantité de commande soit donnée à chaque stock soit un coût de passation de commande est facturé uniquement pour les commandes externes. Ils ont montré que les politiques optimales échelon (*R*, *Q*) des modèles peuvent être estimées par une série de politiques indépendants et optimales à seul stade.Yang et al. (2011) ont également considéré un système en série à deux échelons avec la demande suivant à un processus de Poisson et géré par une politique échelon (*R*, *Q*), ils ont dérivé une condition nécessaire pour l'optimalité d'une politique échelon (*R*, *Q*) et la quasi-convexité de la fonction de coût du système. Sur la base de ces propriétés, ils ont proposé un algorithme heuristique simple pour trouver une politique (*R*, *Q*) quasi-optimale pour le système. Shang et Zhou (2010) ont étudié un système en série géré par la politique échelon (*R*, *nQ*, *T*) avec deux types de coûts de passation de commande: l'un associé à chaque commande de *Q* unités et l'autre encouru lors de chaque inventaire d'un stock. Ils ont développé une heuristique simple pour obtenir les quantités et les intervalles optimaux de commande.

Les étudesde l'approche de Service Stochastique Pour Les Systèmes D'assemblage

Par rapport aux systèmes en série, les systèmes d'assemblage avec la demande stochastique ont attiré relativement peu d'attention dans la littérature.

Schmidt et Nahmias (1985)a caractériséune solution optimale pour un système d'assemblage ǎ deux niveaux avec la demande stochastique. Rosling (1989) ont montré qu'un système d'assemblée générale sans coûtsde passation de commande peut être transformé en un système en série équivalent. Ces deux articles supposent qu'aucun coût de passation de commanden' existe dans les systèmes considérés. L'inclusion des coûts de passation de commande rendles systèmes d'assemblage avec la demande stochastique extrêmement difficiles. De nombreux articles ont étudié l'évaluationet l'optimisation de la politique (R, Q) (Federgruen et Zheng, 1992; Rosling, 2002; De Bodt et Graves, 1985; Chen et Zheng, 1994).Une discussion sur la politique (R, Q) pour les systèmes d'assemblage est donnée dans Axsater et Rosling (1993) et Chen (2000).En pratique, on souvent utiliser une approche simple en deux étapes pour déterminer la quantité de commande Q et le point de commande R d'une politique installation/échelon (R, Q). Dans la première étape, la demande stochastique est remplacée par sa valeur moyenne et la quantité de commande Q est déterminéeselon un modèle EOQ standard. Dans la deuxième étape, le point de commande R est déterminé pour la quantité de commande Qdonnée. Notons que la plupart des travaux précédents, qui étudientla politique (R, Q), présentent des algorithmes heuristiques plutût que des méthodes exactes pour l'évaluation decoût et l'optimisation de la politique pour les systèmes d'assemblage avec des coûts fixes de passation de commande.

Les étudesde l'approche de Service Stochastique Pour Les Systèmes de Distribution

Dans ce paragraphe, nous nous concentrons sur les études sur les systèmes de distribution ǎ deux niveaux avec un entrepôt et plusieurs détaillants.

La plupart des études précédentes avec la politique installation/échelon (R, Q) se focalisent sur l'évaluation exacte ou approximative des coûts de ces systèmes, comme dans Svoronos et Zipkin (1988) et Axsater (1993). Une revue générale de ces études avant 2003 est donnée par Axsater (2003). Kiesmuller et al. (2004) a développé une méthode d'évaluation approximative pour un système de distribution à deux niveaux. Seifbarghi et Akbari (2006) a dérivé la fonction du coût qui est utilisée pour trouver de manière approximative le point de commande d'un système de distribution à deux niveaux. Axsater et al. (2007) a présenté trois techniques pour l'évaluation du coût d'un système de distribution à deux niveaux. Howard et Marklund (2011) ont considéré un système de distribution dans lequel l'entrepôt applique la politiqueéchelon (R, Q)et les détaillants utiliser les politiques base-stock, ils ont développé une méthode exacte pour l'évaluation du coût du système.

Peu d'articles ont étudié l'optimisation de la politique installation/échelon (R, Q) pour les systèmes de distribution. Axsater et Rosling (1993) ont démontré que la politique installation (R, Q) et la poltique échelon (R, Q) peuvent dominer l'un l'autre dans des situations différentes pour les systèmes de distribution. A notre connaissance, le seul articleconsidérant des modèles de vente perdue avec la politique (R, Q) est Al-Rifai et Rossetti (2007). Bijvank et Vis (2011) ont fourni une revue générale de la thé orie de gestion des stocks avec la vente perdue.

Les étudesde l'approche de Service Garanti Pour Les Systèmes de Stocks Multi-échelons

Tous les travaux antérieurs sur cette approche ont utilisé des politiques base-stock pour la gestion des systèmes de stocks multi-échelons sans coûts de passation de commande.

L'approche de service garanti provient du travail de Kimball (1955), qui a été réédité en 1988 (Kimball, 1988). Dans cet article, Kimball a étudié un seul stock avec la demande aléatoire mais bornée, géré par une politique base-stock. Il a prouvé que la borne de la demande durant le délai d'approvisionnement du stock peut être utiliséepour définir son niveau de base-stock (niveau de récomplètement). Simpson (1958) a généralisé le modèle de Kimball à un système en série et prouvé que la politique optimalede stockage du système est une politique "tout ou rien". Sur la base de cette propriété, Grave (1988) a démontré que le problème d'optimisation considéré par Simpson peut être résolu en utilisant un algorithme de programmation dynamique. Plus tard, cette approche a été généraliséeaux systèmes d'assemblage, aux systèmes de distribution, et à des systèmes plus généraux dans Inderfurth (1991), Inderfurth et Minner (1998), Graves et Willems (1996, 2000), Minner (2000), Humair et Willems (2006), et Humair et Willems (2011).

Récemment, Grave et Willems (2008) et Schoenmey et Grave (2009) ont étendu leurs travaux antérieurs (1996, 2000) aux chaînes d'approvisionnement avec la demande non-stationnaire ou avec l'évolution de la prévision de la demande.

Comparaison de l´approche de Service Stochastique et Approche de Service Garanti

Seuls quelques articles dans la littérature comparent les deux approches. L'une comparaison a été faitedans Graves et Willems (2003). Ils ont appliqué deux approches pour un système d'assemblage et a constaté que l'approche de service garanti dominel'approche de service stochastique.

Klosterhalfen et Minner (2010) ont fait une autre comparaison des deux approches sur des systèmes de distributionà deux niveaux et ont montré que la supériorité de l'une des deux approches dépend de leurs paramètres spécifiques et ne peut être établie en général. En outre, ils ont présenté une méthode pour déterminer le niveau deservices in terne approprié, qui est utilisé pour définir les coûts de flexibilité d'exploitation dans le modèle de GSA. Minner et al. (2003) a donné quelques indications concernant l'utilisation appropriée de la flexibilitéd'exploitation. Notons que toutes les comparaisons citées ci-dessus sont axées sur les systèmes de stocks multi-échelons sans coûts de passation de commande.

Chapitre 2 Optimisation de Politiques de Stockage (*R*, *Q*) pour les Systèmes en Série

Aprèsla description des systèmesde stockagemulti-échelons et l'approchedeservice garanti(GSA)dans le dernier chapitre, ce chapitre traite de l'optimisation de politiques de stockage(*R*, *Q*) pour les systèmes en série avecPoissondemandedans le cadre de la GSA. A part la prise en compte des coûtsde stockage à tous les stocks comme dans le modèlestandard de la GSA, nous considérons égalementdescoûts de passation de commandes et des coûtsde flexibilitéd'exploitation. Après une présentation des hypothèses et des notations, nous formulerons un modèle mathématique pour le problème. Ce modèle peut être résolu par une procédure itérative fondée sur deux algorithmes de programmation dynamique (DP). Unalgo rithmeDPest utilisé pour résoudre le sous-problème de détermination de quan tités de commande (Q-problème), et l'autre est utilisé pour résoudrele sous-problème de détermination de points de recommande (R-problème). Les expériences numériques que nous avons faites sur des instances générées aléa toirement démontrent que les algorithmes et la procédure proposés sont très efficaces.

Description du Problème

Un système de stocks en série avec N stades (stocks) dont l'inventaire est fait en temps réel est considéré, où le stade N commande auprès d'un fournisseur externe avec un stock illimité, stade N-1 commande du stade N, stade N-2 commande du stade N-1, et ainsi de suite. Enfin, au stade final, i.e., stade 1, la demande clientèle se produit. Tout stade du système est géré par une politique de stockage (R, Q). La demande clientèle du stock suit un processus de Poisson de taux moyen λ. Le coût de passation de chaque commande et le co ût de stockage échelon par unité de produit par unité de temps du stock i est c_i et h_i^e respectivement, i=1, 2, $\cdots$, N. En outre, le coûtdela flexibilité d'exploitation de p est facturé pour chaque unité de produit rempli ȧ l'aide d'une mesure extraordinaire.

Dans le cadre de la GSA, l'hypothèse clé est que la demande clientèle du stade final est stochastique et bornée. La partie excessive de toute demande supérieure ȧ une borne est satisfaite par des mesures extraordinaires telles que les heures supplémentaires ou la sous-traitance. Donc, pour un niveau de service α ($0<\alpha<1$) donné au stade final, i.e., stade1, la bonne supérieurde $D(\tau)$ de la demande totale durant un délai de τ unités de temps peut être formulée comme suit:

$$\sum_{k=0}^{D(\tau)} \frac{[\lambda\tau]^k e^{-\lambda\tau}}{k!} \geqslant \alpha \tag{2-1}$$

Nous pouvons démontrer que $D(\tau)$ est ni concave et ni convexe avec τ.

Notations

Indices:

i: Index de stade, i=1, ⋯, N, où N est le nombre de stades dans le système,

t: Index de temps, $t \in [0, \infty]$

Paramètres

T_i: Délai de production du stocki, i=1, 2, ⋯, N,

L_i: Délai net du stocki, i.e., $L_i = SI_i + T_i - S_i$, i=1, 2, ⋯, N,

λ: Taux de demande moyenne de la demande clientèle au stock 1,

α: Niveau de service du système,

s_1: Borne sur le délai de service avalau stock1.

A l'instant t,

$I_i(t)$: Stock physique du stock i,

$I_i^e(t)$: Stock physique échelon du stock i,

$IL_i^e(t)$: Niveau de stock échelon du stock i,

$IP_i^e(t)$: Stock disponible échelon du stock i,

$d[t - L_i, t)$: Demande totale durant un délai de L_i unités de temps du stock i,

$\hat{d}[t - L_i, t)$: Demande remplie normalement par le système considéré durant un délai de Li unités de temps du stock i, i=1, 2, ⋯, N.

Variables de décision

β: Taux de remplissage du système,

R_i: Point de recommande du stock i,

Q_i: Quantité de commande du stock i,

S_i: Délai de service aval du stock i,

SI_i: Délai de service amont du stock i, i=1, 2, ⋯, N.

Modélisation du Problème

L'objectif du système en série est pour minimiser le coût total moyen, qui comprend des coûts de passation de commandes, des coûts de stockage et des coûts de flexibilité d'exploitation donnée par

$$\sum_{i=1}^{N}\left(\frac{c_i\beta}{Q_i} + h_i^e \cdot E[I_i^e]\right) + p\lambda(1-\beta) \tag{2-2}$$

Pour chaque stock i, uneéquation d'évolution du niveau de stockéchelon peut être dérivée ci-dessous:

$$IL_i^e(t) = IP_i^e(t - L_i) - d[t - L_i, t) \tag{2-3}$$

Dans le cadre de la GSA, $IL_i^e(t) = I_i^e(t) \geqslant 0$ et $I_i(t) \geqslant 0$,

$$IP_i^e(t - L_i) \geqslant d[t - L_i, t) + IP_{i-1}^e(t) \tag{2-4}$$

Par ailleurs, nous pouvons également obtenir que, ὰ partir du temps $t - L_i$ avec le stock disponible échelon $IP_i^e\ (t - L_i) = R_i + 1$, il existe une réalisation du processus de la demande du temps $t - L_i$ au temps t tel que $d\ [t - L_i, t) \geqslant D(L_i)$ et $IP_{i-1}^e(t) = R_{i-1} + Q_{i-1}$.

Avec ce résultat important, afin d'assurer que l'inégalité (2-4) est valable pour toute ré alisation de la demande dans la GSA, nous devons avoir

$$R_i \geqslant \sum_{j=1}^{i} D(SI_j + T_j - S_j) + \sum_{j=0}^{i-1} Q_j - i \text{ pour } i=1, 2, \cdots, N \tag{2-5}$$

Puisque l'objectifdu problèmeest de minimiserle coût total, il existe une solution optimaleavec R_i, i=1, 2, ···, N donnéspar l'équation suivante.

$$R_i = \sum_{j=1}^{i} D(SI_j + T_j - S_j) + \sum_{j=0}^{i-1} Q_j - i \text{ pour } i=1, 2, \cdots, N \tag{2-6}$$

Selon Hadely and Whitin (1960), le stock disponible échelon $IP_i^e(t)$ est distribué uniformément dans l'intervalle $[R_i + 1,\ \ R_i + Q_i]$, donc, nous pouvons obtenir $E\ [I_i^e]$ comme suit:

$$\begin{aligned} E[I_i^e] &= E[IP_i^e(t - L_i, t) - d[t - L_i, t)] \\ &= E[IP_i^e(t - L_i, t) - \hat{d}[t - L_i, t)] \\ &= R_i + \frac{1 + Q_i}{2} - \lambda\beta L_i \\ &= \sum_{j=1}^{i} D(SI_j + T_j - S_j) - \lambda\beta(SI_i + T_i - S_i) + \sum_{j=1}^{i-1} Q_j - \frac{1 + Q_j}{2} - i \end{aligned} \tag{2-7}$$

Avec l'équation (2-2) et (2-7), nous formulons le problème d'optimisationde la politiquede stockagecommele problème de programmationnon linéaireci-dessous:

P: Min

$$\sum_{i=1}^{N}\frac{c_i\lambda\beta}{Q_i}+\sum_{i=1}^{N}\{h_i^e\cdot[\sum_{j=1}^{i}D(SI_j+T_j-S_j)-\lambda\beta(SI_i+T_i-S_i)+\frac{1+Q_i}{2}-i]+$$
$$\sum_{j=i}^{N}h_j^e\cdot Q_{i-1}\}+p\lambda(1-\beta)$$

Sous les contraintes suivantes:

$Q_{i+1}=m_i Q_i$ pour $i=1, 2, \cdots, N-1$ (2-8)

$SI_i+T_i-S_i\geqslant 0$ pour $i=1, 2, \cdots, N$ (2-9)

$SI_i\geqslant S_{i+1}$ pour $i=1, 2, \cdots, N$ (2-10)

$0\leqslant S_1\leqslant s_1$ (2-11)

$Q_i\geqslant 0$ et entier pour i=1, 2, $\cdots$, N (2-12)

SI_i, $S_i\geqslant 0$ et entier pour i=1, 2,$\cdots$, N (2-13)

Dans ce modèle, la fonction objective est de minimiser le coût total du système qui se compose des coûts de stockage, des coûts de passation de commandes et des coûtsde flexibilitéd'exploitation. Les contraintes (2-8) sont les contraintes de ratio entier entre la quantité de commande d'un stock et celle de son successeur. Les contraintes (2-9) assurent que le délai net de chaque stock est non négatif. Les contraintes (2-10) impliquent que chaque stock peut commencer la production lorsque toutes les matières (composants) nécessaires sont disponibles. Les contraintes (2-11) imposent une borne supérieure s_1 sur le délai de service aval du stock 1. Les contraintes (2-12) et (2-13) signifient que toutes les variables de décision doivent être entières.

Lorsque β est connu, $p\lambda$ $(1-\beta)$ dans la fonction objective dumodèlePdevient une constante qui peut êtreignoré et lemodèlepeut être décomposéeen deuxsous-problèmesindépendants, l'un avecvariables de décision Q_i et l'autre avecdes variables de décision SI_i et S_i. Lesdeux sous-problèmes sont appelés le problè me de détermination de quantités de commande (Q-problème) et le problème de détermination de points de recommande (R-problème)respectivement.

Q–problème:

Min: $\sum_{i=1}^{N}[\frac{c_i\lambda\beta}{Q_i}+h_i^e\cdot(\frac{1+Q_i}{2}-i)+\sum_{j=1}^{N}h_j^e\cdot Q_{i-1}]$

Sous les contraintes suivantes:

$Q_{i+1} = m_i Q_i$ pour $i = 1, 2, \cdots, N-1$

$Q_i \geqslant 0$ et entier pour $i=1, 2, \cdots, N$

R-problème:

$$\text{Min: } \sum_{i=1}^{N} h_i^e \cdot \left[\sum_{j=1}^{i} D(SI_j + T_j - S_j) - \lambda\beta(SI_i + T_i - S_i) \right]$$

Sous les contraintes suivantes:

$SI_i + T_i - S_i \geqslant 0$ pour $i = 1, 2, \cdots, N$

$SI_i \geqslant S_{i+1}$ pour $i = 1, 2, \cdots, N$

$0 \leqslant S_1 \leqslant s_1$

SI_i, $S_i \geqslant 0$ et entier pour $i=1, 2, \cdots, N$

Dès que lesdeux sous-problèmessont résolus, la quantitéoptimale Q_i est donnée par lasolutiondu Q-problème, etlepoint de commandeoptimale R_i peutêtre déterminé par $\{SI_j, T_j, S_j | 1 \leqslant j \leqslant i\}$ et $\{Q_j | 0 \leqslant j \leqslant i-1\}$ selon l'équation (2-6).

L'analyse ci-dessus suppose β que soit connu. Cependant β n'est pas connu, mais elle peut être déterminée par la politique de stockage (R, Q) du système considéré. Par conséquent, deux algorithmesde programmation dynamiqueefficaces sontproposés pour résoudre le Q-problèmeet R-problème respectivementlorsqueαet β sont donnés. Sur la base de la politique optimale de stockage (R, Q), β peut également être calculé. Enfin, le problème d'origine (modèle P) peut être résolu par une procédure itérative fondée sur l'estimation de la valeur optimale de β.

Algorithmes de Programmation Dynamique Pour Les Sous-Problèmes

Pour le Q-problème, nous développons d'abord deux propriétés importantes pour déterminer l'espace d'état W_i de chaque variable Q_i, pour $i=1, 2, \cdots, N$.

Propriété 1: Pour un systèmeen sérieavec N stades, une borne supérieure de Q_1 est donnée par:

$$\overline{Q}_1 = \sqrt{\frac{2\lambda\beta \sum_{i=1}^{N} c_i}{\sum_{i=1}^{N} (2i-1) h_i^e}}$$

Propriété 2: Pour le stock i du système en série, si le point de commande du stock i-1est donné par Q_{i-1}, une borne supérieure de m_{i-1} peut être obtenuepar:

$$m^{-}_{i-1} = \frac{1}{Q_{i-1}} \cdot \sqrt{\frac{2\lambda\beta \sum_{j=i}^{N} c_i}{\sum_{j=1}^{N-i+1} (2j-1) * h^{e}_{i-1+j}}}$$

Nous désignons $U_i(Q_{s(i)})$ comme l'ensemble de toutesles valeurs possibles de Q_i lorsque $Q_{s(i)}$ est donné. Selonla contraintede ratio entier (3-8), $U_i(Q_{s(i)})$ peut être alors s'écrire comme

$$U_i(Q_{s(i)}) = \{k \mid k = Q_{s(i)} \cdot j (j \leqslant m^{-}_{i-1})\}, i = 1, 2, \cdots, N$$

Par conséquent, l'espace d'étatde Q_i (i=1, 2, ⋯, N) peut être dérivécomme suit:

$$W_i = \begin{cases} \{1, 2, \cdots, \overline{Q}_1\}, & i = 1 \\ \{U_i(k_1) \cup U_i(k_2) \cdots \cup U_i(k_n), & o\{k_1, k_2, \cdots, k_n \in W_{s(i)}\}\}, i = 1, \cdots, N \end{cases}$$

Basé surlesdeux propriétés importantes, nous pouvons développer un algorithme de programmation dynamique pour résoudre Q-problème afin de trouver les meilleures quantités de commande pour tous les stocks.

Pour le R-problème, nous avons appliqué un algorithme de programmation dynamique proposé par Graves and Willems (1996, 2000) pour trouver les délais de service amont et aval (S_i, SI_i) optimaux du système étudié.

Procédure d'Optimisation

Le problème d'optimisation original, i.e., l'optimisation de politique de stockage (R, Q) pour le système en série dans la cadre de la GSA, peut être résolu en deux boucles: 1) déterminer le niveau de service optimal α et 2) pour chaque α donné, résoudre le modèle P. Ici, la première boucle appelle la deuxième boucle. Du fait qu'une seule variable décision α doit être optimisée dans la première boucle, elle peut être déterminée en utilisant une recherche linéaire. Dans le cas où la fonction objective du système est convexe par rapport à α, la recherche linéaire peut être effectuée à l'aide d'une méthode telle que la méthode de la section d'or. Sinon, elle peut être faite en discrétisant les valeurs possibles deαsur l'intervalle [0, 1]. A la suite, nous allons discuter de la façon de résoudre le modèle P pour un α donné.

Pour résoudre le modèle *P*, nous avons besoin de calculer le taux de remplissage β, qui peut être déterminépar les paramètreset la politique de (*R*, *Q*)du système considéré. Nous présentons une méthodede calculer βdu système comme suit.

$$\beta = 1 - \frac{1}{Q}\sum_{i=R+1}^{R+Q}\sum_{k=i+1}^{\infty}\frac{(\lambda L)^k e^{-\lambda L}}{k!}\cdot\frac{k-i}{k}$$

$$= 1 - \frac{1}{Q}\sum_{i=R+1}^{R+Q}\sum_{k=i+1}^{\infty}\frac{(\lambda L)^k e^{-\lambda L}}{k!} + \frac{1}{Q}\sum_{i=R+1}^{R+Q}\sum_{k=i+1}^{\infty}\frac{(\lambda L)^k e^{-\lambda L}}{k!}\cdot\frac{i}{k}$$

Dans l'équationci-dessus, on notele délainet au stade 1par *L*. En raison de la simplification, l'indice, "1", qui indiquele stade1,est omis dans *L*, *R* et *Q*.

A la suite, nous proposons une procédure itérativepour résoudre le modéle Pbaséesur l'estimation de la valeur de β à chaque itération. Depuis β est généralementplus grand queαetproche de α lorsqueαest proche de 1, il est initialisé àαdans la procédure. Dès quela valeur de β ne change pas endeux itérations successives, nous avons obtenu le β réelet la politique échelon optimale de (*R*, *Q*) pour le systèmepar la résolutiondu modè lePlors de la dernièreitérationde la procédure.

Notez que lorsquela politique échelon optimale de (*R*, *Q*) trouvéedans laprocédure est transformée enune politique installation optimale de (*r*, *Q*) pour le système en série considéré. Le point de commande de cette politique peut être facilement calculé comme $r_i = D(SI_i + T_i - S_i) - 1$.

Expériences Numériques

Nous avons évaluéles performancesde deux algorithmesde programmation dynamiquepourle *Q*-problème et *R*-problème, respectivement, et la performancede la procédure itérative proposéepar des expériences numériques sur des instancesgénérées aléatoirement. Tout d'abord, nous avons testé les algorithmes de programmationdynamique proposéspour le *Q*-problème et le *R*-problème sur six ensembles d'instancesavec2, 3, 4, 10, 50 et 100 stades, respectivement. Les résultats expériences indiquent que les algorithmes de programmation dynamique sont effi caces pour résoudre le *Q*-problème et *R*-problème. En suite, la performancede la procédure itérativeest évaluéepar des expériences numériques sur les mêmesensembles d'instancesgénérées aléatoirement. Pour chaqueensemble d'instances, quatredifférentes valeurs de α variantde

0,8 à 0,98 ont été considérées. Lesrésultats numériquesont montré quela procédure itérativea une bonnepropriétédeconvergenceetest efficacepour résoudre le problèmed' optimisation de lapolitiquedu stockage avecun α donné.

Chapitre 3: Optimisation de Politiques de Stockage (*R*, *Q*) Pour les Systèmesd'Assemblage

Plus généralement, ce chapitre traite de l'optimisation de politique de (*R*, *Q*) pour un système d'assemblage avec Poisson demande dans le cadre de la GSA. La méthodologie d'optimisation utilisée dans ce chapitre est similaire à celle pour les systèmes en série. Toutefois, un système d'assemblage, qui a plus d'un prédécesseur immédiat pour certains stocks, se distingue d'un système en série qui a un seul prédécesseur immédiat pour tous les stocks, ce qui conduit à une structure de réseau plus compliqué. Par conséquent, l'algorithmede programmation dynamiquepour le problème de détermination de quantités de commande (*Q*-problème) proposédans le dernier chapitrene peut être directementutilisé pour le systèmed'assemblage. Dans ce chapitre, nous développons un nouvel algorithme de programmation dynamique pour résoudre le *Q*-problème du système d'assemblage étudié. *L*'idée clé de cet algorithme est que la procédure récursive de programmation dynamique est effectuée dans les deux directions, avant et arrière. Une procédure récursive en avantest appliquée en premier temps dans le but deréduirel'espace de solutionsdu problème. Sur la base des solutions obtenuespar la procédureen avant, une procédure en arrièreest utilisée pour identifierlasolution optimale.

Description et Modélisation du Problème

Nous considérons unsystème d'assemblage avec plusieurs articles intermédiaires (composants et sous-assemblages) etunproduit finalunique. On suppose que le stock de chaque article est revu en temps réel. La structure du réseau du système est définie par sa nomenclature (bill of material, BOM) qui est un arbre dont le nœud racine correspond au produit final. On suppose N est le nombre d'articles dans le système, $N>3$. Ces articles sont numérotés de 1 à *N*, où l'article 1 représente le produit final. L'article *i* est noté stock *i* pour $i=1, 2, \cdots, N$. En outre, nous supposons que la demande clientèle du produit final suit un processus de Poisson de taux moyen λ. Comme mentionné dans le chapitre 3, lecoût total du systèmese compose detrois types de coûts: coûts de passation de commandes, coûts de stockageet coûts de flexibilité d'exploitation. L'objectif est de minimiser le coût total du système à long terme sujet à un niveau de service α au client donné.

Dans le cadre de la GSA, pour un niveau de service α donnée, une borne supérieure $D\ (\tau)$ sur la demande totale durant un délai deunités de temps peut être formulée comme suit:

$$\sum_{k=0}^{D(\tau)} \frac{[\lambda\tau]^k e^{-\lambda\tau}}{k!} \geqslant \alpha \tag{3-1}$$

Le problème d'optimisationde la politiquede stockageétudiépour le systèmed'assemblage peutêtre formulécomme un problèmede programmationnon linéairesuivant:

P: Mini

$$\sum_{i=1}^{N} \frac{c_i \lambda\beta}{Q_i} + \sum_{i=1}^{N} \{ h_i^e \cdot [\ \sum_{j\in SUC(i)} D(SI_j + T_j - S_j) - \lambda\beta(SI_i + T_i - S_i) + \frac{1+Q_i}{2} - C_i] + \sum_{j\in PRE(i)} h_j^e \cdot Q_{s(i)} \} + p\lambda(1-\beta)$$

Sous contraintes suivantes:

$$Q_i = m_{s(i)i} Q_{s(i)} \text{ pour } i = 1, 2, \cdots, N \tag{3-2}$$

$$SI_i + T_i - S_i \geqslant 0 \text{ pour } i = 1, 2, \cdots, N \tag{3-3}$$

$$SI_i \geqslant \max\{ S_{P(i)} \} \text{ pour } i = 1, 2, \cdots, N \tag{3-4}$$

$$0 \leqslant S_1 \leqslant s_1 \tag{3-5}$$

$$Q_i \geqslant 0 \text{ et entier pour } i=1, 2, \cdots, N \tag{3-6}$$

$$SI_i,\ S_i \geqslant 0 \text{ et entier pour } i=1, 2, \cdots, N \tag{3-7}$$

Dans la fonctionobjective, β esttoujoursinconnu. Nous supposonsd'abord que β soit donné, alors, le modèle P peut être diviséen deux sous-problèmes indépendants, le sous-problème de détermination de quantités de commande (Q-problème) et le sous-problème de détermination de points de recommande (R-problème). Le Q-problème a unefonction objectiveconvexecomposéede tous les termes dépendant de Q et des contraintes(3-2) et (3-6), alors que le R-problème a une fonction objectivenon linéairecomposéede tous les termes dépendant de R et des contraintes linéaires(3-3), (3-4), (3-5) et (3-7).

Algorithmes de Programmation Dynamique Pour Les Sous–Problèmes

Différent d'un systèmeen série quine possède qu'un seulprédécesseur immédiat, le système d'assemblageétudiépeut avoirle stock d'un articlequia plus d'unprédécesseurimmédiat, l'algorithmede programmation dynamiquene peut pas êtredirectementappliqué àrésoudre le Q-problème du systèmed'assemblage. Dans ce chapitre, nous développons un nouveauprogramme dynamiquepour résoudre le Q-problème des systèmes d'assemblage. L'idée clède l'algorithme estque la procédurerécursivede programmation dynamiqueest appliquéedans deux directions, à savoir, à la direction en avantet la directionen arrière. Dans la procé dure en avant, l'état du système est mis en extension en avant à partir du stock du produit final aux stocks des articles achetés auprès de fournisseurs externes, tandis qu'dans la procédure en arrière, l'état du système est mis en extension dans le sens inverse. La procédureen avantest appliquée en premier temps dans le but deréduirel'espace de solutionsdu problème. Basé surles solutions obtenuespar la procédureen avant, la procédure en arrièreest appliquéepour identifierla décision optimalepourchaque stock etensuiteobtenir la solutionoptimaledu problème.

Pour le R-problème, nous avons aussi appliqué un algorithme de programma tion dynamique proposé par Graves et Willems (1996, 2000) pour trouver les délais de service amont (S) et les délais de service aval (SI) optimauxdu système étudié.

Procédure d'optimisation

Après l'introduction dedeux algorithmes DP pour les deuxsous-problèmes (Q-problème et R-problème), nousproposonsune procédure d'optimisationitérative pourrésoudre leproblème d'optimisationd'origine (modèle P).Comme mentionné dans le chapitre2, pour un niveaude serviceαdonné au client, le problème d'optimi sationpeut êtrerésolu parune procédure itérativefondée sur l'estimation de la valeur de β à chaque itération. La procédurecomporte deuxétapes principales danschaque itération:

- Pourune valeur estimée de β, résoudre le modèle P;
- Calculerletaux remplissage β réeldu système considé ré;

Parce que le tauxde remplissage β ne dépend que dupoint de recommande *R* et de la quantité de commande Q du stock du produit fini quiest unique pourle système d'assemblage, son tauxde remplissage β peut être calculésimilairement par

$$\beta = 1 - \frac{1}{Q}\sum_{i=R+1}^{R+Q}\sum_{k=i+1}^{\infty}\frac{(\lambda L)^k e^{-\lambda L}}{k!}\cdot\frac{k-i}{k}$$

$$= 1 - \frac{1}{Q}\sum_{i=R+1}^{R+Q}\sum_{k=i+1}^{\infty}\frac{(\lambda L)^k e^{-\lambda L}}{k!} + \frac{1}{Q}\sum_{i=R+1}^{R+Q}\sum_{k=i+1}^{\infty}\frac{(\lambda L)^k e^{-\lambda L}}{k!}\cdot\frac{i}{k}$$

A noter que, dans la formule ci-dessusl'indice "1" qui indiquele stock1est omise dansL, *R* et *Q*, où *L* est le délai net déterminé parla résolution du problèmed'optimisation de lapolitique de stockage.

Avec laformule pour le calcul de β, nous pouvons proposer une procéduresimilaire àcelle pour le systèmeen sériepour résoudre le modèle *P*. La procédurecommence à partir de la mise enαcomme la valeur initiale de β. A chaque itération, pourune β estimée, la politique échelon optimale de(*R*, *Q*)pourle système considéréest obtenue en résolvantle modèle *P*, etle taux deremplissage β réeldu systèmeest ensuite calculé. Siles deux valeurs de β sont identiques, la procédures'arrête.

Expériences Numériques

Nous avons effectué des expériences numériques pourévaluer les performancesdes deux algorithmesde programmation dynamiquepourle *Q*-problème et *R*-problème, respectivement, et la performancede la procédureitérativeproposée. Enoutre, nous avons effectuéégalementune analyse de sensibilitépour examiner les impacts des paramètres différents du systèmesur la performancede l'algorithme. Toutes les expériences sonteffectuées sur troisensembles d'instances avec 7 article set 3 niveaux, 15 articleset 4 niveauxet 63articleset 6 niveaux, respectivement. Pour le *Q*-problème, nous avons comparé notrealgorithmeavecl'algorithme de WallaceetMichael. Les résultats montrentque notre algorithmede programmation dynamiquepro posé pour le *Q*-problème est plus efficace quel'algorithme de Wallace et Michael, et ils démontrent aussi quenotrealgorithmeest très efficacepour la résolution desgrandesinstances, avecun temps de calculmaximal de moins de 0,0068 secondes pour les instancesavec 63 articles. Pour le R-problème, les résultats numériques démontrent quele temps de calculde l'algorithmede programmation dynamiqueest assez court, ce qui démontre l'efficacitéde l'algorithme. En outre, pour le Q-problème, nous pou vons observerquele temps de calculmoyen diminueen h_i^e, c_i, et augmenter enλ, les résultats égalementdémontrent que leparamètre λa une influence considérablesurle temps de calculde l'algorithme. Pour le R-problème, nous pouvons ob server quele paramètredeλa une influence considérableen temps de calcul, relativement, le paramètre de h_i^e n'a que peu d'influence.

Chapitre 4 Optimisation de Politiques de Stockage (*R*, *Q*) pour les Systèmes de Distributionà Deux Niveaux

Dans ce chapitre, nous étudions un système de distribution à deux niveaux avec un entrepôt et plusieurs détaillants. La caractéristique la plus distinctive d'un tel système est que chaque stock a un seul prédécesseur direct, mais a plusieurs successeurs directs. Dans ce système, toutes demandes finales, qui se produisent chez les détaillants seule ment, suivent de différents processus de Poisson et sont indépendantes. On suppose que chaque stock dans le système a un coût fixe pour passer chaque commande et que chaque stock est géré par une politique de stockage (R, Q) avec l'inventaire en temps réel du stock. Dans le cadre de la GSA, nous supposons que la demande excessive au-delà d'un niveau maximum raisonnable sera satisfaite en utilisant des mesures ex traordinaires avec coûts de la flexibilité d'exploitation. De plus, nous supposons que le système étudié a une condition initiale randomisée. Dans ces hypothèses, nous pouvons établir un modèle mathématique pour le problème d'optimisation et ensuite proposer une procédure d'optimisation pour résoudre le modèle basé sur la décomposition du modèle en deux sous-problèmes qui sont résolus en utilisant un algorithme de programmation dy namique ou en calculant la quantité de commandeéconomique correspondantes. Plus particulièrement, nous considérons cinq différents types de contraintes de ratio entier éventuellement imposées sur les quantités de commande des stocks du système étudié, et comparons leurs efficacités par des expériences numériques.

Description et Modélisation du Problème

Nous considérons un système de distribution dans lequel un entrepôt approvi - sionne N détaillants. L'entrepôt est noté comme stock 0 et le détaillant i comme stock i

pour i=1, 2, ···, N. On suppose que la demande clientèle du stock i suit un processus de Poisson de taux moyen λ_i. Le coût de passation de chaque commande et le coût de stockage échelon par unité de produit par unité de temps du stock i sont c_i et h_i^e respectivement, i=0, 1, ···, N. De plus, nous définissons p_i et β_i comme le coût unitaire de flexibilité d'exploitation et le taux de remplissage du détaillant i (i=0, 1, ···, N) respectivement, où β_0 est le taux de remplissage de l'entrepôt.

Puisque l'approvisionnement de l'entrepôt est utilisé pour satisfaire la demande normale (la partie de la demande en dessous du niveau maximum raisonnable), la quantité moyenne commandée de l'entrepôt par unité de temps est donnée par $\lambda_0\beta_0$.

Dans le cadre de la GSA, pour un niveau de service α_i donnée au client du détaillant i, une borne supérieure D_i (τ) sur la demande totale durant un délai de τ unités de temps de ce stock peut être formulée comme suit:

$$\sum_{k=0}^{D_i(\tau)} \frac{[\lambda_i \tau]^k e^{-\lambda_i \tau}}{k!} \geqslant \alpha_i, \quad i=1, 2, \cdots, N \tag{4-1}$$

Dans les systèmes en série et les systèmes d'assemblage, la borne supérieure de la demandedurant un délai est définie uniquement pour le stock du produit final et tous les autres stocks ont la même borne que celui du stock final. Toutefois, pour le système de distribution, puisque la demande de l'entrepôt est la somme des demandes de tous les détaillants à long terme, la borne supérieure de la demande de cet entrepôt durant un délai doit être différente de celles des détaillants, donc nous devons aussi définir une borne supérieure $D_0(\tau)$ de la demande totale durant un délai de τ unités de temps pour l'entrepôt, et elle peut être formulée comme la suivante:

$$\sum_{k=0}^{D_i(\tau)} \frac{[\lambda_0 \tau]^k e^{-\lambda_0 \tau}}{k!} \geqslant \alpha_0, \quad \text{where } \alpha_0 = \frac{\sum_{i=1}^{N} \lambda_i \alpha_i}{\sum_{i=1}^{N} \lambda_i} \tag{4-1a}$$

Où α_0 est le niveau de service de l'entrepôt aux clients finaux.

Supposons que dans le système étudie, le stock i emploie un politique échelon de stockage (R_i, Q_i), pour son approvisionnement. Dans les hypothèses de la demande bornée et la condition initiale randomisée du système, le problème d'optimisation que nous étudions peut être formulé comme le problème de programmation non linéaire suivant:

P: Minimize

$$\sum_{i=0}^{N} \frac{c_i \lambda_i \beta_i}{Q_i} + h_i^e \cdot [(D(SI_i + T_i - S_i)) - \lambda_i \beta_i (SI_i + T_i - S_i) + \frac{Q_i - 1}{2}] + h_0^e [\sum_{i=1}^{N} D(SI_i + T_i - S_i) + \sum_{i=1}^{N} Q_i - N] + \sum_{i=1}^{N} p_i \lambda_i (1 - \beta_i)$$

Sous les contraintes suivantes:

$SI_i + T_i - S_i \geqslant 0$ pour $i = 1, 2, \cdots, N$ (4-2)

$SI_i \geqslant S_0$ pour $i = 1, 2, \cdots, N$ (4-3)

$0 \leqslant S_i \leqslant s_i, \ i = 1, 2, \cdots, N$ (4-4)

$Q_i \geqslant 0$ et entier pour i=1, 2, ⋯, N (4-5)

$SI_i, \ S_i \geqslant 0$ et entier pour i=1, 2, ⋯, N (4-6)

Dans ce modèle, les variables de décision relatives à chaque stock i sont la quantité de commande Q_i, le délai de service aval S_i et le délai de service amont SI_i; T_i est le délai de production du stock i; s_i est une borné supérieure imposée sur le délai de service aval du stock, s_i, i=1, 2, ⋯, N sont des paramètres donnés.

Dans la fonction objective, β est toujours inconnu, ce qui rend le problème d'optimisation difficile à résoudre. Nous supposons d'abord que βest donné, le modèle P peut donc être décomposé en deux sous-problèmes indépendants: le Q-problème qui a une fonction objectif composée de l'ensemble des termes relatives àQ_i (i=0, 1, ⋯, N), et des contraintes (4-5), et le R-problème qui a une fonction objectif composée de tous les termes relatives àR_i, i=0, 1, ⋯, N et des contraintes linéaires (4-2), (4-3), (4-4) et (4-6).

Dans la suit, nous développons des algorithmes efficaces pour résoudre les deux sous-problèmes pour α et β donnés.

Toutes les analysesci-dessus supposentque β soit connue. Cependant, βesttou-joursinconnue, mais ellepeut être déterminée par les paramètres et la politique de stockage (R, Q) du système. Basé surlessolutions desdeux sous-problèmes, nous avons proposéune méthode pour calculer β, etune procédure d'optimisation pour résoudre le problème d'optimisationd'origine (modèle P).

Contraintes de Ratio Entier Pour le Q–problème

Pour le Q-problème, il peut avoir des contraintes supplémentaires reliant la quantité de commande d'un stock à celle de son fournisseur. Par exemple, on demande que la quantité de commande d'un fournisseur soit un multiple de la quantité de commande de son client. De nombreux chercheurs ont étudié différents types de contraintes de ratio entier dans un système de distribution à deux niveaux, mais aucune comparaison entre ces contraintes n'a été faite en termes d'efficac ité. Dans ce chapitre, nous considérons cinq différents types de contraintes de ratio entier pour le Q-problème.

Les différents types de contraintes de ratio entier dans cinq cas sont décrits comme suit.

Cas 1: sans contrainte de ratio entier;

Dans ce cas, il n'existe pas de lien entre la quantité de commande de l'entrepôt (Q_0) et la quantité de commande d'un détaillant (Q_i, i=1, 2, ···, N). Dans ce cas, le Q-problème a une structure simple, qui peut être divisé en sous-problèmes N indépendants et résolu par la méthode de la quantité de commande économique (EOQ method).

Cas 2: $Q_i=m_i \cdot Q_N$, pour certains entiersm$_i$, i=1, 2, ···, N–1;

Ce genre de contraintes de ratio entier a été examiné par Chen et Zheng (1997) dans leur modèle d'un système de distribution à deux niveaux avec un entrepôt et plusieurs détaillants, où Q_N est considéré comme la taille de lot de base du système. Ici, le détaillant N peut êtreremplacé par tout autre détaillant($i \neq N$)etle choix dudétaillantde référence dépend du tauxmoyen de la demandede chaquedétaillant. Dans l'hypothèse que le stock disponible initial à l'entrepôt est également un multiple entier de la taille de lot de base, ils ont montré qu'une telle restriction n'est pas trop coûteuse.

Cas 3: $Q_i=m_i \cdot q$, pour certains entiersmi, i=0, 1, ···, N;

De même, ce cas suppose une taille de lot de base dans le système de distribution, dans laquelle la quantité de commande de chaque stock (Q_i, i=0, 1, ···, N) doit être un multiple entier de la taille de lot de base notée q. Dans la pratique, qpeut correspondre àla capacitéd'une palettepour la livraison. La capacité estle nombre d'unités d'un produit que la palettepeut porterpour l'expéditiond'une commande.

Cas 4: $Q_0=m_i \cdot Q_i$, pour certains entiers m_i, i=1, 2, ⋯, N.

Ce cas suppose que la quantité de commande de l'entrepôt (Q_0) est toujours un multiple entier de la quantité de commande de chaque détaillant (Q_i, i=1, 2, ⋯, N). Cette hypothèse, qui est couramment adoptée dans la littérature de gestion des stocks, est tout à fait naturelle vu que la politique d'approvisionnement de l'entrepôt est de satisfaire tout ou rien d'une commande de détaillant (Axsater, 1996).

Cas 5: $Q_0=m_0 \cdot q_0$, Q_1, ⋯, $N=m_i$, ⋯, $N \cdot q_1, 1 \leqslant i \leqslant N$, $q_0=k_0 \cdot q_1$, pour certains entiers m_i, i=1, 2, ⋯, N, k_0.

Dans le cas 2et 3, une taille de lot de base est généralement supposéepourl'entrepôt etlesdétaillantsdans le système de distribution. Cependant, puisque l'entrepôt et les détaillants appartiennent à différents niveaux dans la chaîne d'approvisionnement, cette stratégie de coordination peut être difficile à mettre en application. Donc, le cas 5 propose une nouvelle contrainte de ratio entier. Ce cas suppose qu'il existe une taille de lot de base pour chaque niveau dans le système, c'est-à-dire, Q_0 est la taille de lot de base pour le niveau d'entrepôt (niveau 0) et Q_1 est la taille de lot de base pour le niveau de détaillant (niveau 1), et les quantités de commande de tous les stock au même niveau ont la taille de lot de base commune, la taille de lot de base au niveau d'entrepôt (niveau 0) doit être un multiple entier de la taille de lot de base au niveau de détaillant (niveau 1), c'est-à-dire, Q_0 est un multiple entier de q_1.

Algorithmes de Programmation Dynamique Pour les Sous-Problèmes

Pour le Q-problème, nous avons considéré cinq différents types de contraintes de ratio entier, et ont développé des algorithmes de programmation dynamique pour résoudre ce sous-problème, sauf une méthode de la quantité de commande économique (EOQ method) appliquée pour résoudre le Q-problèmeavec le contrainte de ratio entier-du cas 1.

Pour le R-problème, nous avons appliqué l'algorithme de programmation dynamique proposé par Graves et Willems (1996, 2000) pour le résoudre afin de trouver les meilleurs délais de service amont et aval (S, SI) du système étudié.

Procédure d'Optimisation

Similaire aux systèmesen sérieet systèmes d'assemblage, le problème d'optimisation d'origine peut être résolu parune procé dure itérative. La procédure comporte deuxétapes principales: d'une part, pour un taux de remplissageestimédu système, nous calculons la quantité de commande optimale (Q_i) etlepoint de recommandeoptimale (R_i) pour chaque stocken résolvantdeux sous-problèmesà l'aide dedeux algorithmes de programmation dynamique. Deuxièmement,nous calculonsle taux de remplissageréel-dusystème donnésa politique de stockage. Lorsque letaux de remplissageréelest égalau-taux de remplissageestimé, la solution optimale du problè me d'origine est trouvée.

Pour le systèmede distributionà deux niveauxconsidérés, l'entrepôta plusieurs-détaillants et ces détaillantspeuvent avoirdifférents tauxde remplissage. En outre, le taux de remplissageexternede l'entrepôtest généralementdifférent destauxde remplissage desdétaillants.

Pour chaque stock i, (i=0, 1, ⋯, N), si le point de recommande et la quantité de commande du détaillant i sont donnés par R_i et Q_i, respectivement, son taux de remplissage β_i peut être calculé comme suit:

$$\beta_i = 1 - \frac{1}{Q_i}\sum_{j=R_i+1}^{R_i+Q_i}\sum_{k=j+1}^{\infty}\frac{(\lambda_i L_i)^k e^{-\lambda_i L_i}}{k!} + \frac{1}{Q_i}\sum_{j=R_i+1}^{R_i+Q_i}\sum_{k=j+1}^{\infty}\frac{(\lambda_i L_i)^k e^{-\lambda_i L_i}}{k!}\cdot\frac{j}{k},\ i=0,1,2,\cdots,N$$

A la suite, nous utilisons une procédure itérativepour résoudre leproblème d'origine(modèleP) basé sur l'estimation de la valeur de β_i à chaque itération. Quand le β_i réelest égalà sa valeur estimée, la solution optimale du problème d'originepeut être trouvée. La procédureprésente les caractéristiques suivantes: 1) la valeur initiale de β_i est fixéà α_i, 2) la procédures'arrête lorsquela valeur estimée de chaque β_i ne change pas dansdeux itérations successives(i = 0, 1, ⋯, N).

Expériences Numériques

Nous avons évalué les performancesde deux algorithmesde programmation dynamiquepourle Q-problème et R-problème, respectivement, et la performancede la procédure itérativeproposéepar des expériences numériques sur des instancesgénérées aléatoirement.

Pour le Q-problème, afin d'analyser les impacts de différents types de contraints de ratio-entier, nous avons testé un ensemble d'instances de petitetaille(N=4), etensuite nous avons considéré cinq ensembles d'instances de moyenne à grandetaille avec N=9,

20, 50, 100, respectivement, dansune tentative d'analyser plus profondément les perfor mances desalgorithmes proposés. D'après lesrésultats des expériences, nous pouvons observer queles coûts optimauxsont similairesparmi les cinqcas différents, ces résultatsdémontrentque le coûttotal du système est insensible au choixdes quantités de commandedans le système. Lestemps de calculdescinq cassont assez courts, ce qui démontre l'efficacité desalgorithmes. Pour le R-problème, les cinq mêmes ensembles d'instancessont testés. A partir des résultats, nous pouvons observer quepour les petitesinstances (N=4), leR-problème peut être résolu presque instantanémenten utilisant l'algorithmede programmation dynamiquede Graveset Willems, alors que pour les grandesinstances(N=9, 20, 50et 100), le temps de calculde l'algorithmedevient plus long, mais il est encore assezcourt. Cela démontrela pertinencedu choix de cet algorithmepour la résolution du R-problème.

Chapitre 5 Conclusions et Perspectives

Dans cette thèse, nous avons étudié l'optimisation de la politique de stockage des systè mes de stocks multi-échelons avec des coûts fixe de passation de commande ɑ̀ chaque stock. En raison de l'existence des coûts de passation de commande, ce problème d'optimisation devient trè s difficile pour les systè mes généraux de stocks multi-échelons. Dans la littérature, deux approches concurrentes sont u tilisées pour résoudre le problème, l'approche de service stochastique (SSA) et l'approche de service garanti (GSA). Par rapport ɑ̀ la SSA dont le modèle a générale ment une structure très complexe, la GSA modélise un système de stocks mul ti-échelons de manière approximative et peut établir un modèle de programmation mathématique relativement simple pour le système. Ce modèle simplifié permet ɑ̀ un planificateur du système de prendre des décisions stratégiques ou tactiques sur le placement de stocks de sécurité.

L'hypothèse principale de la GSA est que la demande excessive supérieure ɑ̀ un certain niveau est satisfaite ɑ̀ l'aide de la flexibilité d'exploitation. Sur la base de cette hypothèse, la GSA peut formuler le problème d'optimisation de la politique de stockage d'un système de stocks multi-échelons comme un problème de programmation mathématique déterministe. Cependant, dans la plupart des études précédentes de la

GSA, les coûts de la flexibilité d'exploitation n'ont pas été pris en compte dans son modè le d'optimisation. Cela a provoqué la critique de cette approche dans le passé. De plus, les coûts fixes de passation de commande qui existent souvent dans les chaînes d'approvisionnement industrielles ont été ignorés dans le modèle. A notre connaissance, aucun travail précédent n'a utilisé la GSA pour optimiser les systèmes de stocks multi-échelons avec des coûts fixes de passation de commande.Par conséquent, dans cette thèse, nous avons concentré sur deux grands thèmes de recherche: 1) Utilisez la GSA pour optimiser les systèmes de stocks multi-échelons avec des coûts fixes de passation de commande à chaque stock. 2) Généraliser la GSA pour tenir compte des coûts de la flexibilité d'exploitation dans l'optimisation de la politique de stockage des systèmes.

Cette thèse a considéré trois différents types de systèmes de stocks multi-échelons: les systèmes en série, les systèmes d'assemblage, et les systèmes de distribution à deux niveaux. Pour chaque système, nous supposons que la demande du client final est générée par un processus de Poisson, un coût fixe est facturée à chaque stock quand il passe une commande, et chaque stock est géré par une politique (R, Q). Notre objectif est de trouver une politique optimale (R, Q) pour le système de sorte que le coût total du système qui contient les coûts de stockage, les coûts de fixes de passation de commande et les coûts de flexibilitéd'exploitation est minimisé tout en respectant un niveau de service offert auclient.

Après une introduction générale et une revue de la littérature dans le chapitre 1, chapitre 2 aborde l'optimisation de la politique (R, Q) pour un système en série avec la demande suivant un processus de Poisson et coûts fixes de passation de commande. Dans le cadre de la GSA, nous avons d'abord établi un modèle mathématique pour le problème d'optimisation, qui est un modèle de programmation non linéaire. Puisque la fonction objective du modèle dépend de deux niveaux de service (niveau de service α et du taux de remplissage β) du système, nous proposons une procédure itérative pour résoudre le modèle basé sur l'estimation du taux de remplissage β lorsque le niveau de service α est donné. La procédure itérative appuie sur la résolution de deux sous-problèmes du modèle: le problème de déter mination de quantités de commande (Q-problème) et le problème de détermination de points de recommande (R-problème).

Nous avons développé un algorithme programmation dynamique (DP) efficace pour résoudre le *Q*-problème, basé sur deux propriétés importantes sur l'espace d'état de ses variables de décision, ce qui rend notre algorithme DP beaucoup plus efficace qu'un algorithme DP dans la littérature.Le R-problème est résolu en utilisant un autre algorithme DP proposé par Graves et Willems. Les expériences numériques montrent que les deux algorithmes DP sont très efficaces pour résoudre le *Q*-problème et R-problème de grande taille avec un temps de calcul court. Les résultats numériques montrent également que la procédure itérative d'optimisation a une bonne propriété de convergence et un calcul efficace pour résoudre le problème d'optimisation de la politique de stockage.

Chapitre 3 généralise le modèle et l'approche de résolution proposés dans le chapitre 2 aux systèmes d'assemblage. Étant donné que les systèmes d'assemblage étudiés ont une structure plus complexe que les systèmes en série, l'algorithme DP du *Q*-problème pour les systèmes en série ne peut être directement utilisé pour les systèmes d'assemblage. Par conséquent, nous avons développé un nouvel algorithme DP pour résoudre le *Q*-problème des systèmes d'assemblage, dans lequel une procédure récursive avant et une procédure récursive arrière sont utilisés à la fois pour identifier la solution optimale du problème. Les expériences numériques démontrent l'efficacité de l'algorithme.

Chapitre 4 porte sur l'optimisation de la politique (*R*, *Q*) pour les systèmes de distribution à deux niveaux. L'optimisation d'un tel système est plus difficile que celle d'un système d'assemblage. Pour le système de distribution, nous avons aussi établi un modèle mathématique pour son problème d'optimisation de la politique de stockage et développé une procédure d'optimisation pour résoudre le modèle. Plus particulièrement, nous considérons cinq différents types de contraintes de ratio entier éventuellement imposées sur les quantités de commande de l'entrepôt et des détaillants. Pour chaque type, nous avons proposé un algorithme efficace pour résoudre le *Q*-problème. Nous ont comparé les cinq types de contraintes de ratio entier en termes de leurs efficacités par des expériences numériques. Les expériences numériques démontrent l'efficacité de la procédure d'optimisation pour résoudre le problème d'optimisation des stocks du système de distribution étudié.

Cette thèse a étendu le domaine d'application de la GSA du placement de stocks sécurité dans les systèmes de stocks multi-échelons sans coûts de passation de commande ὰ l'optimisation de la politique (*R, Q*) des systèmes de stocks multi-échelons avec des coûts fixes de passation de commandes ὰ chaque stock. Il a également étendu la GSA standard en tenant compte explicitement les coûts de flexibilité d'exploitation et les effets de cette flexibilité dans le modèle GSA du problème d'optimisation.

Bien que le travail de cette thèse ait démontré les avantages de la GSA dans l'optimisation des systèmes de stocks multi-échelons, beaucoup de travail reste ὰ faire. Il ya quelques orientations possibles pour la recherche future. Tout d'abord, la performance de la politique des stockagesconçue par la GSA devrait être comparée avec la performance de la politique des stockages conçue par la SSA.

Dans la littérature, très peu d'études contribuent ὰ une telle comparaison, en parti culier, pour les systèmes de stocks multi-échelons avec des coûts de passation de commande. C'est ὰ cause que le modè le stochastique employé par la SSA a souvent une structure très complexe si les coûts fixes de passation de commandesont prises en considération, et il est très difficile de trouver une politique optimale de stockage pour un tel systè me, seuls les algorithmes heuristiques ont été développées. Donc, la comparaisondes deux approches est encore un problème ouvert.

Deuxièmement, dans cette thèse, le processus de demande clientèle est supposé d'être un processus de Poisson, mais en réalité, la demande peut suivre un autre processus stochastique. À l'avenir, nous étudierons des systèmes de stocks multi-échelons avec d'autres processus de demande, tels que le processus de Poisson composé et le processus de distribution normale.

Troisièmement, cette thèse ne considère que des systèmes de stocks multi-échelonsavecl'inventaire continu de chaque stock. Dans la pratique, l'état d'un stock peut être revu périodiquement. Dans ce cas, la politique (*R, Q*) est généralisée et remplacée par la politique (*R, nQ*). L'optimisation de la politique (*R, nQ*) pour les systèmes de stocks multi-échelons avec l'inventaire périodique de chaque stock dans le cadre de la GSA est également dans la liste de nos sujets de recherche futurs.

Enfin, cette thèse a considéré trois types de systèmes de stocks multi-échelons, i.e., les systèmes en série, les systèmes d'assemblage et les systèmes de distribution ɑ̀ deux niveaux. Dans la pratique, une chaîne d'approvisionnement peut avoir ɑ̀ la fois une structure d'assemblage et une structure de distribution. Un de nos travaux futurs est d’étudier des systèmes de stocks multi-échelons plus généraux dans lesquelles tous les liens entre les stocks sont possibles.

References

[1] Al-Rifai, M., Rossetti, M., 2007. An efficient heuristic optimization algorithm for a two-echelon (*R, Q*) inventory system, 109, 195-213.

[2] Andersson, J, Melchiors, P. 2001. A two-echelon inventory model with lost sales. International Journal of Production Economics, 69, 307-315.

[3] Arnold, T., Chapman, S., 2004. Introduction of Materials Management, 5th edition, Pearson Education. Upper Saddle River, NJ,USA.

[4] Arda, Y., Hennet, J.C., 2006. Inventory control in a multi-supply systems. International Journal of Production Economics, 104, 249-259.

[5] Arslan, H., S. Graves, T. Roemer, 2007. A single-product inventory model for multiple demand classes. Management Science, 53, 1486-1500.

[6] Axsater, S., 1990. Simple solution procedures for a class of two-echelon inventory problems. Operations research, 38,64-69.

[7] Axsater, S., K. Rosling, 1993. Installation vs. echelon stock policies for multilevel inventory control. Management Science. 39, 1274-1280.

[8] Axsater, S., 1993. Exact and approximate evaluation of batch ordering policies for two-level inventory systems. Operations Research, 41, 777-785.

[9] Axsater, S., 1996. Using the deterministic EOQ formula in stochastic inventory control. Management Science, 42, 830-834.

[10] Axsater, S., Juntti, L., 1997. Comparison of echelon stock and installation stock policies with policy adjusted order quantities. International Journal of Production Economics, 48, 1-6.

［11］ Axsater, S., 1997. Simple evaluation of echelon stock (*R, Q*) policies for two-level inventory systems. IIIE Transactions, 29, 661-669.

［12］ Axsater, S., Junti, L., 1996. Comparison of echelon stock and installation stock policies for two-level inventory systems. International Journal of Production Economics, 46, 303-313.

［13］ Axsater, S., 1998. Evaluation of installation stock based (*R, Q*) policies for two-level inventory system with Poisson demand. Operations Research, 46, 135-144.

［14］ Axsater, S., 2003. Note: optimal policies for serial inventory systems under fill rate constraints, 49, 247-253.

［15］ Axsater, S., 2003. Approximate optimization of a two-level distribution inventory system. International Journal of Production Economics, 81-82, 545-553.

［16］ Axsater, S., 2005. A simple decision rule for decentralized two-echelon inventory control. International Journal of Production Economics, 93, 53-59.

［17］ Axsater, S., 2007. On the first come-first served rule in multi-echelon inventory Control. Naval Research Logistics, 54, 485-491.

［18］ Axsater, S., Ollsson, F., Tydesjo, P., 2007. Heuristic for handling direct upstream demand in multi-echelon inventory systems. International Journal of Production Economics, 108, 266-270.

［19］ Bendre, A., Thorstenson, A., 2008. Evaluation of performance approximations for (*r, q*) inventory policies in a lost-sales setting, In : Proceedings of the international conference of flexible supply chains in a global economy, July, Molde University College.Bessler, S. A. and Veinott, A.F. JR., 1966. Optimal policy for a dynamic multi-echelon inventory model. Naval Research Logistics, 13, 355-389.

［20］ Bijvank, M., Vis, I.F.A., 2011. Lost-sales inventory theory: A review. European Journal of Operational Research, 215, 1-13.

［21］ Bossert. J., S. Willems, 2007. A periodic-review modeling approach for guaranteed service supply chains. Interfaces, 37, 420-435.

［22］ Cachon, G.P., 2001. Exact evaluation of batch ordering inventory policies in two echelon supply chains with periodic review. Operations Research, 49, 79-98.

［23］ Caglar, D. and D. Simchi-Levi, 2000. Two-echelon spare parts inventory system with Lateral Shipments, Working Paper, 1, 7-14.

[24] Callarman, T.E., Hamrin, R.S., 1983. A comparison of dynamic lot sizing rules for use in a single stage MRP system with demand uncertainty. International Journal of Op- erations and Production Management, 4, 39-48.

[25] Carlson, R.C. and Yano, C.A., 1986. Safety stock in MRP-systems with emergency setups for components. Management Science, 32, 403-412.

[26] Chao. X., S. Zhou, 2009. Optimal policy for a multiechelon inventory system with batch ordering and fixed replenishment intervals. Operations Research, 57, 377-390.

[27] Chen, F., 1988. Echelon reorder points, installation reorder points, and the value of centralized demand information. Management Science, 44, 221-234.

[28] Chen, F., Y. Zheng, 1994. Lower bounds for multi-echelon stochastic inventory systems. Management Science, 40, 1426-1443.

[29] Chen, F., Y.Zheng, 1994. Evaluating echelon stock (*R, nQ*) policies in serial production/inventory systems with stochastic demand. Management Science, 40, 1262-1275.

[30] Chen, F., Zheng, Y., 1997. One warehouse multi-retailer systems with centralized stock information. Operations Research, 45, 275-287.

[31] Chen. F., Y. Zheng, 1998. Near-optimal echelon-stock (*R, nQ*) policies in multistage serial system. Operations Research, 46, 592-602.

[32] Chen. F., 2000. Optimal policies for multi-echelon inventory problems with batch ordering. Operations Research, 48, 376-389.

[33] Chen, F., Samroengraja Rungson, 2000. A staggered ordering policy for one-warehouse, multiretailer systems. Operations Research, 48, 281-293.

[34] Chen, F.Y., Feng, Y.Y., Simchi-Levi, D., 2001. Uniform distribution of inventory positions in two-echelon periodic review systems with batch ordering policies and interdependent demands. European Journal of Operational Research, 140, 648-654.

[35] Cheung, K.L., Hausman, W.H., 2000. An exact performance evaluation fort he supplier in a two echelon inventory system. Operations Research, 48, 646-653.

[36] Clark. A., H. Scarf., 1960. Optimal policies for a multi-echelon inventory

problem. Management Science, 6, 475-490.

[37] Crowston, W.B., M.H. Wagner, 1973. Economic lot size determination in multi-stage assembly systems. Management Science, 19, 517-526.

[38] De Bodt, M., Graves, S., 1985. Continuous review policies for a multi-echelon inventory problem with stochastic demand. Management Science, 31, 1286-1295.

[39] Deuermeyer, B., L. Schwarz, 1981. A model for the analysis of system service level in warehouse/retailer distribution systems: The identical retailer case. In studies in the management sciences: The multi-level production/inventory control systems. L. Schwarz (ed.), North-Holland, Amsterdam, 16, 163-193.

[40] Dogru, M.K., Van Houturm, G.J., De Kok, A.G., 2008. Newsvendor equations for optimal reorder levels of serial inventory systems with fixed batch sizes. Operations Research Letters, Elsevier, 36, 551-556.

[41] Eppen, G.D., R.K. Matin, 1988. Determining safety stock in the presence of stochastic lead time and demand. Management Science, 34, 1380-1390.

[42] Ellis, S., K. Knickle, P. Manenti, 2009. The modern supply chain: Inventory optimization competitive assessments. URL: http://www.orale.com/comporate/analyst/reports/industries/aim/idc-manufacturing-insights-io.pdf.

[43] Federgruen, A. and Zipkin, P., 1984. An efficient of dynamic algorithm for computing optimal (*s, S*) policy. Operations Research, 32, 818-832.

[44] Federgruen, A. and Zheng, Y., 1992. An efficient algorithm for computing an optimal (*r, Q*) policy in continuous review stochastic inventory systems. Operations Research, 40, 808-813.

[45] Federgruen, A., 1993, Centralized planning models for multi-echelon inventory systems under uncertainty. S.Graves, A. Rinnooy Kan, P. Zipkin, eds. Handbook in Operations Research and Management Science, 4, Logistics of Production and Inventory. North-Holland, Amsterdam, 7-14.

[46] Forsberg, S., 1996. Exact evaluation of (*R, Q*) policies for two-level inventory systems with Poisson demand. Europe Journal of Operations Research, 96, 130-138.

[47] Gallego, G., 1997. New bounds and heuristics for (*Q, R*) policies. Manage

ment Science, 44, 219-233.

[48] Gallego, G., O. Ozer, 2003. A new algorithm and a new heuristic for serial supply chains. Operations Research, 33, 349-362.

[49] Gallego, G., Ozer, O., Zipkin, P., 2007. Bounds, heuristics, and approximations for distribution systems. Operations Research, 55, 503-517.

[50] Graves, S., 1985. A mutli-echelon inventory model for a repair item with onefor-one replenishment. Management Science, 31, 1247-1256.

[51] Grave, S., D. B. Kletter, W. B. Hetzel, 1988. A dynamic model for requirements planning with application to supply chain optimization. Operations Research, 46, 35-49.

[52] Graves, S., S. Willems, 1996. Strategic safety stock placement in supply chain. Proceedings of the 1996 MSOM Conference. Hanover, NH.

[53] Graves, S., S. Willems, 2000. Optimizing strategic safety stock placement in supply chain. Manufacturing and Service Operations Management. 2, 68-83. Graves, S. C. and S. P. Willems. Supply chain design: Safety stock placement and supply chain configuration. A. G. de Kok and S. C. Graves, 2003. Handbooks in Operations Research and Management Science vol. 11, Supply chain management: Design, coordination and operation. North-Holland Publishing Company, Amsterdam, The Netherlands. 3, 95-132.

[54] Graves. S., S. Willems, 2005. Optimizing the supply chain configuration for new products. Management Science, 51, 1165-1172.

[55] Graves. S, S. Willems, 2008. Strategic inventory placement in supply chains: Nonstationary demand. Manufacturing Service Operations Management, 10, 278-287.

[56] Hadley, G., T. M. Whitin, 1961. A family of inventory model. Management Science, 7, 351-371.

[57] Haji, R., Neghab, P., Baboli, A., 2009. Introducing a new ordering policy in a twoechelon inventory system with poisson demand. International Journal of Production Economics, 117, 212-218.

[58] Hill, R., Seifbarghy, M., Smith, D., 2007. A two-level inventory model with lost sales. European Journal of Operational Research, 181, 753-766.

[59] Howard, C., Marklund, J., 2011. Evaluation of stock allocation policies in a divergent inventory system with shipment consolidation. European Journal of Operational Research, 211, 298-309.

[60] Huh, W., G. Janakiraman, 2008. A sample-path approach to the optimality of echelon order-up-to policies in serial inventory systems. Operations Research, 36, 547-550.

[61] Huh, W., G. Janakiraman, 2010. On the optimal policy structure in serial inventory systems with lost sales. Operations Research, 58, 486-491.

[62] Humair. S., S. Willems, 2006. Optimizing strategic safety stock placement in supply chains with clusters of commonality. Operations Research, 54, 725-742.

[63] Humair, S., S. P. Willems, 2011. Technical note: Optimizing strategic safety stock placement in general acyclic networks. Operations Research, 59, 781-787.

[64] Inderfurth K., 1991. Safety stock optimization in multi-stage inventory systems. International Journal of Production Economics, 24, 103.

[65] Inderfurth, K. and Minner, S., 1998. Safety Stocks in multi-stage inventory systems under different service measures. European Journal of Operational Research, 106, 57-73.

[66] Jung. J., Blau. G., Pekny. J., Reklaitis. G., Eversdyk. D., 2008. Integrated safety stock management for multi-stage supply chains under production capacity constraints. Computers Chemical Engineering, 32, 2570-2581.

[67] Kiesmuller, G.P., de Kok, A.G., Smits. S.R. Van Laarhoven, P.J.M., 2004. Evaluation of devergent N-echelon (*s, nQ*) policies under compound renewal demand. OR Spectrum, 26, 547-577.

[68] Kimball, G. E., 1988. General principles of inventory control. Journal of Manufacturing and Operations Management, 1, 119-130.

[69] Klemm, H., 1973. On the operating characteristic " Service Level" . A. Prekopa, ed., Inventory Control and Water Storage. North-Holand, Amsterdam-London, 169-178.

[70] Klosterhalfen, S., Minner, S., 2010. Safety stock optimization in distribution systems: A comparison of two competing approaches. International Journal of Logis

tics: Research and Applications, 13, 99-120.

[71] Lee, H., Moinzadeh, K., 1987. Operating characteristics of a two-echelon inventory system for repairable and consumable items under batch ordering and shipment policy. Naval Research Logistics Quarterly, 34, 365-380.

[72] Lesnaia, E., 2004. Optimizing safety stock placement in general network supply chains. Ph.D. thesis, Massachusetts Institute of Technology. Cambridge, MA.

[73] LI, P., CHEN, H., 2011. Optimal (*R, nQ*) policies for serial inventory systems with guaranteed service, International Conference on Operations Research. Zurich, Switzerland, 1, 7-14.

[74] LI, P., CHEN, H., 2013. Optimal batch ordering policies for assembly systems with guaranted service. International Journal of Production Research (Accepted), 1, 7-14.

[75] Love, S., 1972. A Facilities in series inventory model with nested schedules. Management Science, 18, 327-388.

[76] Magnanti. T., Shen. Z., Shu. J., Simchi-Levi. D., Teo. C., 2006. Inventory placement in acyclic supply chain network. Operations Research Letters, 36, 228-238.

[77] Minner S., 1997. Dynamic programming algorithms for multi-stage safety stock optimization. Operations Research Spektrum, 19, 261-271.

[78] Minner, S., 2000. Strategic safety stocks in supply chains. Berlin Heidelberg New York: Springer.

[79] Minner. S., 2001. Strategic safety stock in reverse logistics supply chains. International Journal of Production Economics, 71, 417-428.

[80] Minner S, Diks EB, de Kok AG, 2003. A two-echelon inventory system with supply lead time flexibility. IIE Transactions, 35, 117-129.

[81] Mitra S, Chatterjee AK, 2004. Echelon stock based continuous review (*R, Q*) policy for fast moving items. Omega, 32, 161-166.

[82] Moinzadeh, K., H. Lee, 1986. Batch size and stocking levels in multi-echelon repairable systems. Management Science, 32, 1567-1581.

[83] Nahmias, S., Smith, S., 1994. Optimizing inventory levels in a two-echelon retailer system with partial lost sales. Management Science, 40, 582-596.

[84] Rezg, N., Xie, X., Mati, Y., 2004. Joint optimization of preventive maintenance and inventory control in a production line using simulation. Taylor & Francis, 42, 2029-2046.

[85] Rosling. K., 1989. Optimal inventory policies for assembly systems under random demands. Operations Research,37, 565-579.

[86] Rosling, K., 2002. The square-root algorithm for single-item inventory optimization. Working Paper, Vaxjo University , 1, 7-14.

[87] Sahin, E., Buzacott, J., Dallery, Y., 2008. Analysis of a newsvendor which has errors in inventory data records. European Journal of Operational Research, 188, 370- 389.

[88] Sahin, E., Dallery, Y., 2009. Assessing the impact of inventory inaccuracies within a newsvendor framework. European Journal of Operational Research, 197, 1108-1118.

[89] Schmidt, C. and Nahmias, S., 1985. Optimal policy for a two-stage assembly system under random demand. Operations Research, 33, 1130-1145.

[90] Schoenmeyr. T., S. Graves, 2009. Strategic safety stock in supply chains with evolving forecasts. Manufacturing Service Operations Management, 11, 657-673.

[91] Schwarz, L. B. and Schrage, L., 1975. Optimal and System Myopic Policies for Multi-echelon Production/Inventory Assembly Systems. Management Science, 11, 1285-1294.Seifbarghi, M., Akbari, M., 2006. Cost evaluation of a two-echelon inventory system with lost sales and approximately Poisson demand. International Journal of Production Economics, 102, 244-254.

[92] Shang, K., Song, J.S., 2007. serial supply chains with economies of scale: Bounds and approximations. Operations Research, 55, 843-853.

[93] Shang, K., 2008. Note: A simple heuristic for serial inventory systems with fixed order costs. Operations Research, 56, 1039-1043.

[94] Shang, K., S. Zhou, 2009. A simple heuristic for echelon (*r, nQ, T*) policies in serial supply chains, Operations Research. 37, 433-437.

[95] Shang, K., S. Zhou, 2010. Optimal and Heuristic Echelon (*r, nQ, T*) Policies in Serial Inventory Systems with Fixed Costs. Operations Research, 58, 414-427.

[96] Shang, K., Song, J.S., P. Zipkin, 2010. Coordination mechanisms in decentralized serial inventory systems with batch ordering. Management Science, 55, 685-695.

[97] Shang, K., 2012. Single-stage approximations for optimal policies in serial Inventory systems with nonstationary demand. Manufacturing Service Operations Management, 14, 414-422.

[98] Shenas, N.Y., Jahromi, A.E. and Yazdi, M.M., 2009. An efficient procedure for computing an optimal(*R*, *Q*) policy in continuous review systems with poisson demands and constant lead time. Transaction E: Industrial Engineering, 16, 128-137.

[99] Silver, E.A., Pyke, D.F., 1988. Inventory Management and Production Planning and Scheduling. John Wiley &Sons, New York, 3rd edition.

[100] Silver, E.A., D.P., Bischak, 2010. The exact fill rate in a periodic review base stock system under normaly distributed demand. Tech. rep., Haskayne Schoo of Business, University of Calgary, Alberta, Canada, 7-14.

[101] Simpson, K.F., 1958. In-process inventories. Operations Research, 6, 863-873.

[102] Sinha, C.S., M.J. Sobel, V. Babich, 2011. Computationally simple and unified approach to finite-and infinite-horizon Clark-Scarf inventory model. IIE Transactions, 43, 207-219.

[103] Simchi-Levi, D., Y. Zhao, 2007. The generic methods for evaluating stochastic mult-ehelon inventry systems. Working Paper, Rutgers University, Neward, NJ.

[104] Simchi-Levi, D., P. Kaminsky, E. Simchi-Levi, 2008. Designing and managing the supply chain: Concepts, strategies, and case studies. 3rd ed. McGraw-Hil/Irwin.

[105] Svoronos, A., Zipkin, P., 1988. Estimating the performances of multi-level inventory systems. Operations Research, 36, 57-72.

[106] Tijms, H.C., H. Groenerelt, 1984. Simple approximations for the reorder point in periodic and continuous review (*s*, *S*) inventory systems with service level constraints. European Journal of Operational Research, 17, 175-190.

［107］ Teunter, R.H., 1998. Economic ordering quantities for remanufacturable item inventory systems. Working Paper, University of Magdeburg, Germany, 1, 31-98.

［108］ Trebilcock, B. 2009. Top 20 supply chain management software suppliers. URL:http://www.mmh.com/article/356221_2009_Top_20_supply_chain_management_software_suppliers.php?q=top+20+supply+chain+software.

［109］ Van Houturm, G.J., 2006. Multi-echelon production/inventory systems: Optimal policies, heuristics, and algorithms. Tutorials in Operations Reasearch, 163-169.

［110］ Van Houtum, G.J., A. Scheller-Wolf, J. Yi, 2007. Optimal control of serial inventory systems with fixed replenishment intervals. Operations Research, 55, 674-687.

［111］ Veinott, A. F., 1965. The optimal inventory policy for batch ordering. Operations Research, 13, 424-432.

［112］ Viswanathan, N., 2007. The supply chain innovator's technology footprint 2007—A benchmark report on companies' technology investment plans for gaining immediate and strategic payback. URL: http://www.aberdeen.com/summary/report/benchmark/3981-RA-Supply-Chain.asp.

［113］ Wagner, H.M., Whitin, T.M., 1958. Dynamic version of the economic lot size mod- el. Management Science, 5, 212-219.

［114］ Yang, L., J. Yang, G. Yu, H. Zhang, 2011. Near-optimal (*r, Q*) policies for a two-stage serial inventory system with Poisson demand. Int. J. Production Economics, 133, 728-735.

［115］ Zangwill, W. I., 1966. A deterministic multi-period production scheduling model with blacklogging. Management Science, 13, 105-119.

［116］ Zangwill, W. I., 1969. A backlogging model and a multi-echelon model of a dynamic economic lot size production system—A network approach. Management Science, 14, 429-450.

［117］ Zheng, Y.S., 1992. On properties of stochastic inventory systems. Management Science, 38, 87-103.

［118］ Zipkin, P., 1986. Stochastic lead-times in continuous-time inventory models. Naval Research Logistics Quarterly, 14, 429-450.

[119] Zipkin, P., 2000. Foundations of Inventory Management. Jeffrey J.Shelstad. The McGraw-Hill Companies, Inc.